The Seen, the Unseen, and the Unrealized

Capitalist Thought:
Studies in Philosophy, Politics, and Economics

Series Editor: Edward W. Younkins, Wheeling Jesuit University

Mission Statement

This book series is devoted to studying the foundations of capitalism from a number of academic disciplines including, but not limited to, philosophy, political science, economics, law, literature, and history. Recognizing the expansion of the boundaries of economics, this series particularly welcomes proposals for monographs and edited collections that focus on topics from transdisciplinary, interdisciplinary, and multidisciplinary perspectives. Lexington Books will consider a wide range of conceptual, empirical, and methodological submissions, Works in this series will tend to synthesize and integrate knowledge and to build bridges within and between disciplines. They will be of vital concern to academicians, business people, and others in the debate about the proper role of capitalism, business, and business people in economic society.

Advisory Board

Books in Series

The Ontology and Function of Money: The Philosophical Fundamentals of Monetary Institutions by Leonidas Zelmanovitz

Andrew Carnegie: An Economic Biography by Samuel Bostaph

Water Capitalism: Privatize Oceans, Rivers, Lakes, and Aquifers Too by Walter E. Block and Peter Lothian Nelson

Capitalism and Commerce in Imaginative Literature: Perspectives on Business from Novels and Plays edited by Edward W. Younkins

Pride and Profit: The Intersection of Jane Austen and Adam Smith by Cecil E. Bohanon and Michelle Albert Vachris

The Seen, the Unseen, and the Unrealized: How Regulations Affect Our Everyday Lives by Per L. Bylund

The Seen, the Unseen, and the Unrealized

How Regulations Affect Our Everyday Lives

Per L. Bylund

LEXINGTON BOOKS
Lanham • Boulder • New York • London

Published by Lexington Books
An imprint of The Rowman & Littlefield Publishing Group, Inc.
4501 Forbes Boulevard, Suite 200, Lanham, Maryland 20706
www.rowman.com

Unit A, Whitacre Mews, 26-34 Stannary Street, London SE11 4AB

British Library Cataloguing in Publication Information Available

Library of Congress Cataloging-in-Publication Data
The hardback edition of this book was previously catalogued by the Library of Congress as follows:

Names: Bylund, Per L. (Per Lennart), author.
Title: The seen, the unseen, and the unrealized : how regulations affect our everyday lives / Per L.
     Bylund.
Description: Lanham : Lexington Books, [2016] | Series: Capitalist thought: studies in philosophy,
     politics, and economics | Includes bibliographical references and index.
Identifiers: LCCN 2016024294 (print) | LCCN 2016027359 (ebook)
Subjects: LCSH: Free enterprise. | Entrepreneurship. | Commerce. | Economics.
Classification: LCC HB95 .B946 2016 (print) | LCC HB95 (ebook) | DDC 330--dc23 LC record
     available at https://lccn.loc.gov/2016024294

ISBN 9780739194577 (cloth : alk. paper)
ISBN 9780739194591 (pbk. : alk. paper)
ISBN 9780739194584 (electronic)

Printed in the United States of America

To Susanne

Contents

Acknowledgments

This book would not have been possible without the magnificent contributions to economic reasoning and theory by prominent and outstanding thinkers and theorists, including but not limited to Adam Smith, David Ricardo, Frédéric Bastiat, Carl Menger, Joseph A. Schumpeter, Ludwig von Mises, and Friedrich A. von Hayek. This book was ultimately made possible by these thinkers, and the author claims no credit for the ideas shamelessly copied from their awe-inspiring works and repackaged into this book. What remains as this book's contribution would not have been possible without the help of Brent Beshore, Kevin Carson, and Saul Benjamin Oxholm. The author has also benefited from thoughts and comments by David Weiner and Jake Cahan, and the assistance of Franco Buhay and Steve Trost is also gratefully acknowledged. Not a single word would have been written, however, were it not for the support and inspiration from my beloved wife, Susanne.

The author's contribution includes the errors and mistakes still to be found throughout this book.

Chapter One

The How of the Market

Consider the question, "Does the market work?" Some would probably answer, with or without qualification, with a "yes." But qualification aside, most would likely adopt what they might characterize as a skeptical view. Their answer would therefore be in the negative or, if positive, with some type of qualification—"yes, it works *if*" or "it works *when*."

Perhaps it is due to political rhetoric that we find the question to have a certain moral or ethical underpinning. Much is blamed on the generic "market," which probably makes many of us think of the financial markets and hedge funds based on Wall Street in New York City. We have learned to adopt a negative view of "the market," as opposed to society. The same is true about competition, which we see as a cornerstone of how markets act, as opposed to cooperation. We are inclined to think not in terms of *whether* to regulate markets, but "how much," or in what manner, in order to get out of the market what we want or need. The assumption many of us tend to hold is that the market is dysfunctional in some sense, and this warrants correction from another party—and there is only one other party: political authority. Overall, there is something daunting or unnerving about leaving things to "the market" and therefore losing control or the pretense of control.

It can be argued that this type of automatic skepticism, if not an entirely dismissive attitude toward markets, is an indication of the great influence on popular thought by the tradition of economic skepticism going back through centuries and including thinkers like Thomas Robert Malthus, Karl Marx, John Maynard Keynes, and, much more recently, Thomas Piketty. These thinkers share a disbelief in markets and primarily see problems inherent in or resulting from its value-creating and production-coordinating qualities. They assume that "the market" is unable to cope with important challenges and may even, at least to some degree, be the *cause* of social unrest, tensions, and conflict. Indeed, Marx claimed that there are inherent contradictions in the market system—more specifically, capitalism—such that capitalist competition will "inevitably" lead to crisis. As markets left unregulated and uncontrolled will tend to cause great inequality, social conflict, and ultimately widespread despair, thinkers in this tradition often place their trust in the political apparatus and its powers of coercion to tame market forces and allow society to resist the temptation of economic incentives. This is a fundamentally pessimistic view of humanity, which assumes that people left to their own devices will not engage in peaceful exchange for mutual benefit and community-building, but will be at each other's throats. Unless people are subdued and controlled, they will resort to shortsighted violence and this will soon degenerate into a Hobbesian war of all against all.

But we need not trace the historical or theoretical origins of popular market skepticism. It is sufficient for our purposes to note that "the market" is often used not only to describe the system, and thereby how the economic organism, to borrow Pierre-Joseph Proudhon's term, actually functions, but comes bundled with a value judgment that often leans toward dislike or pessimism. For this reason, asking the question "Does the market work?" may cloud the fact that we are asking a real and positive question of relevance to how we understand—and can describe and explain—society and humanity. Consider instead the alternative but rather synonymous question "Does the *economy* work?" This question appears different; it seems purely descriptive and neutral. The economy, as everyone knows, is just what is all around us—it is what we work in, what we shop in, what we benefit from and what we contribute to. There is no value judgment involved when talking about the economy, and therefore we have no problem adopting a neutral position with regard to describing or attempting to explain the economy. Yet both questions above refer to the same thing: the economic system or organism. The difference is that "the market," while often misunderstood, may refer to the economic forces unbridled and unhampered, that is the economy without regulation. The term economy, in contrast, seems to refer to the regulated and taxed economy as we're used to in our everyday lives, that is the market plus boundaries and restrictions set through political means. Perhaps this is why many would adopt a basic skepticism toward the market: it is or appears uncontrolled and unmanaged and therefore may seem unreliable, whereas the economy is under political or democratic control. The former, the market, seems to be out of our hands; it is the market forces unleashed and thus "gone wild," whereas the latter, the economy, is something we can influence together—where everybody has a say.

But note that we are really talking about two different kinds of influences or forces here, one being the purely economic or "market" force and the other being the political, restrictive force. When we think of the economy as it is in most if not all countries today, then we are thinking about a mix of these two realms of influence: a mixed economy consisting of both market and political forces. It is difficult to trace the outcome at any point, or any specific phenomenon, to one force or the other. This is exactly why it is important to recognize the difference—and to discuss the market in its pure form. Granted, a purely free market does not exist anywhere in this world—perhaps least of all on Wall Street—but we need to understand what is meant by the market, or the economic organism without any political or other exogenous influences, in order to figure out what is going on around us, how policy affects market actions, behavior, and institutions. This is the sense in which we will most commonly refer to "the market" here: as unbridled, unhampered, unregulated, and unmanipulated *economy*. It is not about the financial markets or fruit stands in the town square, but the *economic organism*: its structure, tendencies, and evolution.

Does it work? Well, it depends on what we mean by "work." If by "work" we mean that the outcome is of a structure that dovetails with what we would personally prefer, then the answer is probably no. But the proper question is not if the economic system, which hardly exists to please only you, fulfills all your wants and wishes. The question is what it brings about—what is the outcome of the economic system as it is structured at a certain point in time? If we answer or at least theorize on this question, then we can begin to explain how it works, why it works this specific way, and what it means for us as individuals—and for society and humankind. Then we can also ask how we can improve it, that is how we can get "more" out of it than we do at present. We can ask how other influences affect the outcome and what would be the consequences of specific proposals to further improve it. We can also ask what causes its existing limitations and misallocations, that is, why we don't already get more.

That the economy, and therefore the market, works in one way or the other—regardless of our personal preferences—should be beyond any doubt. It exists, and therefore it must work in some sense of the word. The reason this question is misunderstood and often answered in a highly emotional manner is that we commonly take a normative position with respect to the market, and then over-politicize the question. So we look at the outcome of the market and compare it with our personal preference or maximum—how we conceive of the most perfect of all worlds, our utopia or nirvana[1] —and blame the difference on "the market." But the question of whether the market "works" is really about understanding the functioning of the processes that make up the economic organism; it is the question of *how* it works, not whether we like the specific outcome—or the structure thereof—that it currently generates. In other words, it is a question about how well we understand the market as a process, which is a necessary precondition for assessing the outcome and, more importantly, figuring out how we get what we get and why we don't get more.

What we will do in this chapter, therefore, is look at *how* the market works. That is, we will look at the fundamental forces that are intrinsic to an economy and that cause specific outcomes, shape behavior, and create patterns of action—and with them expectations of how people will react. We may refer to these forces as institutions. Whether this means that it, the market, really does work, in the normative sense, is something the reader will have to decide for him- or herself. This latter question, by the way, depends ultimately on what the market, or more specifically how the market is perceived, is compared to. It raises the question of whether this benchmark is itself realistic and realizable. Very often, a normative assessment of the market is based on a comparison with some utopia, that is a flawless and unrealistic imagined alternative, rather than the reality of other system practices. Our task here is not to make inadmissible comparisons such as this, or even to make a comparison between the market system and alternative systems. Rather, the purpose of this discussion is to produce an understanding of how the market functions, that is what the uninhibited economic organism would be like and how we can understand it. We may think of it as the unbridled, unhampered "free market," though as we will see this is really an abstraction—often used incorrectly—of a rather simple and quite unprovocative component. To understand "the market," therefore, we must look at what comprises a market. Only then can we understand it as an organism or system. The normative assessment of whether this is an attractive or ethical system is left to the reader.

WHAT CONSTITUTES THE MARKET

The market can be explained and understood using its component: the exchange. A market economy is the overall system that allows for and indeed is composed of any and all exchanges that, by those conducting those exchanges, are considered legitimate. But to see how this is the case, we must first elaborate on what we mean by exchange. And before then, we should discuss what the motivations for individuals to engage in exchange are.

Simply put, an exchange comprises at least two individuals exchanging something that is valuable for something else that is also valuable. If they do so voluntarily, by which we mean that no one is using or threatening to use physical force against one of them in order to get them to engage in the exchange, then it follows that they are both made better off. How so? Because if they did not believe that they were better off by carrying out the exchange, then they wouldn't choose to do so. This is the case because value is fundamentally subjective: how you value something is not necessarily identical to how I value that same thing or how someone else values it. So it can be the case that I value something you have more than what I have to offer in exchange and, *at the same time*, you value what I have more than what you have to offer. If this is the case, then we might choose to exchange those somethings. In fact, it wouldn't make any sense for us not to. And as a result, we both get what we desire more highly—that is, what we value more—and we're better off for it. At least, this is the case unless there is fraud involved, which is a deceitful way of making something appear as more valuable than it actually is.

If both individuals involved in an exchange refrain from coercion and fraudulent behavior—that is, the exchange and the items that change hands are untainted and openly offered and therefore voluntary—then this exchange constitutes value creation because the parties are both better off by doing the exchange than not. The exchange is therefore a necessary component of economic growth. All exchanges taken together constitute, as a composite that abstracts from the specifics of each individual exchange, "the market."

But there is of course more to the market than simply exchanging stuff that we already have on hand with people that happen to cross our paths. For instance, it is often the case that in order to get into a position where a specific exchange is possible, one will first need to make other exchanges or engage in production. This fact is the essence of *Say's Law*, after the French economist Jean-Baptiste Say (1767–1832), who was among the first to express this rather obvious truth. Despite being superficially obvious, the Law is important to understand both exchange and markets. In part, this is because it points to the importance of time and therefore the temporal aspect of economic action: some things must happen before other things are possible. And in order to get something specific that you desire, you must first make sure to have something that the person who has it in his or her possession desires even more. After all, we already saw how voluntary exchanges are possible only when each party has something that the other party values more highly (which is the same thing as saying that he or she finds it more desirable).

With production arises a number of issues that make markets the very complex organisms they typically are in modern, advanced economies.[2] One important such issue is the uncertainty that production necessarily entails, since it is impossible to know how the produced good will be received when it is finally available. With time, things change. Among those things that change over time are people's preferences—something a person values in the present may not be valued in the future. Perhaps the particular want that gave rise to the valuation has been satisfied in some other way, or the person has simply changed his or her mind for no particular reason. Undertaking production therefore comes at very high risk of missing what the potential customers will actually want, since the producer might be producing something that turns out to not be desirable when it is finished.

The problem is exacerbated by the fact that any costs of production are typically incurred in the present, and they must consequently be covered prior to completion of the production process and the final sale of the good—and whether or not the undertaken production turns out to be successful. Someone has to cover those expenses and face the risk of not being able to cover them with the anticipated (that is, hoped-for) future revenue if the good cannot be sold. This task of bearing the uncertainty of production is what we refer to as entrepreneurship: entrepreneurs choose the type of production that they judge has the greatest chance to meet the approval of consumers at the time it is finalized, and they therefore reap the reward if successful (earn a profit) and take full responsibility if it fails (suffer a loss of invested means).

As entrepreneurs are the residual claimants of uncertain business undertakings, which means they get to keep any profits that remain after all costs have been covered, there is a strong economic incentive for those with an entrepreneurial bent to attempt to produce something that consumers will value very highly. After all, if consumers value the product very highly they are willing to pay a high price, which makes it easier for the entrepreneur to cover the necessary expenses to carry out the production process and to earn a return. This simple driving force is what makes entrepreneurs willing to undertake highly uncertain and innovative projects—because they believe that what they will be able to offer will warrant a high price. In other words, if they are able to accurately predict the future market, and align their efforts with this imagined future, they will be mightily rewarded. This includes accurately estimating what consumers value, and how highly, based on the entrepreneur's idiosyncratic understanding for what people desire as well as what wants other entrepreneurs may be able to satisfy. uch entrepreneurship is the driving force of the market, and profit is the economic driving force of the entrepreneur.

It follows from this understanding of the entrepreneur that entrepreneurs do not compete with each other only for opportunities to exchange with consumers—but also for the resources used in production. As resources are scarce, "the market" is engaged in a complex system to establish the trade-offs between different uses of resources. Steel can be used to produce hammers and stoves and automobiles and intercontinental missiles. Steel can also be used to produce a great number of things that we are presently unaware of. The question is then how we can decide to best use the limited quantity of steel that we have available. In other words, how do we get the most value out of the little steel we have?

This question is answered by letting entrepreneurs risk their capital (that is, their resources or assets) in free enterprise and therefore compete with each other for the steel (really, for all resources that can be used productively). By doing this, and therefore by bidding over one another to acquire the limited resources that are available, entrepreneurs guide production overall.

They bid for resources using the capital they have at hand, whether their own or invested by others, and bid as highly as they can while still estimating that their venture will earn a profit. Those who aren't very good at estimating what consumers will want and how much they will want it, and therefore the prices they are willing to pay, will likely lose their investments. Those who are better at imagining what will be profitable get more capital and can therefore expand their business, start new businesses, and invest in innovations that can provide value in the future. This "weeding out" of entrepreneurs with poor judgment, and the rewarding of those with better judgment, amounts to a discovery process: over time, society overall discovers better, more valuable ways to use resources in production. In other words, we become more prosperous and our standard of living increases.

As entrepreneurs engage in this bidding for resources, they collectively determine how each resource should be valued relative other resources. The result of this process is market prices for all resources that approximate their social valuation in production. Prices, as we will see in the next chapter, don't reflect how efficiently resources are used in the present, but how efficiently they could be used—both in the present and in the imagined future. And their basis is not the preference of entrepreneurs, but what entrepreneurs anticipate that consumers will desire. If entrepreneurs anticipate that they will be able to use steel in much more profitable ways in the future, they will bid much more highly for steel and therefore the price of steel in the present will go up. So the price reflects the value that entrepreneurs anticipate the resource could have in production aimed at satisfying future consumers; in this sense, prices tend to approximate the social—that is, everybody in a whole society combined—good or value of the resource and thereby how consumers will want it to be used. Entrepreneurial production is core to what comprises the economic organism, and the aim of such production is to satisfy consumers as best possible—which rewards successful entrepreneurs with profits.

The prices, while determined by entrepreneurs, also guide entrepreneurs when they try to estimate whether a new venture could turn out to be profitable: if its production process depends on using resources with relatively high prices, the chances of earning a profit are slimmer than if it can be realized using relatively cheap resources. So as entrepreneurs bid for the resources they need to produce products that they think they can sell at profitable prices in the future, they establish prices that reveal a social valuation of the resources—and this, in turn, provides entrepreneurs with an incentive to use the resources of lesser value. The cheaper resources—that is, by entrepreneurs collectively deemed less desirable because they are less suitable (and therefore less productive) for satisfying anticipated consumer wants—can more easily allow the individual entrepreneur to earn a profit, which means there is reason to think hard whether the cheaper resources can be used instead of the more expensive ones.

Entrepreneurs, in other words, constantly consider trade-offs and "what if" questions: what if, instead of relying on expensive steel, a production process can be established using a much cheaper resource—for example, wood? Of course, using wood instead of steel would change the production process, and probably the product too, which means the entrepreneur must change the whole calculus and estimate what profit could be earned from this different product produced using another, alternative production process. So while there is a trade-off between resources, there is also a trade-off between production processes and between different variations of the end product. The entrepreneur chooses the combination that he or she judges will maximize the chance for profit, which is what will provide the highest value to consumers—by using the lowest-valued resources possible.

Note that this is all based on simple exchange of goods for mutual benefit—and the fact that to engage in exchange and therefore acquire something you desire, you must have something to offer in return. For this reason, entrepreneurs attempt to produce something they think others—that is, consumers—will want, so that the entrepreneur can thereby get what he or she wants. By allowing entrepreneurs to act on their beliefs about what will or could be, and allowing them to reap any benefits thereof, we have explained an economic production apparatus that amounts to an advanced economy engaged in future-oriented production. With production, the potential to generate real value increases exponentially as compared to the simple, production-less exchanges we started out with. Of course, the production apparatus established by entrepreneurs in their quest for profits also increases the risk for errors, since time is now an important production factor. With only exchanges in the present, time has little impact on economic life except for the time needed to search for the best possible exchange—time is a type of transaction cost. But with production, resources are acquired and used in the present so that entrepreneurs can produce a good to sell in the future. Time therefore becomes a factor of production and a scarce resource, since any entrepreneur chooses between different uses for it: production of different products using production processes of different lengths. The capital (that is, machinery and other assets necessary, or the value thereof) used in a production process awaiting its completion and final sale of the produced good consequently constitutes a cost: the resources could be used in numerous other ways, which means shorter production processes—that is, those that use less time from beginning to end—would allow for using the same capital in more projects in any given time period. The real downside of any choice is what could have been but now cannot be because we chose something different.

This downside—what is not seen—is the *economic* cost of any choice. It applies to any resource and amounts to the benefit that could be generated had the resource not been used in the way it presently is. In other words, the cost of using something in a specific manner in a specific production process is the opportunity foregone—whatever valuable alternative way in which the resource could have been used instead. This true economic cost—opportunity cost—signifies the fundamental trade-off and therefore the choice that was made between all possible valuable opportunities.

MESSY, APPROXIMATE, AND IN PROGRESS

The previous section established the fundamentals of economy and how we can conceive of it in terms of its fundamental component: voluntary exchange. But it does not follow from the discussion how to properly assess the market and its function, or establish whether it can be improved. One can easily conceive of the system of production-for-exchange as either maximizing or not, that is, as optimal or suboptimal. To reiterate the question that we asked above, does the market work?

This question unfortunately has no clear answer. The reason for this is that we must first figure out what is the proper benchmark to compare the market to. And we must also figure out what it is that we're comparing to begin with—the pure form of market as voluntary exchange, and whatever patterns and behavioral structures this gives rise to, or the economic reality, that is market plus political and other influences, that we see around us. From the point of view of modern mainstream economics, and specifically their model of perfect competition, an economy is efficient if there are no gains from trade that aren't being made, that is no gains remaining and that each resource is therefore put to its maximizing use. In other words, each resource is used in such a way that the value it creates exceeds its opportunity cost: there are no better alternative uses available in the present. The economy is in a state of equilibrium, where actions are not taken for the simple reason that any action can only cause a reduction in total value. The whole economy is maximized.

This also means that there can be no change and also no growth, since there are no more opportunities for improvement. Whether consumers are fully content or not, they cannot by any action be made better off. Consequently, the market is in a fixed and maximizing state. As such, there is no production undertaken that has not yet been finalized and the goods sold. If this were the case then it is easy to see that the resources currently bound in a production process—which does not yet satisfy any want, but aims toward future satisfaction—could have been used in a better way, simply by directly satisfying a want, any want, in the present. It is difficult to see any similarity between this economic state and the "pure" market, described above in terms of voluntary exchange and production, or the one experienced in our everyday lives. Rather than a fixed state, the market as we know it includes—if it is not primarily composed of—productive efforts by entrepreneurs and their business firms, which means it is in constant movement, and always aiming for value creation to be realized—if all goes well—at some future point in time. This view of the market as something "in progress" follows directly from our discussion of production above: production is how entrepreneurs create something that consumers find valuable enough to engage in exchange. Whenever this is the case, the market cannot ever be in a maximizing state and this means that an assessment of any temporary state of the market—a snapshot, as it were, taken at a specific point in time—must necessarily be inefficient as compared to a hypothesized full utilization of resources (where none of them can be used in a more valuable way than to satisfy wants in that specific moment).

In other words, the real market—an economy engaged in numerous production undertakings—cannot be anything like the mathematical models we learn in undergraduate and graduate economics courses. Rather than a state, whether this state is efficient (equilibrium) or not (disequilibrium), the market is better viewed as a process that is constantly in progress (that is, disequilibrium) toward the realization of some expected or imagined value that entrepreneurs anticipate are attainable through production. The myriad production processes in progress in a market at any time are at different stages, where some have barely begun while others are well underway or nearing completion. And we know from experience that many of these undertakings will fail. While a heuristic, it can be informative to think of production as a discovery process that serves to weed out most attempts. Indeed, most entrepreneurs fail most of the time. It is not easy to accurately imagine and time the market.

Yet entrepreneurs as a group do just that: they imagine what consumers will want and they bring it to them and offer those things for sale in the open market. What amounts to successful entrepreneurship can be one or more of many things: from cutting costs or responding to existing demands via solving problems that seem pervasive in society to educating consumers in what they should value. Many of our wants are latent and we can neither accurately identify them or imagine how everyday problems—which we may erroneously consider to be simple but unfortunate facts of life—could possibly be solved. Yet entrepreneurs can do this. Many disruptive technologies change people's behavior not because they respond to an observed want expressed by consumers as an unmet demand, but because they solve a problem that many of us have long stopped considering as a solvable problem—or haven't even thought of as a problem to begin with. When we are offered the potential solution, we're made better off because we can change our ways of life.

We change our behavior to one that was not possible while the problem remained. In this way, entrepreneurs can, through disruptive products, educate consumers about their own wants, which until that point remained "hidden" and latent—even to themselves.

Entrepreneurship, in other words, is much more than simply responding to an obvious and known shortcoming in the present state of things. Production can disrupt what was considered obvious, natural, and unchangeable by offering something of great value that we as consumers didn't expect and couldn't imagine. As we have already adapted our behavior to the way the world works—or the way we thought it worked—the introduction of something that ultimately relieves us of the necessity of certain actions has us swiftly changing our behavior to one that is less costly to us or more comfortable.

While this improves how consumers can choose to live their lives, it also adds to the uncertainty that entrepreneurs face in production. A disruptive innovation introduced by an entrepreneur can at any moment pull the rug out from under the feet of other entrepreneurs. Consider, for instance, the entrepreneurs involved in production that aimed to make transportation with horse and carriage more comfortable, cheaper, and perhaps faster. They were all competing for consumers who wanted the best type of transportation possible, and they competed by improving on transportation: better, lighter, more comfortable carriages. Henry Ford's production of automobiles disrupted transportation by offering a reliable means that didn't require ownership of and caring for horses. So whoever was involved in production relating to horse breeding, feeding, shoeing, and so on, as well as in the production and servicing of carriages, stables, and whatnot else that contributed to the production of transportation by horse and carriage, saw a rapid decline in market demand for their services. For most of them, the automobile, and especially its effect on transportation, was an utter and complete surprise; many of those who were unprepared undoubtedly lost everything they had invested in their expertise, customer relations, tools, and so forth.

Yet consumers were made much better off.

With respect to historic disruption such as the automobile, powered flight, the smart phone, or even the wheel, the innovation may seem obvious. But we cannot foresee—and many of us are unable to even imagine—what will change our lives in the years to come, so you can understand how these disruptive innovations changed the very basis for entrepreneurs and their business firms. Disruptive innovations are just that: disruptive. They change the conditions for production by revealing other uses for productive resources and by changing the behavior of consumers. The entrepreneurs affected simply had no idea of what would come or how it would affect people and consumers in general, and their own business in particular. Consequently, even an already existing and profitable type of business—a so-called "proven" business idea—is a fundamentally uncertain enterprise simply because we cannot trust that things will continue to be the way they have been. An apprenticeship in carriage-building would seem like the "sure thing"—a guaranteed job—up until the disruption caused by the automobile was a fact. You wouldn't want to be one of those apprentices having invested years of work at no or very low pay to learn and master a trade that suddenly is hopelessly out of fashion; it is a sure path to unemployment.

The fact that there are and will be disruptive innovations, which revolutionize production and change consumer behavior, means it would be outright dangerous, at least from the point of view of economic prosperity and therefore our well-being, to take the present for granted and then, perhaps through state-of-the-art research, try to maximize based on what we already know—the facts obvious to us—about the status quo. Even if we could get more out of production the way it is currently structured, on a societal or economy-wide level, we cannot know what opportunities for improvement to our lives that we could lose by using existing resources to a greater degree. Indeed, leaving some resources idle is the very reason why some entrepreneurs will be able to use those resources to produce disruptive innovations that can set in motion a vast process of change that affects everybody's lives. Economic optimization and politically preferred ends such as full employment would, if actually achieved, risk undermining the bases for improvements that are yet to be realized—many of which are not even imaginable in the present. Unused resources are not a waste but an investment, unless they are idle because they are forced to be idle, because they're owned by an entrepreneur who expects they will be more valuable in the future. If other entrepreneurs were to think these resources are worth more when used in present production, then they would bid those resource out of the "hoarder's" hands. Since they didn't, leaving them unused should be the most highly anticipated value of the resource. Indeed, the under-utilization of resources may be an important factor in reason why we see disruptive innovations; for this reason, measures taken to increase the short-term utilization of idle resources—what's sometimes referred to as "slack"—could undermine an economy's ability to realize innovation and therefore its ability to grow, which consequently can have an adverse effect on our well-being.

Production is a messy and uncertain business, and it is certainly not optimal in any common sense of the word. The only constant is change, and disruptive innovation can at any time change the conditions for any existing or planned production undertaking. Entrepreneurs therefore live and act in a world of immense uncertainty. Unless they can take into account everything they anticipate could happen, they will surely suffer a loss.

If we take a step back and look at an economy's production structure as a whole, as an aggregate of all entrepreneurs' production efforts, it will appear more slow-moving and path dependent. After all, what is a radical change to some individual entrepreneur and that threatens to put his or her firm out of business, may to the overall economy seem like a minor change. Also, on an aggregate level changes seem to fit into the larger picture and we can talk about economic growth overall while abstracting from the demise of hundreds, thousands, or even millions of entrepreneurs who sadly failed to see that a disruptive change was just around the corner and therefore lost their businesses. This system-wide analysis has its place and provides important insight into the evolution of an economy. But by aggregating we are likely to also miss important changes and, perhaps more interestingly, how those changes come about and develop over time. Indeed, macro level phenomena are comprised of millions of individual choices by entrepreneurs and their customers, by producers and consumers, all of which is the result of those persons acting in their self-interest and doing subjective cost-benefit analyses with regard to both the present as well as the imagined future. In this sense, we're all entrepreneurs to some degree, and we all take part in the changes that happen all around us: as both contributors to and beneficiaries of the productive engine that composes the economic organism.

RECAPITULATING

We have seen in this chapter how the economy can be explained by simple exchange, where value is offered for value. If the exchange is voluntary, then all parties to it are better off—or it wouldn't happen. This follows from the fact that we subjectively value goods and services. Of course, this doesn't mean that there can be no errors: anyone can *believe* that a good is of great value, but then when using it realize that it wasn't quite as expected—or that they were really looking for something else. This could be because of a genuine mistake, because our preferences change soon after the exchange, or for any other reason. It can also be because of fraud or other disinformation, though this would raise questions about whether the exchange was truly voluntary: the party's voluntary decision to engage in the exchange was based on the fraudulent information, which was not supplied in good faith.

We also found that this simple fact about voluntary exchange—that both parties to it consider themselves made better off by it—suggests an incentive to engage in production. By investing time and labor in producing goods *that are valued and thus requested by others*, one's chances of engaging in exchange increases. Also, it is reasonable to expect that one would get more out of exchanges, since a high-quality and properly positioned produced good is valued more highly by others and they therefore are willing to trade greater values in exchange for it. Thus, in discussing production and the role of entrepreneurship we understand the real implications of voluntary exchange and consequently find it necessary to briefly touch on the role of prices—and especially prices in production.

Prices play an immensely important role in advanced economies and price theory occupies a central role in economics. To understand the market and how it works, we must dig a little deeper into the meaning of prices: their determination and role in production and consumption. This is the topic for the next couple of chapters.

NOTES

1. See Demsetz (1969) on the so-called nirvana fallacy.
2. For a more in-depth discussion on the problems arising due to production, see, e.g., Bylund (2016).

Chapter Two

The Price Is Right

In the long-running American television game show "The Price Is Right," contestants compete in trying to get the price of displayed goods "right." Whoever gets closest to the real price of the good without going over wins the round. The idea is simple enough, since we're all used to seeing prices presented to us printed on price tags in stores. The prices are non-negotiable, so we either pay the price or don't get the good. Simple enough. So all the contestants in the game show need to do is guess what is on the price tag. But where does that price come from? And what's to say that this price is "right"? Prices can be different in different stores, and they can vary over time because of inflation, competition, and temporary sales. So which price does the game show use? Perhaps they would say that they use something resembling the "market price" for the good, but this only raises the question: where do market prices come from?

There is something missing to our story. It is not at all obvious how we get to a world where we are presented fixed prices for a multitude of goods in stores from what we discussed in the previous chapter: the simple opportunities for mutually beneficial exchanges of subjectively valued goods. If the reader recalls, we actually touched briefly on prices in chapter 1—but only as something guiding production choices, and arising as a result of entrepreneurs bidding for resources to use in production of goods and services. Those are not the prices we see in stores, however, which are exclusively for goods intended for consumers. So how do we get to the point where goods in stores have prices, and what is to say that those are the *right* prices?

The answer is that there is no such thing as a "right" price. We could also say, which is equally accurate, that *all* prices are right. The reason for this is that goods and services offered for sale in the market do not have a single price, but many. This is easy to understand if we return to the discussion in chapter 1 where individuals exchange goods. In any single exchange, each good has two prices: one for the buyer and one for the seller. For instance, if Adam offers Adele a can of Coke in exchange for an apple, then we know two things about the valuation of these goods: we know that Adam values the apple more highly than the Coke, and, assuming Adele accepts the terms, that Adele values the Coke more highly than the apple. In this case, they're both willing to go through with the exchange since both expect to be better off— subjectively speaking, that is by their own ranking of preferences—with what the other party offers. But it is wrong to conclude from this that the apple "is worth" a can of Coke. It is for Adam, since he's willing to give up a Coke for the apple. But it isn't for Adele, who rather makes the opposite exchange.

Unfortunately, this doesn't get us to a point where there is a price of the goods exchanged. The reason is that for Adam to offer his can of Coke for the apple, all we know is that he values the apple more highly—but we don't know how much more highly. We also know that Adele is willing to give up her apple for the can of Coke, which means that she values the Coke more highly than the apple. Neither means that the price of the apple *is* a can of Coke. To say that this is the case is to claim that they are valued the same, which means a person would be indifferent to which of the two he or she acquires—and this is not the case for either Adam or Adele: they are both very clearly interested in giving up one for the other. So since they're both willing to go through with the exchange, they must both have different "prices" in mind at which they would be indifferent to going through with the exchange. Perhaps Adam thinks the apple is worth two cans of Coke while the Coke to Adele is worth an apple and a half. We don't know, but we do know that they value the goods differently and therefore have different maximum prices for them. That is, they're willing to give value up to a certain point in order to get the other—and more treasured—value.

The same reasoning applies if Adam, instead of negotiating with Adele, would drive to the grocery store to buy an apple for money. However he values his money, in order for him to go through with the exchange—that is, to buy the apple—he must think the apple is "worth" more than the money he gives up to buy it (including the time and effort and gasoline it takes for him to get to the grocery store and back). If he considers the money to be worth more than the apple, then he would be worse off buying it. If that's the case, he won't buy, but if they are worth exactly the same to him, then going through with the exchange means nothing to him—it is a pointless and worthless endeavor.

Indeed, the same goes for the store owner, who wouldn't sell the apples if they were worth more than the money offered in exchange for them. But this isn't obvious when considering large companies such as Walmart, and there is more to discuss about prices before we get to the price printed on the thousands of price tags on goods stacked on numerous shelves in myriad aisles in a Walmart Supermarket. At this point, it is sufficient to note that the prices of goods in Walmart require no alternative logic. The same logic holds as for Adam and Adele, but it requires more elaboration to see it.

The supermarket example introduces a phenomenon that is not present in the example of Adam and Adele: *money*. We tend to think of money as value, but this is a shorthand and not entirely accurate. A dollar bill has little use value except for the fact that you believe that others will accept it in exchange. Were this not the case, it would really just be a piece of paper with ink all over it. In fact, it would probably be more valuable had it not had all that ink all over it, since then it could at least serve as paper for taking notes!

MONEY

As generally recognized by economists, money is a universally accepted medium of exchange. In other words, money is useful—that is, we consider it *valuable*—because we know that we can offer it as payment for goods that more directly satisfy our wants. We know that others will accept money as payment, and that's the whole reason money is valuable. So money has value for its indirect usage, that is for its value in exchange. Now we can see how money is explained using the simple example of exchange that we discussed in chapter 1. We noted that in the simple exchange situation people have an incentive to produce things of value, which can then be offered in exchange for what is more desirable. Indeed, the best good to produce would be one that others value highly—especially if many or all value it—so that it increases the chances of finding someone who wants it in exchange. So the most valuable type of production undertaking is not necessarily to produce what you want yourself, but produce something others really want and that you're good at producing. This way, you maximize your chances of getting as much as possible of the goods and services that you value.

In other words, production is undertaken to increase one's own well-being, that is in one's self-interest, but what is produced is produced to satisfy the wants of *others*. This is what entrepreneurs do, as was pointed out in chapter 1. They produce not what they wish to personally consume, but produce what they are good at producing and believe others will want—and value highly—so that the entrepreneurs can then use the produced good as a means to get what they really want through exchange. It might seem a bit roundabout or indirect, but it makes sense since we all have different skills and abilities and we tend to get better at producing if we specialize and focus on one type of activity. So to get as much as possible out of our efforts, we want to play on our strengths and produce what we're relatively good at producing rather than producing what we actually need but lack the skillset to produce.

By doing this, we soon get to a point where we are all producing for each other and maximizing our own well-being by satisfying other people's needs. So by serving others, we serve ourselves. This is what Adam Smith called the "invisible hand" of the market.[1] It is a fairly simple and intuitive but still powerful concept, but one that is often misunderstood and scoffed at or even forgotten.

Out of this situation where people are busy producing for each other—for the *market*, as it were—it is easy to see that some produced goods are more usable than others to trade. They may be valued by more people, for instance. But they could also be relatively easy to store and to transport, have long shelf life (that is, they don't go bad quickly), and so on. It would then make sense for people to offer their own produced goods for sale with payment in these more easily usable goods rather than directly engage in exchange for what they need personally. For instance, if Adele grows apples for a living, which means she has a lot more than the one apple she offers to Adam, then she would like to use as many apples as possible in exchange for something more desirable before they go bad. She has no use for hundreds of apples, but there may be hundreds of people who want an apple or two each. One possible solution to this conundrum is for Adele to find the people who have something she wants who also want apples, and then offer to trade. But it is much easier to find people who want apples but offer something that fits the description of money: something that a lot of people want and that is easy to store and transport, and so on. Adele would be willing to trade for those things, since she can use them later—she anticipates that others will be willing to exchange them for other goods. Apples, as we know, are a season-al, so Adele is stuck every fall with hundreds of apples and is left with none for the rest of the year. So she needs to make sure she gets whatever she can for them in exchange, and that she acquires something that retains value and doesn't go bad.

This way, some goods will emerge as much more universally usable than others. And as people keep exchanging for certain goods in order to use them in future trades, they become a standard. Whether the goods being traded are sea shells, cattle, or gold coins, what matters is the degree to which others accept them as payment in exchange for their goods, not that you want those particular goods yourself. This is how we can conceive of money being born according to a well-known essay by Austrian economist Carl Menger.[2]

What happened historically is a little more complex, but it doesn't change the use and value of money as a medium of exchange or the advantages of a money economy. Rather than money emerging spontaneously as a way for eager traders to get out of troublesome and costly barter, money appears to have first been used as a unit of account within non-state bureaucracies (such as temples) and legal systems. Money therefore already had an established exchange ratio towards the goods it had been used to keep track of within bureaucracies, which likely made it easier to adopt in outside market trade. Whereas the historical record provides a more roundabout explanation for how markets adopted money for trade, it doesn't change the fact that money has the properties of an accepted medium of exchange and is of value to the economic system (the market) for the reasons explained logically by Menger and others. The latter also allows us to logically establish the value of a money *per se* (or, money *qua* money) in advanced exchange economies by "regressing" to a fictitious time before money. We can therefore move ahead in our hypothetical market to explain prices using money. That money, as a trusted medium of exchange, is an important component of markets as well as economic growth is, as we will see throughout this discussion, beyond doubt.

THE DETERMINATION OF PRICES

With money there is a common unit in the market in which prices can be expressed. This doesn't really change anything with respect to where prices come from or how they are determined, but money makes it easier to express, communicate, and compare prices. It is, after all, a lot easier to figure out one's options with information such as "a dozen apples trade at two gold coins and loaves of bread at one gold coin each" than "an apple was exchanged for a can of Coke and a loaf of bread was exchanged for a dozen three-inch nails." It is easier to see how the former offers many more options, since only two trades are necessary to purchase *any* good—first you sell goods for gold coins, then you buy goods paying in gold coins. In contrast, with the price information just given for a non-money barter economy, Adele would have to find the people with matching wants for each of a potentially long series of exchanges in order to get what she wants (unless she can find someone willing to exchange a loaf of bread for apples). For instance, in order to buy a loaf of bread she might have to first sell an apple to Adam for a can of Coke, then find someone to trade the can of Coke for a dozen nails, and then visit the baker to offer the nails for the loaf. That is, assuming the baker wants more nails than the dozen we know that he already accepted. And, of course, it might be the case that Adele has to sell two apples for two cans of Coke because Adam won't trade for only one apple, and then she can trade the two cans to get twenty nails, of which twelve can be used to buy the bread. But what if she doesn't want the remaining eight nails? Can she buy 2/3 loaves of bread? Or can she find someone willing to trade something she wants for eight nails?

With money as a universally accepted medium of exchange, more trades become possible and each exchange is less costly because there is no need to find someone who has what you want and wants what you have—what we call "double coincidence of wants." Recalling what we learned in chapter 1 about voluntary exchange, more trades means more value is created since through every undertaken exchange all involved parties are better off (or they wouldn't do it). Consequently, more value is created faster in a money economy than in a barter economy.

With money, Adam and Adele don't have to exchange the can of Coke for the apple (though they could, of course, if they wanted to). Instead, if Adam has already traded with others for money he could offer Adele a money price for the apple and save the Coke to enjoy with the apple. Money might be just as good for Adele as the Coke, or even better if she's a diabetic or doesn't like the sweet taste of soda pop. The nature of the exchange between Adam and Adele doesn't change because money enters the picture, however. It will possibly be easier for bystanders to recognize the price paid for the apple, but the logic is exactly the same: Adam will value what he gives up in the exchange less than what he receives, and Adele will value what she gives up less than what she receives. But with money it is perhaps easier to see why Adam and Adele value things differently. They have different personal preferences and tastes, but are also in different positions. Adele, as a grower of apples, wants to exchange apples for something she can use as payment to acquire goods and services when apples are not in season; Adam's occupation as maker of Coke is irrelevant for this exchange, as what he offers in exchange for the apple is simply money. So Adam and Adele only need to have one thing in common: their recognition (or belief) that money is a trusted and universally accepted medium of exchange and therefore will buy other things from other people, which also means they will be able to judge whether the price asked by Adele is reasonable considering the purchasing power of money (how much of other goods can be bought for this money). They may also, for the sake of this transaction, be unknown to each other—perhaps completely anonymous—since what matters is the apple offered for sale and the money offered as payment. Without trusted money, however, Adam and Adele would have had to establish that they both wanted what the other person possessed yet was willing to give up in exchange, and figure out whether Adam's can of Coke was really sufficient payment for Adele's apple, and vice versa.

What is the price of the apple, then? As measured in the trusted unit of account—money—we can observe exactly what Adam pays Adele. With what we know about exchanges, we know that this payment is valued more by Adele than the apple, but we don't know how much lower she is willing to go. We also know what Adam was willing to give up in terms of money for the apple, and that he values that amount of money less than the apple.

Say that Adam offered ten moneys for the apple and this was plenty for Adele so she was glad to accept the offer. This means the price for that apple is ten moneys. At this point, it is impossible to know whether or not this is reasonable. But assume Bart is a baker and that he's recently sold a loaf of bread to Becky the nail smith for eight moneys and that Becky sold a dozen nails to Charles for fifteen moneys. Now we have prices of several goods and thus can compare the revealed money prices to our preference rankings of those goods. We now know that others have traded a dozen nails at a higher money price than the loaf of bread and that the loaf of bread, in turn, traded at lower than Adele's apple. We should also know how much money we have accumulated by selling whatever it is we produce, and therefore how we subjectively value that money—both in terms of the toil and trouble of producing those goods and the purchasing power of the money on hand. Similarly, Adele probably based her decision to sell the apple for ten moneys to Adam on her knowledge of how much bread or nails she can purchase for that money. Adam, in turn, based his decision to pay ten moneys for the apple on what he knew about the purchasing power of money and his subjective valuation of those other goods he could have bought.

So with a medium of exchange everybody is able to figure out the relative value of money in exchange for goods and thereby decide what particular exchanges to pursue, and in what order, to maximize utility. As everybody is engaged in deciding what and how much to buy of each good, a "social" relative valuation emerges. The process is the same as we saw above with the entrepreneurs bidding for resources—an issue we will soon get back to—and has the same result. Depending on the anticipated price situation, each person decides how much to produce: Adam decides how many cans of Coke to produce, Adele decides whether to expand or scale down on her orchard, Bart makes up his mind about how many hours he wants to spend by the oven, Becky in the forge, and so on. Their decisions are based on how much money they expect to be offered for their produced goods, and—more importantly—how much of other goods those moneys will buy in return. In other words, they consider the tradeoff between different courses of action, and use the purchasing power of the moneys they anticipate that their products will buy to compare the alternatives. With money, it is easier to consider one's true opportunity cost and therefore to decide on production, consumption, and the value of time.

The price thus goes both ways. Considering the particular exchanges mentioned above, an apple was traded for ten moneys; a loaf of bread was traded for eight moneys; and a dozen three-inch nails were traded for fifteen moneys, and vice versa. Because we have prices of all goods (except the money) in a common unit—money—we can compare their prices: we know, for instance, that a dozen nails are almost twice as expensive, in moneys, as bread. If we had not had any money prices, we could not use anything but our own preference about each good to rank them in terms of value. Thanks to the money prices we can estimate their market value and consequently plan our actions better.

Money also allows for bidding so that Adam, Bart, Becky, and Charles can all offer to buy Adele's apple(s) using the same type of payment. Before money was introduced, they would all have to—assuming her exchange with Adam was an expression of exclusive preference—go through intermediate exchanges in order to get cans of Coke to offer Adele in payment. Now, however, they do not need to pursue specific chains of exchanges to get something Adele prefers, but can simply offer their products in the market for money—and then use that money as offered payment for Adele's apple. This means that Adele's potential customer base has expanded drastically; anyone in this little society would now, in principle, be able to offer payment for apples. In other words, customers would be able to bid for apples. As Adam offers ten moneys for an apple, Becky could offer eleven and Bart twelve. The same goes for all other products, so perhaps Bart offers fifteen moneys for a dozen of Becky's nails whereas Adam offers sixteen and Charles, who values nails most highly, offers the highest price of eighteen moneys.

This type of bidding to buy products forces buyers to offer as much as they can for each product in order to buy them. While they wouldn't bid any higher than they think is worth it, which means they will always offer prices in money that they value lower than they anticipate the product they aim to purchase is "worth" to them, they would probably offer higher prices than they otherwise would have. They are still better off, but not as well off as they would have been had they been the only customer. What this means, from a societal point of view, is not a loss but a gain: the person who values a good most highly, in terms of his or her subjective valuation of money, will come out on top in each bidding. The *realized* value of each good, therefore, is the highest possible.

How so? Let us consider as example the bidding for nails above, where Bart offers fifteen, Adam sixteen, and Charles eighteen moneys for Becky's dozen nails. The only thing this tells us is that Bart values the nails more than fifteen moneys, Adam more than sixteen, and Charles more than eighteen. If none of them are willing to go higher and Charles therefore wins the bidding, we know a little more. We know that Bart values sixteen moneys more highly than the dozen nails and therefore that he values the dozen nails somewhere between the fifteen moneys he offered and the sixteen moneys he didn't offer. The same goes for Adam, who offered sixteen moneys and therefore values the dozen nails higher but not as highly as the eighteen moneys he would need to bid in order to match Charles' bid. So Adam values the dozen nails at between sixteen and eighteen moneys. Only Charles values the dozen nails higher than eighteen of his moneys, so he is the one who values them most highly (in moneys).

This doesn't mean, of course that Charles *objectively* has the highest valuation of (that is, the greatest need for) the nails, only that he *subjectively* values them most highly *in terms of money*. This is not completely arbitrary, however, since his valuation of money is based on the purchasing power of money, and therefore how he values all other goods available in the market as well as his own time and labor that goes into earning the moneys he spends. While it's still an approximation of valuation, it is the most accurate we can get.

If we also have several sellers so that Adele is not a monopolist but has to compete with Agnes and Anton, who also have invested in orchards to sell apples to the customers, then they will bid prices *down* for the chance of selling their apples. The result is an established "price" that, because it incorporates all of the involved individuals' valuations at that moment, reflects the joint subjective valuation of apples with respect to the subjective valuation of money—for both buyers and sellers. It means that, in equilibrium, no apple buyer who values the apples higher than the final price is left without and no apple seller who values the final price higher than the apples is left with apples. This is the determined market equilibrium price, which is a "maximizing" price from the point of view of social value. At this price, the market clears; there are no more gains from trade possible.

This is nothing new, but is actually the standard supply-and-demand diagram taught in Econ 101 classes in college. But it is important to understand the dynamic that precedes it and is only implicit to the snapshot shown in the diagram, as well as understanding that it is based on the many subjective valuations and the consequent actions taken by people who have some form of interest in the products exchanged: in this case, apples and money. The situation we ended up with is one where all involved get as much as possible—that is, they maximize their utility. Why? For the simple reason that whoever values the money necessary to buy an apple more than the apple will keep their moneys, and whoever values an apple more than the money necessary to buy it is able to buy an apple.

This "equilibrium" situation doesn't mean everybody in this economy is fully content with what they have, of course. There may be many who really want to buy an apple or two but who value the money necessary to buy it more than the apple. Or to put this differently: they would really like the sweet taste of a newly picked apple *had the price been lower*. What this means is that their opportunity cost for buying an apple exceeds that of not buying it. So they are—based on their own, subjective valuation—better off not buying it, no matter how good they think the apple tastes. If it were any other way, they would be willing to give up more for an apple. And if the reason they "can't" buy an apple is that they don't have enough moneys, they should be willing to work harder or longer hours or do other things (and perhaps not buy other things with the money) in order to accumulate the moneys needed. In our limited example, there is nothing keeping them from producing and exchanging the goods for money to then use for the purchase of apples. So the reason they don't have the money now, when they want to taste an apple, is that they made another decision previously: they either valued leisure more highly than labor, which is why they couldn't accumulate the funds necessary, or they labored enough but spent the money earned on buying other goods that they, at that point, considered more valuable to them than apples. There are other concerns as well, especially if we compare this model with the real economy that we live and work in, but we will touch on those issues in a later chapter.

SUMMING UP

What we have seen is that the price of a good has very little to do with the actual good, or goods, as it were, since the issue of trade—and therefore price—is one about exchange: one value is given up to acquire another value, which means the other party does the same. The price, therefore, is expressed in what is given up, which is different for each of the parties involved in the transaction. When Adam offers Adele a Coke in payment for an apple, if she accepts, then the price of the apple is a Coke and the price of a Coke is the apple. These prices, in turn, are based on the valuations for Adam and Adele, respectively. Adam offers the Coke because he values the apple more highly and Adele offers the apple because she values the Coke more highly. Both pay a price that they consider to be lower than the value of what is acquired, so they're both better off.

This type of market price between Adam and Adele is a market-clearing price because the transaction happens and therefore exhausts the available gains from trade. If they were not mistaken in their initial judgment of value or immediately after the exchange change their minds, neither Adam nor Adele will be willing to go back, that is to exchange the goods again, because it would make both of them worse off. Indeed, we already saw that Adele values the Coke higher than the apple, so why would she give up the Coke for the apple? The same is true with Adam. In other words, with respect to Adam and Adele and the apple and the Coke, the market has cleared: there are no more gains from trade.

This is equally true in a market with many participants, which could see different prices between each pair of exchangers, that is, in each trade made. But if the prices offered for products differ a lot, other traders would realize they are missing out—that they could be even better off trading with someone else, who would be satisfied with lesser value in exchange. In other words, the exchange parties may change or "rotate" because each of them seeks the better deal. As there are (at least) two parties to each exchange, and both see the transaction as a way of acquiring greater value than they're giving up, they will naturally try to increase the value they're getting. This creates a pressure toward a "standard" market price for each good that is the same across all exchanges. At this level, the market clears for the simple reason that supply meets demand: the number of apples offered at exactly this price equals the number of Cokes offered at exactly this price. So if Adam and Adele have it exactly right, which means they happen to have exchanged at the going market price, then it means other transactions happen as well at that price: 1 Coke = 1 apple. At this price, all owners of apples get to "sell" as many apples as they want for Cokes and all owners of Coke cans get to "sell" as many cans as they want for apples.

While the "standard" or equilibrium price seeks the exact exchange ratio where the market clears, it may fluctuate across a market as well as over time because people value things differently and change their minds, and because finding out the exact price may be costly. Nevertheless, even considering this cost, the price that becomes "standard" in the market suggests that, at the end of the day, all trades that could happen will have happened. Another way of putting this is that all gains from trade have been made, and therefore no one is left out. This doesn't mean, however, that anyone who wants an apple or a Coke got one. It also doesn't mean all of those who have a Coke but would like an apple (and vice versa) got an apple through trade. But this is not a matter of willingness and ability to trade, which would have made it possible for them to get what they desire more highly. Rather, the reason they didn't exchange was that they consider the price too steep. For instance, there may be many owners of Coke cans who would love apples, but who value an apple less than a Coke can. Similarly, there may be many owners of apples who would love to have Coke, but who value a Coke less than an apple. They may have the taste for apples and Cokes, respectively, but their valuations show very clearly that they *prefer* what they have to what they could get. The fact that something is valued is not the same thing as it being valued more, but the point of the market price is that everyone—whether or not they engage in exchange—ends up with what they value more. This is an important lesson to remember when analyzing the economy and market.

NOTES

1. Smith, 1776.
2. Menger, 1892.

Chapter Three

What Prices Communicate

What has been said so far about prices only relates to goods offered for sale that directly satisfy wants: apples and bread satisfy hunger, Becky's three-inch nails can be used to repair one's shelter, and so on. The prices of those goods are determined through an implicit bidding between consumers and producers. Or, more accurately, between potential consumers and potential producers. Why potential? Because consumers may express an interest in a certain good. Whether this leads to an exchange to acquire that good depends on the price one has to pay and all the options present: there may be myriad goods and services that can be bought for money, and whatever good the consumer ends up buying depends on his or her subjective valuation and ranking of all of those goods—and the subjective valuation of the moneys necessary to buy them.

The same is true for producers, but the issue of production necessarily leads us to entrepreneurship and therefore—as we saw in chapter 1—future-oriented action. We already established that production must precede consumption, but whereas this point could seem obvious there is more to it than the fact that you have to bake bread before you can eat it (a lesson Bart could probably tell us more about). Indeed, we saw in the previous chapter that the people bidding to buy apples from Adele and her competitors can bid because they have already engaged in production and sold the produced goods for money. So production is not simply the process that is necessary to make a good available, but also the process that makes it possible to demand other goods. Had Becky not produced and sold three-inch nails, she could not offer to buy apples for money; had Bart not produced and sold bread, he could not offer to buy apples for money. And the same logic applies for everyone else in an economy.

So we see that this example of simple one-stage production when we have a universally accepted medium of exchange—money—means production is highly interdependent because it is a means to some other end. All of our friends in this economy *produce in order to consume,*[1] and they all produce something that they know (or, more accurately, anticipate) will be demanded by others and therefore sold for money. The point of producing is not because labor itself is fun (though it can be) or because what is produced will be immediately consumed (though it might be)—but to sell for money, which can be used to buy what each of these people really want. As producers produce for individuals other than themselves, they don't need to stop when they've produced only what they themselves need—they can keep producing, since they're producing for a lot of people. So we can see how this means that it is likely that more is produced because production is a means used to raise each producer's own standard of living by increasing their purchasing power (that is, money on hand after selling the produced goods). With the money acquired through selling the produced goods, practically any goods produced by anybody are available and can be purchased.

VALUE OF THE MEANS OF PRODUCTION

For our little economy, this means that all consumers are also producers and—therefore—entrepreneurs. Adele doesn't wake up one day surprised to find an orchard full of ripe apples. The orchard is the result of her investment of labor—and possibly other things—over a long period of time. So the apples she now has for sale, and that Adam and Bart and Becky are competing to buy using money, are really the "fruits" of her labor. She probably started years ago to clear the land, plant the seeds, and then care for the seedlings so that they grew into productive apple trees. The reason, as we've seen, is that Adele believed that she could sell apples to Adam and the others for sufficiently high prices to provide her with the purchasing power to get what she needs in turn. By producing and selling apples, she acquires the money she needs to buy nails from Becky to repair the house, bread from Bart to feed herself and her family, and so on.

It may be the case that Adele has discovered an opportunity in the market, by which we mean that there was unmet demand that nobody had seen before.[2] So Adele, alert to this opportunity, acted to profit from it. Or, equally likely, Adele believes she has a certain knack for growing apples and that this would therefore be the most productive use of her time. In both cases, the point is that Adele doesn't have an insatiable hunger for apples and therefore plants apple trees, but that she thinks it is a good use of her time—because it gives her the best possible means to procure what she actually needs from other producers.

Since growing apples takes time and the outcome of the endeavor is in the future, it is uncertain. Since Adele bears this uncertainty, which means she will suffer the loss if it doesn't work out, she's the entrepreneur.

The same is true for all the others in our little society: they invest in the production of goods that they hope to sell for money so that they can then purchase the goods and services they really want. They all, therefore, bear the uncertainty of their undertakings. For Adele, the uncertainty involves a lot of different things: from rabbits and deer eating the seedlings to storms breaking the trees or insects destroying the apples, to competitors—like Agnes and Anton—undercutting Adele's prices to customers or people simply not desiring apples anymore. So there are several parts to the uncertainty that Adele must consider and attempt to deal with. The easiest to deal with is technological uncertainty, which relates to the production process and includes anything that can go wrong with it. Adele can minimize the problems by being very careful, acquiring skills, and perhaps buying insurance to make sure she's protected if something goes wrong.

It is much harder to deal with market uncertainty, which is the uncertainty of what the market will be like when the apples are ready to be picked and sold. Maybe consumers will not be interested in apples anymore. Perhaps everyone has succumbed to a fancy trend of eating gourmet pears instead of staple apples. So it could be the case that Adele has simply misjudged the situation and what people will want. But it could also be the case that Agnes and Anton, who also thought of selling apples, offer their ripe apples for sale before Adele's trees are ready to bear fruit. Or perhaps Anton is a master apple grower and can produce apples at much lower cost than Adele, and is willing to sell apples for so little money that Adele can't cover her costs. So customers willing to buy apples will buy from Anton instead. In these cases, Adele was right about people desiring apples but didn't quite get the production right—she was too slow or too inefficient. She estimated the demand correctly but underestimated the supply. There was less of an opportunity *for her* than she imagined, and therefore she may fail in her endeavor.

These problems alone would probably be enough to deter many of us from starting our own businesses and becoming entrepreneurs, but instead to seek seemingly more stable and safe careers as employees—that is, suppliers of labor to an entrepreneur. By doing this, we escape some of the downside of uncertainty by giving up the upside: instead of the possibility of profit and the threat of suffering losses, we earn a fixed salary. Of course, if the entrepreneur fails, we won't get to keep our income or our jobs, so employment doesn't make us uncertainty-proof. It only means we do not directly have to bear it in the sense that Adele does.

The uncertainty of entrepreneurship gives rise to another issue that follows directly from our example of Adele's investment in an orchard to sell apples. But the conclusion may not seem entirely obvious. We know that

Adele invests in the orchard because she believes it will allow her to sell apples and thereby earn money in exchange, which will allow her to purchase the things she really wants. She believes the outcome is worth more than the time, effort, and resources she puts into it. But what, then, is the "value" of the orchard? There is only one way it can have actual value and it is only recognizable after its production process has been brought to completion: if the entrepreneurial undertaking works out and the orchard produces plenty of apples that Adele then sells for money, then the orchard has value. Its value is directly imputed from the value consumers place on the apples it produces. In other words, if consumers are desperate for apples and willing to give up loads of money for Adele's apples, then that makes the orchard highly valuable because it is the means to producing those apples that provide income. But if consumers are flocking towards gourmet pears instead, so that Adele doesn't get to sell any of the apples, then the value of the orchard is practically zero.[3] Since the orchard isn't consumed directly, its only value is as a means of production—for Adele in our example, the production of apples. Consequently, the value of production goods consists only of its contribution to the value consumers place on the consumption good. In our example so far, there are only two means of production: Adele's labor tending to the apple trees and the orchard (that is, the land, trees, and so on). The value of both is entirely due to the fact that Adele has put them to good use: they were used as means to produce apples that consumers desired and were willing to give up money to buy. The realized value of Adele's invested labor and the orchard is the value it produced for consumers.

Of course, Adele put labor into making the orchard too. The value of this labor, an already incurred and therefore sunk cost, is its contribution to the orchard, whose value is the contribution of apples that directly satisfy consumers' wants. So Adele's labor was invested in two ways: first, to produce the orchard, and then to tend to the trees and make sure the orchard produced apples. Her labor must be valued accordingly, by how much each type of labor invested contributed to the value realized for consumers. If Adam and others did not value the apples and were not willing and able to buy them, Adele's investments would be for nothing—and they would also be valued nothing, unless they could be used in some other way to satisfy other consumer wants. Adele's undertaking was therefore a *speculation*, since she could not in advance know the value of the outcome of her effort. She bears the uncertainty of whether it is a successful undertaking, that is whether she judged the situation correctly.

PRICES OF THE MEANS OF PRODUCTION

What matters to us here, however, is not the theoretically derived value of the means of production, but rather how this gives rise to real *market prices*. As we discussed in the previous chapter, prices of consumption goods are directly related to the value consumers place on the goods and their ability to satisfy real wants. That is, each consumer has his or her subjective valuation of each good and each producer has his or her subjective valuation, and by allowing all of the consumers and producers to bid for goods and money, respectively, their subjective tradeoffs bring about prices for the goods that reflect the joint or social valuation of the goods. The "final price" ends up where it is not too expensive for enough consumers, and where it is sufficiently high for enough producers—considering the alternative uses for the productive resources. But there are no consumers of an orchard just like there are no consumers of labor or an automobile manufacturing plant; these are means of production, not consumer goods, so their pricing is a little different. We already touched on how production goods can be valued above, and in chapter 1 we cursorily discussed entrepreneurial bidding for such resources, but we need to understand this in greater detail to understand how an advanced economy produces goods and allocates scarce resources toward one end over the other.

Let's continue with the example of Adele and her apple-growing business. But we need more details about her entrepreneurship experience to make the logic clear. When Adele's apple trees bear fruit, the seeds have already been in the ground for three years. During these years, Adele has worked on pruning and watering and otherwise tending to the trees in order to make sure they bear as much and as tasty fruit as possible. And before this time, she needed to clear the land and she also readied it for the seeds that she then planted. So let's say she's been working on this for a total of exactly four years, which makes a round and easy number to work with, when she finally gets to pick those ripe, beautiful apples from the trees. Three of those years consisted of waiting for nature to have its course as well as to tend to the orchard, including use of fertilizers and water to make sure the trees developed in the best way possible. Most of the hard labor was invested during the year prior to the tending, however, after Adele planned her undertaking. When she knew what she needed to do, she got to work clearing a piece of land from the wild bushes and trees already growing there, putting in an irrigation system, adding fertilizer, and so on. Then she planted the seeds and kept watering and pruning and otherwise making sure to ready the orchard for picking the apples when ripe. After four years, she's ready to sell the apples to Adam and the others.

All Adam sees, of course, is the apples offered for sale. He neither knows about nor needs to know about the process and all the toil and trouble that

Adele has gone through to be able to offer the apples for sale. He might not even care, for all we know. But he cares about apples, and that's all that really matters—to him, to Adele, to the economy, and therefore to us. So we can see, then, the truth of how the means of production are valued in an economy: they are valuable only because they contribute to producing something that is directly valued by the consumer who consumes it. If they do not, they have no value.

In our example, as there is a market for apples, there are several valuable inputs. Economists traditionally categorize them as land, labor, and capital, but another important category that also contributes to production is time.[4] Our example makes it clear that time—the waiting for the trees to mature and bear fruit—plays an important role. Whether or not we rely on "nature" to take part in the production process, production always takes time and as we cannot use unlimited time to produce what we later hope to sell. It is a scarce resource that we must use efficiently—that is we must *economize* on time spent in our production projects. In fact, time makes a huge difference in terms of opportunity cost: if production was instantaneous, we would only need to consider the different possible uses for resources. But as production extends through significant periods of time, and during this time requires that a certain subset of productive resources is committed to the specific production process, the calculation of opportunity costs is much more difficult. So when Adele chose to clear the land to begin her multi-year production process of apples, she must have estimated the time it would take to complete the process—and then compared the total cost, including the time element, with other possible alternatives of different temporal length. This is of course very difficult, which means Adele is better off the more she can rely on market prices rather than her own work. In other words, the more she can rely on purchasing, rather than producing by herself, the needed seeds, shovels, fertilizers, irrigation systems, and water from other producers in the open market, at anticipated market prices, the easier it is to appraise the value of her apple-growing project—total proceeds compared to her total expenditures, that is, the net value—and compare its profitability to other projects. Again, we see the value of having a money as the universally accepted medium of exchange and unit of account; it simplifies things a great deal for entrepreneurs, both by providing a common denominator for economic calculation and by facilitating trade, thereby making it easier to distribute the tasks that comprise production processes onto multiple separate entrepreneurs.

For Adele's entrepreneurial undertaking we have several inputs used in each of the categories already mentioned: the land (which includes any natural processes such as the growing of planted apple trees), her labor at different stages of the production process (to clear the land, plant the seeds, tend to the orchard, and pick the apples), capital to assist in production (the seeds, fertilizer, water, etc. that she purchases from others and that are therefore made available through other entrepreneurs' production processes), and time (the four years it takes to complete the process). All of these categories have distinct market valuations: there is a market value of land, which depends on its quality and therefore usability for production; of labor, which depends on how it could otherwise be used productively; of capital, which is the price Adele pays; and of time, which is noticeable through the discount rate we must use to compare expenditures in the present with revenues in the future. The discount rate is the valuation of time—or, more accurately, of *waiting*— according to Adele's subjective *time preference*; it is the difference in valuation that Adele would attribute to receiving a certain good now or the exact same good at a later time. Time preference is important in any individual's comparison of values in a temporal world (that is, a world as time-dependent world as the one we live in) and is aggregated into the social cost of waiting through the market's natural interest rate. It is therefore part of all other valuations, since we are all temporal beings.

We'll begin by explaining the prices that Adele pays for the inputs she uses in the process. Of those, we'll first discuss capital or the "produced means of production," i.e., the seeds, fertilizer, irrigation system, and water that she buys in the market. This discussion will shed light also on the valuation of land and labor. In order to procure inputs such as apple seeds in the market, how does Adele figure out how much she can pay without incurring a loss? The answer is that she must begin by estimating how much she will be able to charge for the apples and how many apples she will be able to sell at that price. From this anticipated income, she can then subtract estimates of the expenses she will have for each input, including her own labor. This, of course, includes considering alternative inputs and their effects on the quantity and quality of the produced apples, which could mean she might have to reassess her anticipated sales. If her calculations for the chosen production process end up in the black (that is, a profit), she can decide whether she thinks the whole thing is "worth it" based on the time difference between the present and the time when she completes producing and selling, and compared to alternative uses of her time. In other words, Adele calculates—even if it is only roughly and far from exact—the present value of the four-year enterprise and compares this with the present value of alternative uses of those four years. Her calculation may not be explicit. For instance, she probably doesn't have a discount rate in mind to calculate an exact present value, but she nevertheless considers whether the future income is "worth" the trouble, including the necessary investments and waiting and uncertainty involved. Theoretically, we can understand her subjective valuation as involving a discount rate, and her decision is in fact based on one— but this doesn't mean that she has an exact figure in mind. The same is probably true for most consumers, who don't have a price in mind when entering a store, but react to the prices on the price tags as "too expensive" or "worth it" (or even "a bargain!"). Many of the valuations we do on a regular basis are implicit in this way—and Adele's discount rate, her valuation of time, may also be this way.

Having decided that she will pursue the career of apple-growing, she already has an idea of how much she can spend on inputs without suffering a loss. It doesn't really matter to her whether she spends 99 percent on apple seeds and 1 percent on everything else—or vice versa. She wants to minimize her expenditures and keep the total cost below the money amount she believes is her breakeven point (where the revenue covers all her costs, but offers no profit). The lower the costs she has to cover, the lesser her subjective cost of uncertainty since the chances of profit would appear greater. There is more wiggle room if she can keep outlays that happen in the present—the investment, whether in monies or labor—lower, and therefore a profitable outcome appears more attainable. In every decision, she adds to her entrepreneurial calculus to estimate the outcome and whether the undertaking is still "worth it." In other words, she could bid for resources and pay for them as long as she doesn't exceed what she deems is the max she will be able to afford without losing value through the process. She and other budding apple-growers therefore, to borrow a phrase from twentieth-century economist Ludwig von Mises, "appear as bidders at an auction, as it were, in which the owners of the factors of production put up for sale land, capital goods, and labor."[5] Whether the process actually looks like an auction or not is beside the point: the fact is that these entrepreneurs compete to buy the apple seeds in the same way that consumers will bid to buy the picked apples. In the same sense, sellers of apple seeds compete to sell those seeds by offering them at low prices. Most trades will take place somewhere in-between the high- and low-price extremes. The result is a market price for apple seeds.

There is a major difference between the determination of prices for the factors of production and consumer goods, however, and it has to do with timing. Consumers bid for and therefore help determine prices of products they can consume in the present, and producers likewise bid for consumers' money expecting to cover their already incurred costs or satisfy other wants in the present. But means of production have value only because they will contribute to producing a value arising *in the future*. So whereas consumers in some sense speculate due to their having incomplete knowledge about both their own wants and the product's ability to satisfy those wants, entrepreneurs bid because they expect the capital good (a produced means of production) to contribute to an undertaking that they anticipate will realize value for consumers and therefore generate revenue at a future time. In other words, entrepreneurs do not bid for inputs based on their own value but based on the anticipation of how it contributes to the salability of the *final* good. It is thus based on the entrepreneur's judgment of the future market situation in which the final good will compete with others to satisfy consumer wants. More specifically, entrepreneurs place their bids based on their estimates of what price the final good can be sold for to consumers.

The prices of the means of production are therefore future prices, whereas prices of consumer goods are present prices. The former are pure speculation based on the entrepreneurs' judgment of the market and their belief that their undertaking will earn a profit. This doesn't mean that factor prices are random or arbitrary, only that they are based on anticipations of what will (that is, what *could*) happen. As entrepreneurs risk their own money they have a very strong incentive to be careful rather than haphazard, and because only those entrepreneurs who are better at anticipating what consumers (will) really value will earn a profit—remember, those entrepreneurs who fail won't get a second chance since they will have lost their investment—these should be close to our best possible guesses. It doesn't mean entrepreneurs are superheroes with insights that others don't have, only that investments aren't made at random. Investments are made exclusively when an entrepreneur is convinced that there is very good reason to believe they'll turn out profitable. Over time, those entrepreneurs with inferior judgment will tend to get weeded out since they lose their capital and those who are better earn profits and thus get more capital for future investments.

The price of a means of production therefore comes to reflect the guesses of entrepreneurs competing to satisfy consumer wants. Note that there are entrepreneurs at both ends of each exchange: entrepreneurs who sell the factor and entrepreneurs who buy the factor. The former won't sell at prices that are much lower than what they estimate that they will be, which means they will not go down so much in price that they would—based on their own judgment—be better off waiting and selling at a later point. How much resources they invested in producing the factor is not properly part of this calculation—this cost is sunk and the investment is therefore lost no matter what happens thereafter. The only thing that matters is whether the entrepreneurs will be able to sell their product (the factor) at the best possible price they can get. It is all about their anticipation, in other words, not what their expenses were: either they anticipate the price that they can sell it for will go up, which means they are unwilling to go down in price to sell now, or they think it will go down, which makes them more willing to accept a lower price.

The buying entrepreneurs equally depend on their anticipation of the price of the factor, since they might prefer waiting if they expect the price to fall. They will also be more eager to buy in the present if they expect prices to go up. And their bids ultimately depend on how much they anticipate that they can charge for the final good. For Adele, therefore, this means she will make bids for buying apple seeds based both on how much she thinks she can make from selling the apples, adjusted for her other costs and her required rate of profit, as well as whether she thinks the price of apple seeds will rise or fall at a sufficient rate that she would prefer waiting (or increase her bid in the present).

As the prices are set by apple growers like Adele, on the one hand, and apple seed producers, on the other, all of whom are entrepreneurs, the final market price signals how entrepreneurs collectively value apple seeds— which is based on their joint anticipation of what consumers will value. The price therefore embodies the knowledge and judgments of all the entrepreneurs, revealed through their bids placed for specific means of production. This price, determined through such entrepreneurial bidding, is what we can refer to as a combined "market valuation." It is a collective effort that represents the social value of apple seeds. Or, to say the same thing in layman's terms, the market price is our best collective estimate of what apple seeds "are worth."

CHOOSING YOUR COSTS

Another aspect of the pricing of the means of production is what choices entrepreneurs make with respect to choosing between different means and methods of production—and different production undertakings. This is something that is often overlooked in discussions about production and the pricing of capital, but that is of fundamental importance to understand the dynamic within which entrepreneurs act and how they make choices. In short, entrepreneurs don't price their products—they choose their costs.

We have already seen that the price of the ultimate good, which is made available for direct consumption (in our example, the apples), is priced by "the market" in the sense that consumer valuations decide what they're willing to pay. This price that consumers pay is relative to other goods and services made available to them, so it reflects society's overall relative value realized through the production of apples. As we indicated above, if consumers think pears are tastier and therefore a more effective way of satisfying their wants, then they will shift their "demand" toward buying pears. Pears may cost more per item in money terms, but they will be relatively cheaper because they provide greater value (satisfaction when consumed). All an entrepreneur-producer of apples can do about the market price of apples is to make them available at a price that makes consumers prefer apples to pears, oranges, other fruits as well as other types of goods and services that promise to satisfy their wants in relatively better ways—as well as their valuation of money as a means to acquire goods and services in the future. So whereas entrepreneurs like Adele can have a reservation price of the consumer good, which means she believes she could get a higher price if she waits, still implies that entrepreneurs are subject to consumers' whims. Entrepreneurs are servants of consumers and make money by satisfying whatever wants consumers have.

Entrepreneurs do not actually set the price of what they produce, other than perhaps having a reservation price. Their reservation price is the minimum they're willing to accept as payment in the present for the simple reason that they expect they'll get at least this price in the future—and that it is therefore worth more to wait rather than sell.[6] Without being able to set the selling price, which is a function of consumers' subjective valuations of the good, entrepreneurs choose whether they want to go into a certain line of business and how to produce those goods. In other words, *they choose their costs*. This sounds backwards, but it is part of what entrepreneurs must do in order to run a business profitably. And this is where the future-oriented market prices of the means of production are so important.

Let's again use Adele's entrepreneurial undertaking to illustrate this. Her decision to go into apple-growing is based on her calculation that it will allow her to earn enough money to lead a comfortable life. She estimates the prices she could get from selling apples and the number of apples she could offer and on the market—and when. The price that can be charged depends on the value her apples offer for consumers and she estimates the number of apples she'll need to produce and sell in order to make the whole orchard business worth it. The production quantity necessary of course depends on how costly a production process she chooses. For instance, she could hire a dozen workers to plant and tend to the trees from day one, and thereby produce thousands of apples that will be ready for the market as soon as is physically possible (which, as we know, is about four years). Or she could do it all herself and produce much fewer apples but at lower initial cost (she doesn't have to pay any wages, so there is less of an initial investment). Or she could rent or buy machinery, for instance get a couple of diesel-powered excavators instead of the dozen manual laborers with shovels and rakes. Or she could get only one excavator instead of perhaps four or five laborers and still employ a few workers with shovels and rakes to complement the excavator. The number of possible alternatives for how to produce the apples is limited only by her imagination of how she can do it—there could be hundreds or thousands of ways to produce apples, which affect the per-item cost as well as the quantity produced.

So for Adele to figure out whether the orchard is profitable requires that she consider the alternatives that to her seem like reasonable ways of producing apples. The only way of doing this is to first estimate the price consumers will be willing to pay for the apples, and then estimate the different cost structures that follow from different production processes (the combinations of machinery and labor and so on). Estimating the cost of the different alternatives Adele faces in apple production would be impossible if she couldn't rely on the market prices established by entrepreneurs bidding for all the resources available. As each resource can be used for different things—think of the many uses of labor, for instance, or the many different types of production that could find use for excavators—the value can only be estimated considering the contribution in each use to consumer wants satisfaction. This is why entrepreneurial bidding for the means of production is so fundamentally important in a market economy. Without such bidding, there would be no prices—and therefore it would be impossible for Adele to figure out the "best" use of productive resources. She might know apple-growing well, but without real market prices of the means of production she would only be able to figure out how many apples she would get out of each production alternative. So her economic calculus would be limited to how much work it is for her in each production alternative and how many apples she might get in the end. She wouldn't be able to figure out the best way of using machinery, using labor, or structuring the production process. So she would likely end up with a process that is relatively inefficient—because it isn't guided by market prices that represent the social estimates of the value of the respective means of production. But with market prices, which reflect society's total knowledge of the relative value of the different uses of the means of production, she can take those prices as given and thereby rather easily figure out what is the socially efficient way of producing apples—that is one that generates a profit because the cost of producing is much lower than the value created. This, in turn, provides some insight into how many apples she *should* produce in order for the economy to satisfy as many and highly valued consumer wants as possible. To put this differently, with market prices for the means of production Adele can figure out the most efficient way of producing them—and then maximize the outcome of her use of resources.

Adele, with access to established market prices for the means of production as well as an estimate of what price of apples the market will bear (that is, what consumers will be willing and able to pay), can make an *informed* decision with respect to how to best produce those apples. She can calculate the cost of each different type of production process because she can compare prices of her inputs. She can easily find out what excavators trade for in the market, the cost of labor, the cost of diesel, shovels, rakes, and so on. The prices are readily available because she and other entrepreneurs are involved in bidding (that is buying and selling) for these resources, which then assume prices based on everybody's best guesses of how much they will contribute to the price of the final good—thus, the value offered to consumers. In other words, Adele's situation as an entrepreneur is made a lot easier when there is a market with prices because she can engage in *economic calculation* with respect to different types of production.[7] She'll still bear the uncertainty of her endeavor, but she's assisted in figuring out what's the most efficient use of land, labor, and capital by the prices that she and other entrepreneurs determine through bidding. And she's also assisted in her personal evaluation of time, since entrepreneurs' collective time preference is necessarily incorporated in the determined market prices of the means of production: entrepreneurs of course bid for resources keeping their respective cost of waiting in mind (it is simply not "worth it" to wait too long for too little return). Other entrepreneurs' time preferences therefore play into Adele's decision-making by affecting her calculus. If Adele's personal time preference makes her waiting very costly, she'll have a harder time getting the necessary resources at prices that would make her undertaking "worth it." Similarly, if she doesn't mind waiting at all then the resources will be comparatively cheaper and then she has more options that will still seem to offer a sufficient rate of return. As this applies for all entrepreneurs when they bid for resources, the time component is always incorporated into the prices: the bidding process finds a "golden middle"—the social rate of time preference—for how to most efficiently use society's productive resources and how long to wait for the final goods to be made available.

Adele can therefore, if she decides to go ahead with planting the orchard, choose her costs for apple-growing just like she would choose between apple-growing and other types of production. She can do this only because prices of the final goods are set by consumers—whether or not they are known or just anticipated—and the prices of inputs used in the production process are determined by entrepreneurs collectively. So the only thing that is actually variable in her entrepreneurial undertaking, and therefore the only thing that she can really choose, is, first, whether to produce apples at all, and, second, the cost structure to use in production. In other words, *she chooses her cost*, as do all other entrepreneurs, based on the price she anticipates consumers will pay.

Whereas the ultimate guidance of production is the value consumers see in the final good, and therefore sets the boundaries of what types of production are possible, the cost of production *facilitates* this final price. Indeed, the only reason a consumer want is satisfied through market production is because the final good can be sold (that is, entrepreneurs anticipate it to be salable) at a certain price—or at least within an estimated price range—and that entrepreneurs are able to choose a process for producing this value that incurs lower cost per item than the final price. The price, in this sense, suggests the costs entrepreneurs should be willing to assume in production, which means there is a cost aspect to price—but only indirectly. Both the production cost and the final selling price therefore influence entrepreneurs' production choices and therefore their bidding for the means of production that determines their respective market prices.

What we have now said about prices is that they carry as well as aggregate information about the state of the world and its expected future. Indeed, if prices of apple seeds go up it is because each seed is considered relatively more valuable than before. The reason for this could be an expected rise in future sales due to an anticipated increase in consumer demand. When entrepreneurs anticipate that they will be able to sell more apples or at higher prices, more entrepreneurs will consider becoming apple growers and therefore bid up the prices of inputs used in growing apples. The reason could also be that something has happened further "up" in the chain that makes apple seeds harder to come by. Perhaps there has been a severe infestation of orchards used specifically for seed production so that there are not as many seeds available. With fewer seeds for sale, the sellers will receive higher prices as the buyers bid them up. This will lead to higher profits per seed among seed producers, which in turn attracts more entrepreneurs (and this increases future supply, which forces prices down again), and lower profits among apple growers. This leads entrepreneurs to leave this trade (it is not sufficiently profitable, so they will choose to grow other things—or not grow at all). Production overall can thereby be continuously adjusted to make the best possible use of each resource based on the information revealed through changes in the relative prices of resources. [8]

Prices consequently reveal what entrepreneurs as a group anticipate the future will bring with respect to a specific good. Entrepreneurs can of course be wrong in their anticipations, and many of them are, but this is of little consequence as what matters in price determination is not cheap talk but what is revealed through their *actions*. In other words, entrepreneurs literally bet their money that they are right so there is no reason to think they don't do their utmost to avoid mistakes and errors; they are, after all, the ones who suffer if they are wrong. Consequently, their actions speak louder than words. Indeed, their actions are likely to be more accurate than their expressed opinions. And where they're wrong, they will quickly redirect their efforts to again occupy profit-generating positions—or stop production altogether before it is too late and all capital is lost. So they take much care to get the initial investment right but then also constantly reassess their choice to avoid losses.

THE INVISIBLE HAND IN PRODUCTION

Okay, so we now know that prices reveal information. Prices of consumer goods reveal consumers' real valuation of the goods bought and not bought in the present: if they're not bought, their value is zero or at least lower than the sellers are willing to go (i.e., lower than the sellers' reservation price, which means the sellers anticipate they may get higher prices elsewhere or at a later time). When such prices go up, they reveal that entrepreneurs have made a mistake by producing fewer goods than they should have; when prices go down, they reveal that entrepreneurs have made the obverse mistake: they have produced too many. "Too many" and "too few" aren't objective magnitudes, but an indication of production value relative to other goods produced. So if prices paid for apples go up relative to pears, it simply means that entrepreneurs as a group have produced too many pears relative to apples—that is, too few apples relative to pears. They *should have*, in order to maximize value for everyone, produced more apples.

Changes in consumer prices also signal to entrepreneurs what to do. If prices of apples rapidly go up, it is an indication that there are way too few apples produced in the economy. For an entrepreneur, this means that there is an opportunity to earn profits by entering the business of apple growing, but only if the entrepreneur sees the change in prices and anticipates that this will continue. It could also be something ephemeral or a fluke. If entrepreneurs believe prices reveal a real shortage rather than a temporary mismatch between supply and demand, then we will likely see some of them change their line of business. In this case, with increasing apple prices, they will go into apple growing because that is what the prices say they should do.

Prices of the means of production, in contrast, reveal what entrepreneurs anticipate will be valued by consumers in the future. They could be a result of changing consumer prices, but this is not always the case. In the example above, for instance, if consumer prices for apples rapidly increase then Adele will make a much larger profit than she expected. This means she can use this additional income to go on vacation, but more likely—if she expects the higher prices to last—is that she will use this additional money to expand her business to increase the output and thereby make more money. What this means in real terms is that she will buy more apple seeds and fertilizer, she might buy more land to expand her orchards and hire more people to work for her. By demanding more of these specific means of production traded in the market by entrepreneurs, she bids up their prices. If she is large enough a player in the market or if there are more like her doing the same thing, then this will have a noticeable effect on the market prices for apple seeds, fertilizer, land, and labor—and this will attract other entrepreneurs to produce apple seeds and fertilizer. It will also incentivize entrepreneurs to use other means of production, which due to the price changes will appear as more cost effective. So when the prices are bid up, some entrepreneurs will consider working to increase the supply (and thereby satisfy the increased demand) whereas others will choose different means of production (and thereby lessen the demand).

For land and labor, neither of which can be produced (so supply cannot be increased by production of new land or new labor), their higher prices mean other uses will become relatively more expensive—some such uses will no longer be profitable even though they used to be. This causes resources to shift from their current uses that are made relatively unprofitable to producing the more profitable factors that Adele and her competitors use when growing apples. In other words, the change in what entrepreneurs anticipate consumers demanding will bring about a change throughout the economy's production apparatus; a single change causes ripple effects in production just like the waves around a stone thrown into a pond.

From the point of view of the economy, therefore, we would see a shift of resources from their previous uses toward producing the means necessary for growing apples. Note that this shift is not really about the higher prices offered for apples, the final product, but the anticipation that this higher price will continue for some time—and this anticipation justifies the investment in new or increased production capacity by expanding existing orchards or establishing new ones. The changing prices of the means of production are therefore still purely speculative and based on entrepreneurial anticipations of what will be. The real implication is that entrepreneurs overall now anticipate to better satisfy consumers by growing apples than they previously did. So laborers involved in growing pears and oranges may find that employment on apple orchards to help with growing apples pays them better. Likewise, more land will be made available for planting apple trees than was previously the case. Land cannot be produced, of course, but the land that was used for other things will now seem more profitable if used for apple-growing—because the market price for land used for growing apples is higher. Exactly what the land was used for before, whether it was for growing pears or farming or grazing cattle or parking cars or simply being idle—is of little importance. What we know is that other uses for land, after the price increase for land due to more entrepreneurs bidding for land to plant apple trees that are now relatively less profitable will diminish whereas apple-growing will increase. This is a result of individual entrepreneurs responding to the incentive of higher profits—indicated by the price signal, but based on their anticipation that prices will remain higher than previously.

In this way, despite each decision being made by an individual entrepreneur, the overall usage of resources in a market economy continuously shifts away from the relatively less profitable toward the relatively more profitable. And resources tied up in production of goods that turn out to not have sufficient demand will soon be released as those entrepreneurs realize their mistakes and either move into other types of production or go out of business. At the same time, new types of production that entrepreneurs anticipate will earn higher profits relative to other lines of production will attract resources and will therefore be able to satisfy more consumers. The market, in aggregate, therefore responds to anticipated consumer demand by shifting scarce resources toward the uses where they are believed to be of greater value. Entrepreneurs make these decisions in light of the existing prices, and by changing their buying and selling they, at the same time, influence those very prices. For this reason, prices tend to represent entrepreneurs' joint anticipation of what the future holds. Prices are determined by entrepreneurial bidding and at the same time are used by entrepreneurs when assessing their options. While it might seem like a circular argument, it is not: Adele considers the already determined market prices (and how she anticipates that they will change) for inputs necessary for apple-growing before she decides to go through the trouble of establishing her orchard (or, if it seems cheaper, buy an existing orchard from someone else); only thereafter will she bid for those resources and change their prices. A nascent entrepreneur takes existing prices as they are in his or her initial profitability calculus, and then—when already having decided whether to start the business and how—joins the other entrepreneurs in determining changes to those prices by bidding and not bidding for resources, respectively.

The price system, that is the combined entrepreneurial bidding for resources to use in production and therefore the continuous determination of factor prices, is what Adam Smith referred to as the "invisible hand" that directs production in a market economy. This "hand" consists of the prices that are determined by the constant shifting of resources from one line of production to another—which in turn directs production. A market economy, in other words, is *endogenous* in the sense that its production apparatus overall is automatically adjusted toward satisfying as many wants as possible for the simple reason that people act in their own interest, that is to better serve themselves—this is done through serving others, which generates a profit, and consequently provides the means for greater want satisfaction. Production is undertaken for the purpose of consumption.

It is important to understand that production is continuously adjusted to better meet consumer demand—that is, to satisfy consumer wants. This is the case both *within* production processes, as entrepreneurs adjust their production to new and revealed prices and consumer behavior, and *between* production processes in the market. These are two forms of the same thing: changing production towards better serving consumers, which generates profits. This overall adjustment to production happens without anyone being in charge, and we can now understand how this is possible and why this occurs. We can also understand why Smith referred to this mechanism as "invisible," because while prices are visible the aggregate shift from one production line to another is not: there are no orders issued, no directives made, and no one who makes the final call. Instead, the mechanism is the aggregate phenomenon arising from decentralized, individual decision-making; it consists of the choices of myriad entrepreneurs who are trying to align their efforts with the best possible anticipation of where there will be consumer wants that remain unsatisfied. In other words, they seek opportunities for producing where they will earn profits. So they do indeed, as Adam Smith noted, work in their own self-interest—but by doing this in a market setting, and therefore bidding for productive resources in competition with other entrepreneurs, it is in their interest to serve consumers by offering what is valued by the consumers themselves. And for this reason, markets tend to perform very well as measured by consumer want satisfaction or growth because markets reward finding valuable uses for scarce resources. They also punish those who commit resources to less valuable uses. In short, entrepreneurs earn profits or suffer losses based on how well their actions satisfy real consumer wants. And through their productive efforts they generate the prices that guide other entrepreneurs. In other words, the unhampered market aligns incentives in such a way that it is in the individual's interest to serve the interests of society, which empowers the individual to seek ways of providing even greater want satisfaction.

We've looked specifically at production, which is core to any economy because production simply refers to how society's scarce resources are used. But it is important to remember that while entrepreneurs create and respond to the prices they themselves create, the purpose of production is to facilitate consumption. It is only through consumption that the true value of production is revealed, and with it what entrepreneurs were better than others—and what entrepreneurs were simply wrong. Entrepreneurs in the last category will not be able to participate as entrepreneurs in future production, since they will have lost their invested capital. Whereas the promise of profit is kept in check by the threat of loss, the constant succeeding and failing entrepreneurs competing with each other for the sake of profit taken together amounts to a discovery procedure: by finding better ways of producing, which increases the chance of profit, better ways of satisfying consumers—and therefore the needs and wants of "common people"—are found and tried.[9] The market is therefore best understood as an open-ended, undirected process rather than a system or "machine." What matters is that it serves people by satisfying their wants, and ideally the market should tend to do so increasingly. But this doesn't mean that the market is efficient in any objective sense, which is an issue we will discuss in greater detail in the next chapter.

NOTES

1. This is Say's Law as referred to in chapter 1. For a more elaborate discussion on the meaning and use of Say's Law, see, e.g., Kates (1998).
2. Kirzner, 1973.
3. Menger, 2007, p. 63–67.
4. Rothbard, 2004, p. 13–17.
5. Mises, 1998, p. 332.
6. An entrepreneur's reservation price can have other bases than economic calculation, such as psychological or emotional, but even though those aspects are not purely economic they still play into the entrepreneur's subjective valuation—and therefore their subjective value calculus. In other words, from a theoretical point of view it might seem as though the psychology or emotional aversion to a lower price is "irrational," but as we're dealing with subjective

valuations all things that matter to the individual also matter to our analysis. Whatever the person considers relevant in the valuation of a good or service—or its production process—*is* relevant. Our job is not to make judgments about whether their behavior is rational, but to explain their actions—and the economic implications thereof.

7. This argument about economic calculation and market prices was developed in an essay by Ludwig von Mises, which instigated the so-called Socialist Calculation Debate. See Mises (1935).

8. Hayek, 1945.

9. Hayek, 1978.

Chapter Four

Unbeatable, Imperfect Markets

Production, as we saw in the previous chapters, is undertaken for two reasons and, as it turns out, with two very different implications. First, production can be undertaken with the intention of making possible immediate and personal consumption; it is, in essence, the means by which individuals manage to survive in a world that doesn't exist solely for their own benefit. Such production is akin to what the shipwrecked Robinson Crusoe, to borrow the main character from the 1719 novel by Daniel Defoe, would necessarily spend his time doing—it is focused on survival and living day to day. Without engaging in production, Crusoe would starve to death. To survive, though he leads a lonesome life, he will need to produce the foodstuffs necessary. Thus, he spends his time finding and picking berries, edible leaves, coconuts, and such things. He might attempt to fish or catch animals to eat. It is likely that he will spend most of his time trying to find enough food to survive; he leads a very poor life, especially when considered from the perspective of the modern world. Crusoe's existence is hand-to-mouth and it is unlikely that he will be able to save or find time for leisure. Nevertheless, his best option is to keep producing.

Even if we add other people to this situation, such as the equally fictional Friday, this doesn't change the situation much with respect to production. Whereas some tasks are easier for two people than for one (such as moving timber or large rocks, hunting prey, picking berries, and so on) simply because it includes more man power, the *types* of production they can undertake together is also more plentiful than what Crusoe can do alone. For instance, two people can do things that one person simply cannot. Crusoe and Friday may furthermore feel more secure together and are probably better off by cooperating in other ways than simply doubling the man power when carrying out the same tasks as Crusoe spent his time doing alone. For instance, they can divide tasks between themselves, which would allow them to focus on their respective responsibilities, develop specific skills that help them carry out those tasks, and perhaps even make simple tools to assist them. Such simple division of labor increases their chances of survival and might even award them some leisure time.

They nevertheless lead a life that is similar, at least in terms of production and material comfort, to that of the nomadic people living in the historic Stone Age. Even if Crusoe and Friday are joined by several other people, they would still produce to satisfy their own need for consumption—they would produce in order to survive even if they now would tend to produce different things (so some hunt, others fish, yet others collect nuts and berries, and so on). Through living in and producing for their community, they would collectively be able to produce a surplus and thus reach a greater level of comfort and prosperity, which might be well beyond what is required for survival. So they're probably not starving, but may even find time for a little leisure. Yet whereas producing in a small group for the group's own benefit, with joint ownership (if any) and communal sharing of what is produced, makes for a richer and more plentiful life than that of the lone, autonomous "noble savage," it is not a scalable model of production as it is still intended for direct consumption and therefore sustenance for the group.

The larger the group gets, and therefore the more manpower it has, the greater the problem of figuring out who does what and, consequently, what's a fair and just distribution of what's been produced. Imagine there is a group of well over a hundred people living together. Even if they are able to lead relatively comfortable lives—relative to Crusoe being alone, that is—due to the sheer manpower involved in finding sustenance, the problems of dividing the fruits of their combined labor would tend to increase in both number and magnitude. After a bad day or week, who decides who gets to eat and who doesn't? There are collective action problems involved in larger groups, which give rise to frictions and problems such as free-riding.[1] This, in turn, provides the group with an incentive for centralizing decision-making or finding ways of overriding the individual will (such as majority rule through voting), and with collective decision-making comes bureaucracy for control and management—in other words: politics.

There may be ways for groups to overcome such issues through forming institutions and a culture that sets limits to what is morally and ethically permissible. An obvious "solution" to the large-group problems of collective decision-making is to simply not allow the group to grow too large. However the group manages to handle these issues, the second type of production—intended for *indirect* consumption—offers a solution. As we will see, scalable production is attainable through specialization and division of labor, which in turn is facilitated by markets.

The relevant production for our purposes is market-based in the sense discussed in previous chapters, in which production primarily aims to satisfy one's own wants *in*directly. This separation of production and consumption, with respect to what the individual him- or herself consumes, has positive effects on production in the economy. First, it makes it possible to invest one's time and effort where it is most useful or produces the most output rather than where one has wants that need to be satisfied. Where Robinson Crusoe needed to pick, collect or catch all the food he needed to eat, market-based production can make available a wide variety of foods even to those who aren't involved in its production. What this means is that you can work full time on engineering or in an automobile factory, neither of which may have much to do with food production, yet still have access to plenty of foods. Second, the separation of production and consumption brings about a greater variety and increased appeal of goods produced and offered for consumption because what drives their salability is the ability to satisfy remaining wants (that is, *unsatisfied* wants, either because existing production quantity is insufficient to satisfy existing wants or because those wants have not yet been discovered) as well as their attractiveness in the eyes of consumers, both of which are incentives for product differentiation. But most importantly, the separation of production and consumption leads to social cooperation through markets. Such cooperation is much less prone to have the problems that we saw could arise in groups producing for their own consumption, because it develops and evolves through bottom-up emergence. It is also a much more scalable model that allows for more economic production and, consequently, affluence.

PRODUCTION: SMITH, RICARDO, AND SCHUMPETER

We saw examples of producing for indirect consumption in the previous chapters, where each of our friends focused on producing a single good that they didn't intend primarily for their own consumption (such as Adele and her apple orchard). In comparison to the self-sustaining production of Robinson Crusoe or the communes discussed above, each person's labor is released from the necessity to produce to satisfy their immediate need for consumption. For instance, had Crusoe had access to a market on the island where he was stranded he could simply have focused on producing any one good that he believed would be salable in that market in order to then use the proceeds to acquire what he needs or wants to consume from other sellers. In other words, in such a situation he can rely on both his observation of what people reveal as highly demanded in that market (that is, what they're currently buying at relatively high prices), his understanding of what people will find valuable (that is, goods or services he thinks will better serve consumers), and his own abilities (that is, what he's good at producing). And based on these things, and anything else that he considers relevant, he can choose to focus his efforts on the production of one or a couple specific goods. This means major savings in effort and time used in production for Crusoe as well as for everybody else producing for this market.

Another way of expressing this is to say that actors in a market benefit individually and collectively from specializing. The Scottish "father" of economics Adam Smith noted in his eighteenth century magnum opus *Wealth of Nations* that specializing through the division of labor, that is by concentrating on a specific trade or specific tasks within a production process, offers three primary benefits: it saves time because each worker no longer needs to switch between different tasks, workers develop expertise by repetition which further increases their productivity, and it allows for automation through the development of capital because single tasks tend to be much simpler than the whole production chain.[2] It is easy to see, even intuitively, that Smith was justified in making this conclusion; specializing through the division of labor produces an absolute advantage in production. Modern studies confirm that so-called multi-tasking can have detrimental effects on productivity and effectiveness[3]; we easily understand that "practice makes perfect" and have personal experience that would appear to confirm that this is so; and, finally, the great use of tools, machinery, and robotics in our modern production economy speaks clearly to the productive power of automation.

Add to this situation of specialization the great lesson of *comparative* advantage offered by the British nineteenth century economist David Ricardo.[4] While Ricardo's lesson is often taught and explained as a "two countries, two goods" mathematical exercise, it is a fundamentally important insight that doesn't actually require math. The essence of the lesson is that specializing in production and then trading for access to the diverse goods produced by everybody else makes each actor and therefore society overall more productive and thus better off. The real takeaway from the comparative advantage doctrine is that even where some producers are inferior in every line of production, it is disastrous to shut them out. Indeed, total production increases if they too specialize in producing what they're relatively better at—even if others are more productive in absolute terms. So even if it is the case that some productive people are extremely productive in everything they do, they and society overall are better off—in terms of production, at least— if they specialize in producing where they are relatively better and then let those with overall and thus absolute inferior productivity complement society's production by specializing in what they're relatively better at. Where this happens, society uses its resources to the highest degree possible—and we therefore get the greatest possible value out of people's combined efforts.

The absolute and comparative advantages through specialization that Smith and Ricardo teach us don't reveal the whole picture, however. They don't include the great advancements possible through innovation. While Smith indeed mentions automation as one of the three reasons for the productive powers of specialization through the division of labor, productive innovations are not limited to automating already existing tasks by developing simple machinery to replace manual labor. As twentieth century Austrian economist Joseph Schumpeter famously argued, innovations in the form of what he called "new combinations" can take five different forms: new goods (or new quality of goods); new methods of production; opening of new markets; new sources of inputs; and new types of organization.[5]

Smith's automation through machinery is a subcategory of Schumpeter's second form of new combination: new methods of production. But new methods of production refers to much more than simply developing tools and machines; it also includes different types of processes, which may include completely different tasks and different ways of doing things. Also, Schumpeter's fifth and final point about organization is an important observation that has turned out to be almost prophetic. By organization, Schumpeter means the organization of an industry rather than a single business. In other words, he's talking about how the production apparatus changes over time, a process that he described as "creative destruction"—that is, a "process of industrial mutation . . . that incessantly revolutionizes the economic structure *from within*, incessantly destroying the old one, incessantly creating a new one."[6] What he suggests is that production evolves as new and better ways of producing are introduced into the market and ultimately replace the older and, from the point of view of consumers, less efficient forms. This includes business firms coming and going, entrepreneurs disrupting the market, and with these "revolutionizing" events come changes to the very structure and extent of the market.[7]

Nonetheless, both Smith and Ricardo's examples point to exchange through trade as a necessary facilitator of specialized production and, consequently, the increased satisfaction of consumer wants. Similarly, Schumpeter notes that the reason innovation can disrupt production in markets is not the innovation itself but what it reveals about possibilities in production. Following a successful innovation, competitive pressures compel existing market producers and nascent entrepreneurs to adopt the better method or suffer losses. In other words, voluntary trade, as we discussed cursorily above, is core to understanding market production—including the productive powers of and social cooperation through decentralized, market-based decision-making. It is also core to this book's exploration into the real effects of regulation. Indeed, the lessons from Smith, Ricardo, and Schumpeter each offer insights into how we can (and should) extend our market example in chapter 3 to produce a model of advanced production in a more highly specialized market. We'll look at how their insights contribute to our understanding in the order presented above.

The previous chapter already makes use of the basic division of labor into different specialized employments alongside distinct trades. Indeed, we have each user specializing in a separate trade: Adele as apple-grower, Bart as baker, Becky as nail producer, and so on. We saw how this is more effective in production because each person gets to focus on a specific kind of production, which is exactly what Adam Smith suggested. We also found that the most effective way of serving one's own interests is by focusing production efforts on serving others. This, quoting Smith, brings about "a proportional increase of the productive powers of labour. The separation of different trades and employments from one another, seems to have taken place, in consequence of this advantage." According to Smith, the step from self-sufficiency, where each and every person or family produces what they consume, just like Robinson Crusoe above, to specialization to separate trades is due to the increase in productivity. This may very well be the case, for the three reasons Smith argued makes the division of labor more productive.

But we can also see that while employment in specialized trades like farmer, baker, and blacksmith makes sense and indeed increases productivity, a greater improvement in standard of living is made possible through trade rather than production for consumption in the immediate family or community. Perhaps this is the reason Smith, who suggested that the productivity increase due to specialization under the division of labor is "proportional," doesn't linger on specific trades but immediately moves into industrial production. He thereby goes directly from a situation where individuals or groups such as families and small communities produce for their own consumption to a specialized exchange economy with advanced production structures. Even though he calls his example, the pin factory, a "very trifling manufacture" the step from producing for direct consumption to producing for indirect consumption—where satisfaction of one's true wants is possible through voluntary exchange with other producers—is far from trivial. In fact, if we think logically about the step it appears to be something of a "catch 22." For who would begin producing something that only indirectly satisfies their own wants before there is a market in which to exchange goods? But, at the same time, why would there be a market if everybody produces for their own consumption? This seems like a paradox.

The paradox is probably exaggerated, however, for the simple reason that different families and communities likely have different interests, skills, access to resources, and so on. So there would be a natural variation in what they produce, and there would be both surpluses and shortages that are reasons to seek exchange. For instance, in a year with weather highly beneficial for cotton, the producers of cotton might produce much more than they can or want to use for clothing and other things, so they might seek to exchange their surplus cotton for other goods with families or communities who value the cotton. Some years or seasons—or perhaps due to luck—beaver hunters find and kill plenty of beavers, perhaps so many that they produce hides that they would be willing to use in exchange for other goods. And similar things can be said for other trades.

This means that there can still be markets and market places even though production is primarily undertaken for one's own, or one's family's, consumption. In other words, there is no catch 22 in how markets develop. Rather, the apparent paradox is due to thinking it is necessary for an individual to take the step from production for direct consumption to production for indirect consumption. This is not the case, and history shows that there were plenty of market places and even long-distance trade despite large parts of the population being self-sufficient.

Nevertheless, both the solution to the apparent paradox and the logical leap Smith takes from specialization into trades to a specialized exchange economy point to the importance if not necessity of exchange as a means to distribute the goods produced: specialized production in separate employments, where the goods produced are not only or primarily for one's own consumption, necessitates trade. This is what we saw above with Adele's orchard, which she invested in because she anticipated that it would be a good use of her time—in terms of her ability to satisfy her own needs as a result of first producing for and thus supplying the market with goods that "it" values. In other words, she recognized that the best way of serving herself was to serve others, and she imagined, if not anticipated, apple-growing to be one of if not the best opportunity for her to do so. Of course, as we also saw, there are many ways in which Adele can establish the orchard and run her apple-growing business. This is core to the Smithian lesson of productivity gained through the division of labor. To further illustrate this we'll consider another example that is very similar to the illustration preferred by Smith (the production of pins in a specialized "manufactory"): Becky's production of three-inch nails.

As with Smith's original illustration, Becky's business is also in many respects, as is the case for most of the examples in our simple, small-scale economy, a "very trifling manufacture." Indeed, as is suggested by the limited scope of our example, Becky is probably doing all the work herself, possibly with an apprentice or two, using simple tools for heating, shaping, and cutting the metal into three-inch nails. However, as Smith teaches us there are productivity gains to further specializing so that different people do different things in her nail-producing workshop: a further division of labor. With greater division of labor comes increased productivity per labor unit, and therefore more "bang for the buck." In other words, through a more intensive division of labor Becky could get more output per unit of input.

But this suggests important limitations to the possibility of increasing productivity. First, Becky would need to figure out if it is "worth it" in the same sense as Adele had to do in the example above: is it worth the additional investment, and thus the uncertainty of profitability, to take on a number of workers, invest in blast furnaces, and so on? This question hints at the problem of anticipated demand. Even if there were laborers available for Becky to employ, increased productivity per labor unit means little if there is not a sufficiently sized market that can demand the produced goods. In our little economy, this is an obvious limitation: after all, how many nails could she possibly sell to apple-grower Adele, baker Bart, and the others? She could probably sell a few. But how about hundreds of thousands? Probably not. The increased productivity, which really means there are increasing returns to investments in production, means there is less cost to each produced nail (that is, more nails are produced for each unit of input, whether input is labor, materials, or machinery). But lower cost *per nail* doesn't mean it makes sense to produce millions or billions or even trillions of nails. It only makes sense if there is a chance of actually selling those nails. So productivity through specialization under the division of labor is mitigated by the size of the actual market, that is the possibility of selling what is produced. Or, as Smith put it, the division of labor is limited by the extent of the market.

So when Becky decides on how many to employ in her nail-producing business, how expensive (and productive) machinery to buy, how large a production facility she needs, and so on—that is, the scale of her business— she must anticipate not only whether the goods she intends to produce are valuable to consumers but what quantity would be demanded at what prices. This, in turn, helps her make decisions about the type of production, scale of process, and what magnitude of investments are reasonable. If she anticipates that there is a large untapped market for nails, then she wouldn't have a problem investing in large-scale production. In fact, she would have to in order to maximize her returns. To put this differently, she cannot afford to produce in smaller quantities if she anticipates that there is sufficient demand. The reason is that with increased investment, which she of course would take on only if she anticipates that it will increase productivity, the return on that investment is higher. Choosing small-scale over large-scale makes no sense if profitability—the percentage return on investment—is increased with the higher investment. The other side of anticipated higher return on large-scale production is that it makes small-scale production relatively more costly. So with increased production, Becky can either increase her profits (if she has sufficient pricing power, that is if consumers are willing and able to pay a sufficiently high price) or, in a competitive situation, charge lower prices while maintaining a certain level of profitability. Scale can therefore be an advantage to her business as well as to consumers.

But this requires, of course, that there is a sufficient quantity demanded, without which the undertaking is useless and she'll suffer a loss.

If we attempt to look inside Becky's nail-producing enterprise, or the way it *could* look, using Smith's pin factory as a lens, we'll get an idea of the productive powers of the division of labor within production processes in addition to between employment specific to separate trades. Whereas Smith refers to the specialization through the division of labor into trades as different from similar developments within trades, it is important to note that they are not in principle different. "Dividing" labor presently dedicated to do all the different kinds of operations necessary for self-sufficient production for direct consumption into different trades such as hunter, baker, and blacksmith is not different from dividing the trade of hunting into different trades: trap-maker, spear-maker, trapper, tracker, and so on. The only difference is that we think of hunting, farming, baking and so on as different and naturally separate production processes. But this was not the case when division of labor occurred among self-sufficient individuals or communities—it is only "obvious" with the power of hindsight. Just like it today appears to be a separate trade to be an accountant or manager or welder—all of which are highly specialized trades. All trades, no matter how intensive the specialization, are separated through the division of labor with a single purpose: to bring about increased production for the satisfaction of wants. What this means is that whether we choose to see separate production processes within the market, or instead see the whole market as a production *structure* dedicated to satisfy a variety of wants, is irrelevant. All production is related and in fact interdependent (as we shall soon see), and specialization through the division of labor is intensified when entrepreneurs find a way of doing so and anticipate that it is "worth it"—that is, when it appears to be profitable.

Becky's nail-production business could very well have been organized using much more intensive specialization within, as Smith calls it, a "manufactory." Smith contrasts Becky's type of business as discussed above (where she works alone or with only little help) with the industrialized process: "in the way in which this business is now carried on [in the 'manufactory'], not only the whole work [pin-making] is a peculiar trade, but it is divided into a number of branches, of which the greater part are likewise peculiar trades." Those parts are specific (though not necessarily unique) to the process of pin-making, which itself of course is a specialized process, and labor workers can thereby specialize to carry out one or only a few of those parts. To use specialization through the division of labor within an already specialized process includes separating operations sequentially so that one operation, carried out by one worker, is and must be followed by one other operation, carried out by another worker. This means there is a serial interdependence in the sense that if someone messes up, the whole chain of operations will be affected—not only the separate operation. Or, in Smith's words, "One man draws out the wire, another straights it, a third cuts it, a fourth points it, a fifth grinds it at the top for receiving the head; to make the head requires two or three distinct operations; to put it on, is a peculiar business, to whiten the pins is another; it is even a trade by itself to put them into the paper; and the important business of making a pin is, in this manner, divided into about eighteen distinct operations, which, in some manufactories, are all performed by distinct hands, though in others the same man will sometimes perform two or three of them."[8]

From the point of view of the community producing for direct consumption, the difference between specializing into trades (Becky produces nails, Bart bakes bread, Adele grows apples, and so on) and specializing even more intensively is not much different. What differs is the nature of what is produced and thus the relationship between the individual worker and his or her work. In a factory, we'd see the connection between a workman and the result of his work become weaker, what Karl Marx referred to as alienation. The connection between one's production efforts and what is produced is strongest when producing for direct consumption. But even if producing for indirect consumption, for instance when Becky specializes to produce three-inch nails or Adele grows apples, the connection is obvious: a satisfaction in the sense of "I produced this" can be felt with respect to the very thing produced. In other words, there is only very little alienation, even under intensive specialization.

Interestingly, alienation appears to only occur within "manufactories." The reason for this is, from our perspective of specialization, that the process carried out is more intensively specialized than general market trade. Becky is not alienated with respect to her production of three-inch nails for the reason that they are nails and therefore separate good, but because they are goods *traded in the market*. Nails are not consumed as nails but make inputs in the construction of houses and other things. If Becky had been specialized toward making nails in an economy where nails were not traded as separate goods, which means she would probably be an employee or subcontractor in a house-builder business with in-house production of nails (because they couldn't be bought in the market), the connection between her labor and the product would be much less obvious and, as a result, she would suffer from alienation.

Interestingly, this addresses the Smithian point, discussed above, about how the division of labor is limited by the extent of the market. Indeed, specialization under the division of labor is not possible in more intensive · forms than are already supported by the market. Alienation follows from pushing specialization further so that an integrated process is formed where each specialized operation is entirely interdependent on the other operations in the sequential process. In other words, alienation would only arise in situations with very intensive specialization under the division of labor, that is, not in the general market but as "islands of specialization" brought about by entrepreneurs trying to implement what they anticipate to be superior productive solutions (innovations). Such "islands" step outside the extent of the market and therefore appear integrated, and we can refer to them as firms (like the pin factory).[9]

A more pressing concern for our present purposes, however, is how Becky's nail-producing business relates to Ricardo's insight about comparative advantage. In other words, how do we put the "right" people to carry out each specialized operation in a production process. To Smith, at least in the example of the pin factory, who does what doesn't really matter—his example explicitly relies on uneducated workers rather than specific skills, innate or acquired, and thus specifically uses unspecific labor power. Under such circumstances, it is obvious that repetition (on the job training, as it were) will soon lead to increased productivity (what Smith refers to as "dexterity"). His other two reasons why productivity increases through the division of labor are equally easy to see. Using only basic labor power, Smith's example shows astounding returns to specialization: one workman, he says, "could scarce, perhaps, with his utmost industry, make one pin in a day, and certainly could not make twenty" whereas "ten men . . . could, when they exerted themselves, . . . make among them upwards of forty-eight thousand pins in a day." In other words, working alone each worker cannot make even twenty pins; working together, they make almost five thousand pins each.

Of course, people have different inherent and learned skills. They also have different interests and therefore find it easier to learn different things. Surely this makes a difference in production as well? Of course it does. So if we assume that Becky needs to employ a dozen workers in her factory, she would benefit from picking the most hard-working men and women she can find—and then use them in the best possible ways in the production process. She would fit their already existing skills and their interests with the different operations that make up the nail-making process. Needless to say, she's best off employing the "best" workers out there and then using them where they are most productive. The workers, conversely, are more productive if their skills and work tasks are aligned, and with the increased productivity they are worth a higher wage. This, in effect, is what Ricardo teaches. Even if the workers Becky employs are not productive to the same degree so that some of them, say the newly employed David and Deborah, are so excessively skillful that they are better than for instance Eric and Edda at any and all tasks that need to be carried out in the nail-production process, then the total outcome is better if Becky keeps Eric and Edda employed and uses David, Deborah, Eric, and Edda where they are each most productive.

It may not be obvious in Becky's nail factory because she would likely select the best suited for the job. But if this were not the case, say her business is a family firm and she needs to rely on family members for producing the nails, some of them would be highly productive whereas others might be lazy, and some may have plenty of skills and others have only a few. Furthermore, some of them have experiences that make them productive in many types of positions whereas others have neither experience nor interest in working and therefore won't contribute much to the bottom line. With such a fixed population, Becky would produce more nails by including all of them than not. Obvious? Yes, but it also applies in trade, and that was Ricardo's point.

Say Becky is an extremely productive individual and that she's much better than Bart at both making nails and baking bread. So why wouldn't she produce the nails and bake the bread, and simply exclude Bart? The reason is that they both have limited time and energy, so even if Becky is better at both tasks in absolute terms—or even *much* better—they're both better off if Bart is better at baking bread in relative terms and consequently labors as a baker. So if Becky can produce a dozen nails in an eight-hour work day (which makes her quite productive, considering Smith's pin factory example) or bake twenty loaves of bread, and Bart can produce a miserable four nails or bake seven loaves of bread, then they're both better off specializing and then exchanging with each other to get what they want. We're not here including the productivity gains from production that we learned from Smith, but treat productivity as though it is unchanging. This is unrealistic, of course, but makes the point clear: even without the benefits of learning, saving from not switching between tasks, and automation, individuals are still better off specializing and trading than not.

Using the example above, we can see that Becky is, relatively speaking, more productive when producing nails than when she's baking bread as compared to Bart. For Becky, the choice for a workday is either twelve nails or twenty loaves of bread, so her productivity ratio nails-to-bread is three to five. For Bart, the choice is four nails or seven loaves of bread, making his productivity ratio four to seven. In decimal terms, Becky can produce 0.6 nails for each loaf of bread, and Bart can produce approximately 0.57 nails for each loaf. In other words, Becky has a relative advantage producing nails whereas Bart has a relative advantage producing bread (he can produce fewer nails per loaf than Becky). Another way of looking at this is that to produce a single nail, Becky will have to "give up" (as opportunity cost) the one and two-thirds loaves that she otherwise could've produced while to Bart, who's relatively better at baking, producing a nail means he has to give up one and three-quarters loaf. So it is "cheaper" for Becky to produce nails than bread, as compared to Bart. It is similarly "cheaper" for Bart to produce bread than nails, as compared to Becky. So to get as much as possible out of this situation, Becky should do what she's relatively better at and Bart should, similarly, do what he's relatively better at. At the end of the day, they can get together and share the dozen nails that Becky produced and the seven loaves of bread that Bart baked.

In the real world, of course, productivity is not a constant. Adam Smith showed this as we noted in the discussion above. If we add the Smithian lesson to our Ricardian discussion on what Becky and Bart should do, then it is clear that the relative advantage of Ricardo provides guidance to what is the better starting point in terms of "who does what"—and then, if we add what we learned from Smith, we see that simply by focusing their efforts rather than both Becky and Bart doing both things, we increase productivity even further. If we had more people and let them specialize under the division of labor, then we could see explosive increases in productivity.

But we should add to this picture the lesson we learned from Schumpeter. Whereas Smith includes limited innovation in his discussion on the pin factory, primarily through "automation" of simple tasks by the construction of machinery, this is not what Schumpeter had in mind. Instead, he was talking about revolutionizing innovations that do much more than relieve a worker of his or her simple production task (which, from an economic point of view, means this worker is now a resource available for other productive tasks, and therefore can contribute to economic growth). Schumpeterian innovation changes how production is done; it doesn't just simplify processes that have already been implemented.

An example of such an innovation would be Henry Ford's use of the assembly line technique for mass production of standardized automobiles. Prior to this innovation, each shop could produce only one automobile at a time. The production crew was involved in production from beginning to end, since specific tasks needed to be carried out in a certain order. Alternatively, an automobile factory could have separate crews focused on one part of the production sequence each, and they would then move from car to car in order to finish the job. The assembly line did two things: it standardized production for both workers and consumers. Workers specialized on certain tasks in the sequence and the car was moved between stations, placed as close as possible, using conveyors. As a result, consumers were offered a standard product.

Whatever our views on assembly line production, it was a vast improvement in productivity over the production method used earlier. For this reason, it completely changed the industry and production of automobiles.

As another example, take the printing press. It didn't change the importance of books as sources for knowledge, but it made their production so much more effective and cheap. Rather than reproducing books by hand, the printing press allowed for printing numerous copies at once. This meant new knowledge could be made available to a lot more people a lot quicker; it was therefore easier to educate people and, at the same time, harder for protectors of the status quo to stop new knowledge from spreading. And each book could be made available at a fraction of the price, making advanced knowledge available to more than the elite. This fundamentally changed society and made arbitrary rule much more difficult; the printing press democratized society.

Another effect of the printing press was the new business opportunities through publishing houses, the greatly increased demand for paper to print on, and the circumscribed use for scribes. Productivity in books production of course increased greatly, but an important part of Schumpeterian innovation is the changes caused to other types of production, to what's being offered to consumers, and how this changes things overall. Schumpeterian innovations revolutionize the market by disrupting it. Much of this is accomplished by finding new ways of satisfying consumers, which reshuffle resources and change specializations. With the invention of the automobile, transportation became much cheaper and more reliable. But it also meant that factories and workers specialized to horse carriage production were no longer needed; they could instead be used to satisfy other wants. Likewise, the numerous horses used to pull the carriages could be used toward some other end. While the process can be painful for many of those affected, the effect to the economic system is that resources are released from their present occupations and therefore can be put to other and, presumably, better uses elsewhere—the value they were used to create is better generated through the new innovation.

Taken together, we can see the immense productive power available through specialization and innovation, neither of which would be possible without voluntary exchange. Without a separation of production and consumption, specialization under the division of labor couldn't go very far. Without trade, we cannot take full advantage of relative comparative advantages, as Ricardo teaches. And without trade, a Schumpeterian innovation wouldn't have much effect, since exchange facilitates the innovation's revolutionary improvement to the totality of production. Trade, however, is much more than buying goods for consumption. It is the lifeblood of both production and the enormously productive powers of decentralized markets.

PRODUCTION AS SOCIAL COOPERATION

What has been said so far about specialization under the division of labor in production has focused on separate production processes: from what is conceivable as the start of the production process (as when Adele planted the apple trees in her orchard) to its completion by offering consumers a completed good or service (apples). But market production cannot be properly understood as a sequential process, even if we often intuitively think of and may even observe it as such. Rather, production is an intricate network of interconnected and interdependent productive actions and processes that build off and support each other, and that connect all production efforts into what we in a previous chapter referred to as an "economic organism."

The issue of productive capital is key to understanding how market production is more of an organism than a sequential process. Consider again Adele's undertaking as apple-grower. We already established that her business, and thus the "separate" production process that it entails, starts with clearing the land and planting seeds or saplings, and then continues with tending to the trees, picking the apples, and so on. But is this really a separate process? Hardly. And this is obvious from our previous discussion.

Consider Adele's clearing of the land, which means cutting down trees and thicket. While we would consider both the land and the labor as "original factors" of production, whether or not she does all the work herself or employs helpers, clearing of the land is almost impossible without tools. To cut down trees, remove rocks, and so on, Adele and her helpers will use chainsaws or handsaws, shovels, picks, and possibly sledge hammers. As we discussed previously, Adele would consider using excavators and machinery instead of some of the labor. All of these tools and machinery constitute capital: they're *produced* means of production. In other words, for Adele's production process to even begin, she first acquires the outputs from *other* production processes. For each input used in Adele's apple-growing business there is a separate production process. Indeed, this is the case not only for the tools and machinery used to get started—with different processes for producing the saws, shovels and picks as well as processes for assembling machinery—but also for producing the apple seeds or saplings she plants, the irrigation system she purchases and installs, the ladders and tools used for pruning the trees, the carts and whatever else she needs for picking and transporting the apples.

Whereas these inputs used by Adele have their own production processes, so do the inputs used in *their* production processes. The saw-maker, for instance, relies on other entrepreneurs to make the steel and plastic used to make the saws available; moreover, the tools used for shaping the steel into saws, sharpening them, etc. are also inputs that have been produced using other and separate production processes. And so is the case with the buildings used in the production process (the factory or workshop), to store the steel and tools, and so on. Add to this the vehicles used for transportation and delivery, the automobiles used by workers to get to and from their work in the factory, the heating and ventilation systems along with the electricity and oil or natural gas used to maintain a decent temperature in the factory, and so on. There is, in fact, no end to the number of production processes that tie into and are necessary for Adele's apple-growing process.

Nevertheless, we can think of production as taking place in "stages" from virgin land and labor to the product offered to consumers. For instance, we can think of the production of automobiles as consisting of the sequential stages of mining, smelting, steel-making, and automobile assembly. There are supporting production processes to make these "stages" happen, but they are not core but peripheral to the "flow" of intermediate goods that eventually are offered to consumers in the form of an automobile. In this simple example, the intermediate goods would be iron ore (from mining), iron (from smelting), and steel (from mixing iron and coal). The steel is then used in assembly of automobiles that are the final good.

We can see, then, how we might conceive of the production of each intermediate good as a separate production process, perhaps carried out by a separate business entity or entrepreneur, whereas when combined they constitute the "full" process of production necessary for automobile manufacturing: from farm to table or, as is here the case, from rock to automobile. Seeing market production as consisting of separate but interdependent "stages" is an important insight that helps us understand the effects of changes in an economy. The reason for this is that the production of one stage, for instance steel production, is not only used as input into automobile production but many other types of production. Indeed, ships, airplanes, railroads, and skyscrapers are all in part produced from steel. But so are machines used in producing them. So the steel produced in the stage adjacent to automobile assembly in our example is used for automobiles as well as in the production of machinery used in the automobile assembly process. Some machinery made using this steel could also be used to assist in mining the iron ore that is eventually turned into steel, for blast furnaces smelting the iron, and in steel production itself. So while for the purpose of automobile production we can conceive of production in stages, what is produced in one stage—for instance, steel—can be used in many other stages, and even in steel production itself.

Steel, of course, is widely used so we would expect steel to be part of numerous types of production. But this is the case only partly because steel has valuable properties, that is that steel can easily be used for many different things. Usefulness is only part of the explanation, however. We can think of other materials that could be used in the place of steel, or perhaps other ways of producing that would not require steel. The reason steel is used is because it is useful *and cheap*. If steel was sold at the price of gold, then much of the production that presently uses steel would be directed toward using other materials, different processes, and perhaps cease altogether. So we can imagine that if the price of steel suddenly rises, the relative cost of using steel would go up and entrepreneurs would therefore choose to use different (cheaper) materials, different (cheaper) production processes, or go into different lines of business. By seeing production as stages, therefore, we can track the effects of changes as they affect each stage, and then follow how this affects other stages step by step. If we were to think of production as uniform with indistinct operations that cannot easily be separated, we would not be able to track the specific effects brought about by certain changes. For instance, we would not be able to explain why a sudden and substantial increase in the price of steel leads to automobiles made out of plastic or aluminum, why the laying of railroad tracks is slowed down, or why new and different construction techniques for the building of skyscrapers are suddenly adopted.

Seeing production in stages is therefore an important theoretical tool for understanding how production is coordinated in an economy. But this is not necessarily how entrepreneurs see it, and they do not make decisions based on our conceptualization of production stages. Rather, they respond to prices. So when the price of steel suddenly goes through the roof, individual entrepreneurs do not need to know what happened or why the price dramatically increased; they only need to know that it did.[10] And if they believe that it is not simply a temporary effect or fluke, they will adjust how they carry out their production processes based on this information. If they can raise the prices they charge to their customers, they might try doing so. But under competitive pressures, no one wants to be the first to raise prices since this means customers will likely buy from those not raising prices instead. So they will attempt to cut costs to maintain profitability without raising prices. Part of cutting costs can be to adopt other production processes that don't require as much steel—or no steel at all. As steel is relatively more expensive than it used to be, these alternative production methods, which used to be costlier than using steel, are now better options. So as entrepreneurs try to tackle the problem of rising steel prices, they attempt to find better ways of producing—and thus production overall is shifted away from the now relatively more expensive steel and toward alternative methods, techniques, and materials.

In a competitive market, this type of adjustment is undertaken all the time—even if specific prices do not suddenly go through the roof. Indeed, entrepreneurs compete by keeping their cost down and by figuring out better production techniques, and will shift their production efforts toward the best possible—at least, the best possible technique they know about or can imagine—alternatives. Part of the driving force in this constant and continuous effort is to beat the competition, but part of it is also the chance for profit. By keeping costs down, finding more effective production techniques, or by figuring out more highly valued products to offer to consumers, entrepreneurs can reap profits—by becoming better at satisfying wants. So even without existing competitors, they still have an incentive to improve (though the incentive might not be as strong) for the simple reason that they have a chance of earning higher profits. In this way, production shifts in ways we might not be able to predict. And each shift produces "ripple effects"—like the waves on a pond when a rock is thrown into it—through the stages of production: each change will have some effect on prices, since both demand and supply shift, and this will in turn cause other entrepreneurs to shift their production. In other words, production in a market is in constant flux. It is never stable.

What holds this economic organism together is exchange. The constant adjustments or shifts within the market's entire production apparatus are possible because it is possible for actors to trade. For instance, rapidly increasing steel prices could mean that Adele instead of investing in machinery chooses to hire more labor to satisfy growing demand. Also, she might employ someone dedicated to taking care of and servicing the tools used to prune and tend to her apple trees so that they don't have to be replaced as often. This constitutes a shift in response to some unknown event that effectuated a sharp rise in steel prices. And Adele's choice to avoid this added cost that is reflected in higher tools prices, by employing someone to take care of the tools already in use so that they can be used longer, is one of the effects of the change in steel price. But it is not obvious to an observer, and other entrepreneurs may choose different ways to deal with this change.

While Adele's choice to employ more people—perhaps because she knows someone who is great at taking care of tools—has very little effect on the market overall, how all entrepreneurs combined react to such changes makes a difference. Say many producers are in the same situation as Adele and choose, like she does, to respond to higher steel prices and the resulting higher prices on tools by employing tool service experts or buying this service from companies offering it. This increased demand for such services causes a shift from tools production to tools service and care. As entrepreneurs choose to no longer invest as much in new tools and instead use those funds to increase the time existing tools can be used, the effect is twofold: producers of tools will find it more difficult to sell tools, which means they will be forced to lower their prices (prices of tools, therefore, go down); and servicers of tools will see a similar *increase* in their demand, which means they can raise their prices and many of them probably figure it is worthwhile to invest in increased capacity, and so on.

This, in turn, has effects elsewhere in the market. As tools manufacturers cannot sell as many tools as they used to, they will cut back on their operations and thus use less materials. Some of them will move to smaller offices and production plants, and they will buy less steel from steel producers. In other words, the larger offices and plants that are now too large for tool manufacturers will be made available to the tool servicers who experience increased demand. Tool experts previously employed by tool manufacturers are laid off and instead employed by tool servicers. The steel previously demanded by tool manufacturers can be used by entrepreneurs in other industries or types of production. For instance, they may find better uses in tools and machinery used by tool servicers in servicing the tools that were previously sold by the now downsized tool manufacturers.

This will also have an effect on businesses that seem to be more remote from the production and servicing of tools, such as transportation services, heating and cooling for plants (for instance, perhaps manufacturing requires more high-capacity cooling than does servicing), fuel used to run the machinery, and so on. It also affects which types of trucks are used for transportation, since tool servicing might need to transport the tools from the customer to the plant and back whereas tool manufacturing only transported them one way. So it may increase the use and therefore value of roads, diners, and gas stations. Many of these changes are far from revolutionary in scale, only minor increases or decreases. But they are necessary to properly adjust overall production toward where resources are best used. And it follows from entrepreneurs' anticipation of how they can best satisfy consumers.

In the case of steel prices surging, for whatever reason, Adele chooses to not buy as many tools because the prices of those tools also go up. This is a decision she makes based on her anticipation of how consumers value the apples that she produces. If she would be able to raise prices for apples without consumers shifting their demand to other fruits or edibles, or simply not buying at all, then she might afford to keep buying new tools. But there is no reason why she wouldn't have already increased her prices if she knew— or at least felt confident—that the market could bear higher prices. Also, there is no reason why she would choose to pay for tools when it is more cost effective to service the tools she already has on hand—why would she accept the higher cost unless it is necessary? Prior to the increase in steel price, Adele had concluded that buying new tools but not investing too much into servicing them was the best investment: it provided most anticipated service to her apple-growing business at the lowest estimated cost. After the price of steel increased, however, the tools became more valuable and thus costlier to replace, which in turn increased the relative value of tools servicing; it suddenly made economic sense to invest in taking care of the tools, so Adele shifted her investment from buying to servicing. She will still have to buy tools when necessary, but with proper servicing this will not be as often as it used to be.

Only through exchanging with each other can entrepreneurs bring about the changes we've seen. In Adele's case, she now purchases servicing rather than tools; servicing, in turn, uses slightly different resources than manufacturing, which leads to a shift from producing for manufacturing to producing for servicing; and this, in turn, leads to different uses of the resources used for those kinds of production. Very few of these changes are large enough to bring about revolutionary changes to the overall production apparatus, but it is also likely that the change in steel price affects more than tools manufacturing. Entrepreneurs' everyday decisions, and especially their shifting from one type of operation, along with the inputs and resources used, to another, affect what other entrepreneurs are able to sell and at what prices. If steel prices go up enough, many entrepreneurs in widely different industries that use steel will shy away from using as much as they did—and thus the market for steel shrinks.

"Shying away" from using is here the same thing as not buying as much as before; in other words, the quantity demanded diminishes and steel can therefore be used in greater quantities for more highly valued uses. But note that what is now more highly valued is not necessarily the same as before. While we used the increase in price for a commonly used resource as a starting point for our example, it could also be brought about by a shift in how consumers value goods. The economy is endogenous, which means the market adjusts in response to changes that are not external to it: consumers constitute an important part of the market, and it is quite possible that what they demand—that is, what they *value*—can change for no apparent reason. Entrepreneurs involved in production will need to anticipate and properly adjust their undertakings to this change in order to not go out of business.

The same is true if an entrepreneur innovates a product previously unseen and therefore not demanded. But offering this new product could educate consumers about their true valuations, and therefore cause a shift in demand. Many "disruptive" innovations do this: they fulfill a demand we as consumers didn't know that we had. But when we learn about it, we of course update our behavior and buy this more highly valued good or service in lieu of what we used to buy. So the market needs to continuously adjust and respond to changes that occur both among consumers and within the different kinds of production being undertaken for their benefit, and no matter where the change originates (some changes can be exogenous to the economy as well, such as changes in weather or climate) it causes a chain reaction within production as entrepreneurs respond as best they can to how the change affects their business.

We can see, then, how market production, even though it is highly decentralized, and spontaneous rather than planned, can be thought of as an organism: all of its parts are interconnected in myriad ways, many of which may not be obvious and may not be explicit, and production overall adjusts to changing conditions automatically because each individual entrepreneur makes decisions and chooses what they anticipate to be their best course of action. This way, and as we discussed in previous chapters with respect to producing one's ability to consume, market production is undertaken with the purpose to satisfy others'—consumers'—real and anticipated wants, an activity that is aligned with the producers' quest to satisfy their own wants through earning profits that facilitate consumption.

As production becomes increasingly specialized and therefore, through the division of labor, a whole chain of individual producing entrepreneurs will be necessary for the production of goods for consumption, the entrepreneurs become dependent upon each other. But they are also freed through this process, since they can rely on other entrepreneurs—the "market," as it were—to supply the resources, tools, and inputs necessary. As is the case for Adele, she can specialize in apple-growing because many of the resources necessary to establish and tend to an orchard are already available. She can buy from other producing entrepreneurs what she needs to get started with her own production. This means she will not have to start from scratch, and it also means she will not have to acquire complete knowledge. Rather, she can begin with advanced tools and machinery, each of which requires plenty of skills, expertise and capital investment to produce, and she therefore need not bother with how they are produced, why they are produced, or if there are better ways of producing them. She can in this sense act as a consumer toward the producing entrepreneurs who precede her in the chain of production activities necessary for Adele's customers to be offered ripe and sweet apples. Entrepreneurs are therefore engaged in cooperation in the same way cells or organs cooperate and are interdependent in a body, and it is in this sense we can think of the economy as an organism.

As the purpose of entrepreneurs' undertakings is their own consumption, however indirectly through production that satisfies others' consumption, they are involved in contributing to the public good of value creation. By serving others, they serve themselves. This "invisible hand" of market production, which auto-adjusts to changing conditions, changing consumer preferences, and discoveries of new products, production techniques, and resources, is made possible because of specialization under the division of labor, competition for profit between producers, and the whole process is facilitated through exchange. So while the production apparatus as a whole is interdependent and organism-like, it actually consists of tiny and separate parts: entrepreneurs and laborers who independently make choices in their own self-interest. Competition between them for the purpose of satisfying consumer wants, which facilitates their own wants satisfaction through consumption, therefore constitutes cooperation: by competing to serve consumers in the best way possible, they cooperate in providing value to consumers.

This being said, the market should not be considered efficient. Rather, it is redundant and every entrepreneurial failure constitutes a loss not only for the entrepreneur him- or herself, but to society as a whole because more wants *could have* been satisfied. This is why the weeding out of unsuccessful entrepreneurs, and the resultant shifting of productive resources away from the less productive and toward the more productive, is a core part of what constitutes a functioning market. Without the very real threat of losing what's been invested, there would be nothing to balance the lure of profits— and the order of the market would consequently fail.

OPPORTUNITY COST AND OPTIONALITY

What we have established now is the order that arises from a simple insight: that production precedes consumption or, another way of saying the same thing, that one must produce in order to consume. In the simplest case, all produce what they themselves consume. But production is much more effective if producers can specialize and thereby develop skills and expertise, make use of machinery, and increase the depth of their knowledge with respect to specific (rather than general or wide-ranging) production. We saw how the arguments of Smith, Ricardo, and Schumpeter individually, but more forcefully when used together, show the immense productive powers of decentralized production that utilizes specialization under the division of labor. With increased productivity and therefore production capacity, many more wants can be satisfied. And with more wants satisfied, even more wants arise as worth satisfying. We say that people's wants are insatiable, by which we mean that we will never be fully content—there is always something that could be easier, taste better, look more beautiful, and so on. The reason this is the case is because there is a cost to any achieved value. It doesn't mean that cost incurred and value created balance out, but that there is always something given up in order to gain—there is a tradeoff in every choice.

This tradeoff is what economists refer to as opportunity cost: the real cost of any choice is the value of that which is *not* chosen—because you lose that option when choosing something else. The real cost of a value is therefore the value that is foregone and can no longer be created (unless the opportunity still exists, but then only at the cost of foregoing something else). This is not, of course, production cost. In fact, outlay and expenses for production are practically irrelevant for the opportunity cost of any item. Yet opportunity cost is still core to production decisions.

If Adam has the choice between eating an apple or a pear, then his cost of eating the apple is the pear and the cost of eating the pear is the apple. It doesn't matter to us what fruit he actually chooses, but if it turns out that he chooses the apple we know that he must value it—and the satisfaction he anticipates it will offer him—more highly than the pear. And vice versa. His personal, subjective gain from eating the apple is of course whatever value he gets from eating the apple. But what is more important for our purposes is the economic "profit" of doing so, which is the difference between how he values the apple—which we know must be higher than the pear—and the pear—which we know he values less, since he didn't choose it. Adam had to forego the pear to eat the apple, since he needed to choose between them, and therefore his cost—the loss of satisfaction by choosing the apple—is the satisfaction he would have gained from eating the pear.

Why is this important? It is important because it indicates people's true valuations *as revealed through their actions*, and this is in turn what directs

production. Anyone's stated but not acted-upon opinion may influence people's perception and actions, but in terms of real effects—what actually
affects the outcome of production undertakings, that is profit or loss—only
action and not what is uttered matters. Entrepreneurs invest in what they
anticipate consumers will want, but it is unknown whether they are accurate
in their anticipations before consumers act. The ultimate outcome of how
consumers choose to act generates the profit entrepreneurs earn or the loss
they suffer. If they accurately anticipate consumer valuation and use resources prudently in producing it, then they will earn profits; and if they
don't, they will lose their investment. The real loss, however, is the value that
is forgone—not the prices paid for the resources used to produce that which
wasn't sold. What matters is therefore the relative value of what entrepreneurs do: in order to succeed, they must provide to consumers something that
is not only valuable but relatively more valuable than what other entrepreneurs have to offer. If they fail, the real loss is the opportunity cost of their
production: the time, skill, and resources used to produce that which was not
sold. These resources could have been used in some other way that would
have created value for consumers. All resources are scarce, which means we
do not at all times have exactly the quantity and quality we want of each
resource, which is why we have opportunity costs. The opportunity cost thus
indicates what our options are.

Consider an example as illustration of this point. Adam is given an apple.
As he didn't pay for it, he is strictly made better off by the gift. So what
should he do with this value that he has received? He could eat it, which
would provide him with some sort of satisfaction. Eating the apple is something that he would value. But in order to understand the economic decision
of what to do with the apple, we must also consider his options—the opportunity costs of the apple. It is intuitive to conclude that a gift apple is free and
thus has no cost. But this is not, strictly speaking, true. Because by choosing
to eat the apple, Adam necessarily foregoes other values. What does he
forego? Say that in our little economy, an apple currently trades for the
equivalent of three loaves of bread (Bart is willing to exchange a nice apple
for three loaves of bread) or a half dozen three-inch nails (Becky is willing to
exchange the apple for a half dozen nails). In other words, even if Adam was
given the apple there is an opportunity cost to eating it. This cost can be
expressed as three loaves of bread or a half dozen nails. So in order not to
miss out on the opportunities available to him, he must consider the tradeoff:
apple, three loaves, a half dozen nails. Which is more valuable to him? If
eating the apple is more valuable to him than the alternatives presented to
him, then he should of course eat it—that's how he maximizes his satisfaction in this situation. If not, then he should figure out which option offers him
the greatest pleasure and choose that instead.

This is what economists mean when they say there is no "free lunch." It may not be possible to resell an offered lunch on the open market, but the time you spend dining could be used in some other way. If you have a job with an hourly wage of $10, for instance, and you could without problem choose to work an additional hour instead of spending the hour on a paid lunch, then the lunch cost you the $10 that you could have earned. The concept of opportunity cost is powerful because it reveals what your real options are, and it also emphasizes what you are truly giving up. Interestingly, the opportunity cost is much greater in a market, because only in markets is it possible to trade what you have to acquire alternatives. As in the case of Adam's apple, had there been no market—and therefore no market price for the apple he received as gift—he would have been restricted to the uses he could find for the apple: eating it raw, using it to make apple pie, plant it in the ground to grow an apple tree, give it to somebody else who might find it more useful, etc. But because Adam has access to a market, there are many more options available to him, so *his opportunity cost increases.*

A high opportunity cost for some good or action means there is at least one alternative use that is almost as good. While this could make choosing a bit more difficult, since the alternatives are valued almost the same, it also means that the choosing individual enjoys freedom in the form of optionality: there are valuable alternatives available. As opportunity cost is not only applicable on goods and services, but on any actions and decisions made, we can easily see how high opportunity cost suggests a freedom to choose. Where the opportunity cost is relatively low, meaning the second best alternative is not very valuable as compared to the best, there is no real choice: the one alternative is so much better than all other alternatives that there is no reason to even think about the "alternatives." Indeed, whereas the choice is still formally a choice, which means *it is possible to choose otherwise*, one is so obviously the better alternative that all other options do not matter in the individual's choice calculus.

For this reason, we should in our everyday lives wish to have as high an opportunity cost for our choice as possible. We are in fact better off the more highly we value our alternatives ranked second and third and fourth, since it indicates that there are abundant choices we can make that are of similar value—and therefore that people's differing wants and preferences can be satisfied to a much greater degree than if this were not the case. Unless our wants are unique and even distant from other people's, the fact that we're experiencing high opportunity costs means that many variations of our valuation can be satisfied. This means that other people, with similar wants and needs, will find it easier to satisfy their wants too. It also means that should we lose the ability to choose the most highly ranked alternative—because it is lost or destroyed, sold to someone else who is willing and able to pay a higher price, or some other reason—we are not left much worse off. In other words, we can in some sense measure our well-being and prosperity in terms of the opportunity cost we experience in our choices—we're well off because we must make choices between many similarly valued goods, not between one good and many bads.

This does not mean, of course, that we should consider the opportunity cost itself as something valuable; it is not, since it by definition is the value we do *not* get. It is valuable to us if we somehow fail to choose the best alternative, and it is valuable because it suggests that there are many similarly valued alternatives available to us. But foregoing a high value is not in and of itself valuable, so it is a poor decision to choose the second best alternative for the reason that this raises the opportunity cost of the choice beyond the value attained. We should consider the opportunity costs of all available options when making choices so that the outcome is maximized—so that we do not inadvertently miss out on value that is available to us—but not for the purpose of raising the cost. There are always opportunity costs, and the occurrence of high opportunity costs is valuable only because it implies many good alternatives: optionality. [11]

It follows that markets tend to empower the individual as they increase optionality in consumption through improved and specialized, and therefore also differentiated, production. By engaging in producing for other people's consumption, engaging in specialization under the division of labor, exchange, and innovation, overall production is greatly increased. We saw how this was the case in the previous section, and it follows from this that the producing individual's purchasing power—his or her ability to procure the means to satisfy wants using the value attained through production—is greatly increased through market-based production. By producing more, we can afford to consume more. It also means there are more goods and services offered for our consumption, because by increasing productivity the quantity and variety of offerings that can be made available also increases. By specializing and engaging in market production, therefore, we increase our productivity and that makes us richer, while also contributing to the vast multitude of goods available for purchase in the market. This too makes us richer: improved and specialized production increases our purchasing power, while other people's production increases the number of ways we can satisfy our wants—that is, it increases our optionality—and therefore raises our opportunity cost. Part of the "power of the market," and especially market *production*, is therefore the freedom that is offered in terms of *choices*. This is an insight that we will return to throughout the remainder of this book and that will prove important to understanding the concept of the "unrealized."

Despite this power of the market to generate overall prosperity through production, it would be false to claim that it is a perfect or optimal system. Indeed, we have already noted that entrepreneurs (actually, producers in general) act under the threat of suffering losses if they incorrectly anticipate what consumers demand. This is a necessary implication of not being able to know the future, but it is also one that causes inefficiency: many investments that, with the power of hindsight, should not have been made were made anyway and therefore caused individuals to lose their accumulated funds— and society to lose the alternatives that would have existed had the entrepreneurs not erred. Also, the market will not ever fully utilize all the productive resources available toward providing satisfaction in the present, because some of them will necessarily be dedicated to uses in production processes that will be concluded at different points in time. The investments made today for the purpose of offering goods in the future, as Adele's planting of apple trees or Bart's building or buying an oven for baking, could also have been used to satisfy wants in the present. So market production will not at any single point in time be "maximized," because it constitutes a process of myriad production undertakings that will mature at different times and satisfy different wants. As production takes time, there is always some fraction of productive resources bound in the production for future wants satisfaction.

The unknowability of the future means there is no way around this state of things. There will always be waste and failure and redundancy in market production. Waste will arise due to mistakes and errors; costly failures will be caused by errors or because competing entrepreneurs may turn out to be more successful in their endeavors to satisfy consumer wants; and redundancy in production is necessary to maintain some degree of flexibility to be able to readjust and therefore salvage production processes in the face of unexpected change. The market system, consequently, is never at any point in time *efficient*. Yet at the same time, it is unbeatable in its long-term contribution to human well-being through using and developing scarce resources that allow for satisfying people's real wants and needs.

NOTES

1. See Olson (1971).
2. See Smith (1776).
3. See, for example, Rogers and Monsell (1995) and Rubinstein, Meyer, and Evans (2001).
4. See Ricardo (1817).
5. See Schumpeter (1934).
6. Schumpeter, 1942, p. 83.
7. See Bylund (2016).
8. Smith, 1776, p. 8.
9. I discuss this phenomenon in detail in Bylund (2016).
10. Hayek discusses this information-bearing quality of prices in production (Hayek, 1945).
11. Optionality is discussed by e.g. Taleb (2012), in terms of risk assessment and establishing anti-fragility and is a core part of Williamson's (1985, 1996) Transaction Cost Economics (as asset specificity).

Chapter Five

The Seen and the Unseen

What was stated in the previous chapter about optionality and choice has another dimension, especially as relates to the wealth-generating powers of exchange. As we have already discussed, both parties to a voluntary exchange must expect to become better off or the exchange would not happen. In other words, exchange for consumer goods must by definition *create value* because it increases overall want satisfaction among consumers. But such exchange also causes ripple effects through the economy's production apparatus, since carried out exchanges signal where consumers see real value; obversely, not-made exchanges, and the surpluses that follow, signal where consumers find the value offered is insufficient—in relative terms. What this means is that the totality of exchanges affects how entrepreneurs anticipate that they will be able to satisfy consumer wants; to put it differently, it affects where and how entrepreneurs anticipate makeing adjustments to production plans as entrepreneurs revise their expectations and thus their investments in production plants, which changes the quantity supplied in the market and therefore affect prices of the means of production, which in turn reveals the new social valuation of the means of production and thus allows entrepreneurs with lesser ability to properly adjust their production plans. Indeed, as the more highly responsive or alert entrepreneurs react to changing conditions, they augment consumers' signaling and therefore force other and less alert entrepreneurs, who may not otherwise have realized the change, to follow suit.

These endogenously caused adjustments bring about a productive structure that is highly responsive to change and, as changes happen frequently and responses take time to complete, is best thought of as a process in constant flux. While a production process itself may not be easily changed, the productive capability of the market overall thus remains responsive to the changes revealed by actions taken by consumers as well as the changes in how entrepreneurs anticipate what consumers will value at future points in time. Another way of saying this is that the market is in constant disequilibrium, that is, it is in constant search for and adaptation to bring about a better (more valuable) allocation of productive resources, rather than in stable equilibrium. Changes to the market happen both from within production, primarily because of what actors learn as a result of engaging in Smithian specialization under the division of labor, Ricardian comparative advantage, and Schumpeterian innovation, and in the form of changing consumption patterns as consumer preferences change. The latter change in response to novel offerings in the market (that is, in response to innovative product offerings or changing prices) and in response to consumer experience as well as seemingly arbitrary changes in fads and fancy. But the reasons for what consumers prefer, that is the needs and wants they actively attempt to satisfy through exchange, is beyond the explanatory power of economics. In fact, *why* they want something is quite irrelevant since the task of entrepreneurs is to satisfy the wants that exist, or the ones that will emerge, in an economizing way— not explain why people want this or that.

The interconnectedness of decentralized market production, and thus the ripple effects that result from changes, suggest that the highly responsive market system can also be manipulated. For instance, by temporarily boosting demand for a certain type of product (or producer) or by prohibiting goods and services or production techniques that are valued by consumers (whether for good reasons or not, whether rightly or wrongly), can have a major change on what is actually produced. This is why it is important to properly analyze the effects of regulation on the market, and identify the ripple effects as correctly as possible. As many variables change at the same time and, indeed, all the time, this is a very difficult task and it is likely impossible to perfectly predict the outcome. This does not mean that we are blind to the future and therefore ignorant of what will or may be. The exact state of the future is unknown and may even be unknowable in the present, but it is not unimaginable. This means that we should be careful in making predictions, but can make educated guesses of what to expect.

More specifically, we can imagine the outcome of certain actions by tracing the likely ripple effects and therefore estimate the changes in terms of shifts in emphases: if the price of apples surges, we should expect more investments in apple-growing (as higher prices should mean higher profits) and increased demand in substitute goods (pears, oranges). We cannot say, however, that if the price of apples increases by 10 percent we predict the demand to go down by 8 percent and the demand of pears and oranges to go up by 3 percent and 6 percent, respectively. These numbers may be estimated using how consumers have acted in the past, but we don't know what choices and tradeoffs consumers will face if the apple price goes up in the present or future, which are changes that occur in a new and significantly different economic situation. In other words, the numbers themselves are not valuable as predictions—they are not even indications of what "will or should be." They are, in fact, closer to arbitrary, since the future is very unlikely to be an exact copy of the past.

To get an idea of what to expect from the future, we can reason about what a certain change will lead to in terms of the resultant ripple effects. It is important to be careful, however, not to fall victim to fallacious reasoning by arbitrarily omitting important variables or focusing on only one side of the issue at hand. Such a common such fallacy was masterfully explicated by the nineteenth century French economist Frédéric Bastiat in his parable of the broken window, and is therefore often referred to as the "broken window fallacy." Bastiat here illustrates the error of following the ripple effects that do happen following a certain change—what is seen—but failing to acknowledge what would have happened—what is *not* seen.

As we noted above, but will now go into a little deeper following Bastiat's reasoning, a change brings about changes that in turn bring about changes. For instance, if Adele from our previous chapters thinks it is a great idea to grow wheat on the land between her apple trees in the orchard, and anticipates that this would have no noticeable effect on her apple-growing business, then the added wheat will, because it increases supply but we have no reason to expect an equal increase in the quantity demanded, lower the price of wheat in the market. The miller will therefore be able to get his inputs (the wheat) at a lower price than before, which means he can offer wheat flower to Bart at a lower price—so Bart can then bake more bread or take time off to do something he gets more satisfaction from than baking. This effect is what we observe—the seen, as Bastiat has it. But there's another effect: something that would have happened but now might not happen because of it (the opportunity cost of this new action, as it were)—the unseen. Perhaps the farmer who produced the wheat the miller ground into flour was planning to expand his business by acquiring more land or investing in machinery. As prices fall, this is no longer a viable option; it is not an opportunity for increased return, but would seem to generate a loss at the prices formed after Adele goes into wheat farming. What we do *not* get is as important as what we *do* get when we analyze specific changes in the market. The tradeoff indicates the combined and resultant opportunity costs of a specific decision.

Bastiat's example makes this point very clearly, which is why it is still referred to in research and scholarly debate as well as assigned reading for students.

THAT WHICH IS SEEN

Bastiat tells the story of a shopkeeper whose son has happened to break a glass pane.[1] Furious, the shopkeeper notes that the window needs to be replaced. His no-good son has, through his careless actions, caused a loss that needs to be covered. The shopkeeper has lost value equal to what it will cost him to replace the window pane, an amount that he likely had intended to not pay the glazier. But now he has to. How does Bastiat analyze this? He begins with what is readily observed and that is easily understood by everyone:

> Suppose it cost six francs to repair the damage, and you say that the accident brings six francs to the glazier's trade—that it encourages that trade to the amount of six francs—I grant it; I have not a word to say against it; you reason justly. The glazier comes, performs his task, receives his six francs, rubs his hands, and, in his heart, blesses the careless child. All this is that which is seen.

Indeed, it is easy to see that this analysis is correct: the glazier increases his income thanks to the shopkeeper's son's carelessness. With this additional income, the glazier may be able to pay his employees a higher wage, take time off to spend with his family, or invest in new tools to improve his business. So the positive effect of this trade, which of course makes both the shopkeeper (who values to have a window that is not broken) and the glazier (who happily trades a new window pane and labor for the 6 francs) better off, continues through the economy. Six francs may not be enough to cause far-reaching ripple effects in the economy, but consider if there were more sons breaking windows or an earthquake that destroyed all windows in a whole town (we'll discuss the economic consequences of such disaster in chapter 6). This would have a much greater effect, and we can trace the likely impact this would have on the economy by applying sound economic reasoning. We do not, of course, know exactly what people would choose, so each step away from fixing the broken windows would be more uncertain about where the value actually ends up. Just like we saw above, the glazier can find many uses of his increased income, and whoever gets the value in the next stage depends on the glazier's choice, which of course depends on his subjective assessment of the situation—that is, what he deems of greater value to him in that moment. To be able to follow how the value spreads therefore quickly becomes a hopeless task if we wish to make exact predictions.

Some try to calculate the total effect on the economy by using standard estimates of how much of the increased income the glazier will spend, how much of that money the person who earns it will spend, and so on. Such "multiplier" effects are commonly used when evaluating the effects of policy. Questions asked are, for instance, "what is the real effect on the economy if the government invests $20 billion in infrastructure?" or "how many jobs are created if taxes are cut by 2 percent?" To come up with an answer, we must assume that we know approximately how much of the increased income is spent in each stage, either as an estimate or based on historical analysis of empirical data. So if the glazier will use part of his new income to buy ice cream, the ice cream seller uses part of that new income to buy fresh milk from the farmer, the farmer in turn invests in a better breed of cows, the breeder . . . and so on. Say the fraction spent of any additional income is estimated to be approximately 50 percent across the board, then the glazier will spend 3 francs on ice cream, the ice cream maker will pay 1.50 francs to the farmer, who pays 0.75 francs to the breeder. It is obvious, then, that the real effect on the economy as the shopkeeper buys a new window frame from the glazier for 6 francs is much in excess of 6 francs. In our example, which stops with the breeder but could continue for as long as we wish to follow the fractions of a franc, the 6 francs have an effect of 11.25 francs. The ripple effects through the economy therefore amplify the effect of any investment or trade, the magnitude of which is what the "multiplier" is intended to estimate.

The "multiplier" is based on the concept of economic activity, that is on the production and exchanges that are made within an economy and for economic purposes. Increased activity, as it includes both voluntary trade for mutual benefit and production of goods and services (which, if sold, are valuable), is supposed to approximate value creation and therefore is directly linked with economic growth. For this reason, the "multiplier" effect is used to support stabilization policies in line with the theories of macro economist John Maynard Keynes, which state that the government should use fiscal policy to attempt to stabilize business cycles. According to Keynesians, government should increase taxation and withdraw subsidies during booms to make sure the economy doesn't "overheat," and similarly invest in infrastructure improvements and education and other social goods during slumps for the purpose of increasing economic activity. The discussion in this book can be used by the reader to evaluate Keynes's theory.

The argument is also used by some economists to suggest that everything about war is not dire. Imagine a city devastated by bombings during a time of war. It is easy to see that as soon as the bombing stops, the city will experience immense economic activity to rebuild and restore all that was broken and destroyed in the war. This is not to say, of course, that wars are necessarily good—only that there may be an economic upside following the destruction and devastation of war. Or so the argument goes.

So we can see the direct relevance of Bastiat's parable for public policy, both in terms of fiscal policy intended to stabilize the supposedly natural "mood swings" of a market economy and as an analysis of post-war booms. But Bastiat doesn't tell the story about the broken window to show how great it is that the shopkeeper's son broke the window. No, he uses it to illustrate that focusing only on the seen—that is, the effect of the shopkeeper needing to get a new window—is in fact a fallacy. The reasoning is poor and perhaps even harmful because it is decidedly one-sided. There is more to the story that is essential for a proper analysis: what is *not* seen.

THAT WHICH IS NOT SEEN

Bastiat's point is that a proper economic analysis of the broken window, and therefore the analysis of the real effect of breaking the window, needs to take into account the alternative outcomes. In other words, Bastiat argues that there is an opportunity cost to the broken window. Were this not the case, then we would be a lot better off by smashing people's windows. In fact, considering the analysis of post-war booms—wouldn't occasional wars be a really good idea? At least from the point of view of economic growth, bombing stuff would increase economic activity, set the "wheels in motion," and thus create both jobs and value. Not so, says Bastiat, because we haven't considered the opportunity cost—and that's the proper way of figuring out the real economic effect. Continuing the parable of the broken window, he addresses the issue of opportunity cost as follows.

> [If] you come to the conclusion, as is too often the case, that it is a good thing to break windows, that it causes money to circulate, and that the encouragement of industry in general will be the result of it, you will oblige me to call out, "Stop there! Your theory is confined to that which is seen; it takes no account of that which is not seen."
>
> It is not seen that as our shopkeeper has spent six francs upon one thing, he cannot spend them upon another. It is not seen that if he had not had a window to replace, he would, perhaps, have replaced his old shoes, or added another book to his library. In short, he would have employed his six francs in some way, which this accident has prevented.

Indeed, the opportunity cost to breaking the window (or, really, to replace the broken one) is the *other value* that is foregone by this action. This is the reason why it makes no sense to smash windows to create income for glaziers—it doesn't make society better off. It makes the glazier and whoever the glazier then trades with better off, but at the expense of whoever would have received the income. Yes, *at their expense*. But how does this make sense—haven't we already argued that the market is not a zero-sum game?

Yes, we have. But imagine the alternative scenario where the shopkeeper's son had not happened to break the window. Then the shopkeeper would have a whole window *and* the 6 francs. If he would have used that money to buy shoes, then he would have a window and the shoes, and we would have the "multiplier" work its way through the economy through the shoemaker rather than the glazier. The major difference, of course, is the window: the multiplier effect, assuming we use a standard fraction for consumption/investment, is the same for the 6 francs whether or not the window is broken. The difference between the scenarios, from the point of view of the economic organism, is the window.

The difference is greater if we consider the individual level rather than the system as a whole. The shopkeeper has reason to be furious, because he just lost 6 francs because of his son's careless action. Had the son behaved, the shopkeeper would have a window and the shoes, but because of the broken window the 6 francs are spent to undo the damage. Destruction, of course, is not a means to become rich. This suggests an answer to the implied question about war above: Is war beneficial? No, of course not. Wars destroy, and destruction is a loss. If we for a moment disregard the suffering and death experienced by people affected by war, the economic effect of war may be a post-war boom through increased economic activity and therefore increasing GDP statistics (what is commonly thought of as economic growth). But if we apply Bastiat's lesson on wars, we immediately realize that there was value in the form of houses, roads, infrastructure, and supply chains that were destroyed in the war. The reason we see increased economic activity is that people have lost their homes and need to rebuild them quickly to have shelter, so they might work day and night for a while just to restore what they used to have.

What we don't see, of course, is what these people would have done had they instead kept their homes and if the infrastructure and supply chains were intact. They may not have worked as many hours, simply because they wouldn't need to, but they would start from a much higher level in terms of prosperity. So whereas the economic activity after a destructive war may increase, it increases primarily because the value that has been lost must be restored. It is not actual value creation, but value restoration. All this work would not be needed had the war not destroyed the value that was already created. This means they would have more options had the value not been destroyed: had they not lost their homes, they would have plenty of optionality because the opportunity cost would be relatively high for many alternatives. But since they are without shelter, the value of any action other than rebuilding their homes is so much lower that it makes no sense to even consider it. In fact, the need for shelter is so pressing that leisure or even sleep is not an option, so they may choose to work day and night to restore what was destroyed.

Note that the take-away here is that there is an opportunity cost to economic activity as well. Had there not been destructive bombing of their city, the inhabitants would be relatively richer, they would be presented with several alternatives of similar value—and the value of leisure may be one of them. At some point, of course, we are satisfied with what we have accomplished and value time off higher than more time working. This is also an important tradeoff, and therefore relevant to our discussion on choice and optionality—and the cost of choosing, or opportunity cost. But with your home flattened by bombs, the value of having it restored is so much higher, relatively speaking, than alternative uses of your time, such as leisure. Most of us would not even consider working normal hours to restore it, but it would be an obvious choice for us to work day and night to regain a certain standard of living. The relative value of leisure is very low when you and your family have no place to live.

DESTRUCTION AND OPTIONALITY

As we have seen above, and that we learned with the help of Bastiat's discussion on the seen and unseen, destruction has different implications depending on one's level of analysis—and where one looks. For the economic system, the effect of the broken window is approximately the value of the window. The "multiplier" effect acts in both the seen and the unseen, and unless we know that destroying the window will lead to a much higher fraction of consumed/reinvested income in the chain of actions that begin with the glazier than the chain of actions that begin with the shoemaker, then both effects are approximately the same. Of course, for this to be the case, we must also assume that the replaced window pane is sold at the same cost as the shoes. Nevertheless, it would be erroneous to assume that there is a "multiplier" effect on one side but not the other, so even if they are not exactly the same they will to some extent balance out.

But if we instead look at the individuals involved, and therefore focus on each person, then it becomes obvious that the shopkeeper's son has cost his father six francs by breaking the window. This is a loss that the shopkeeper will have to cover by either accepting lower profits, raising prices, or cutting costs in his business. In Bastiat's example, the shopkeeper is assumed to forego part of his profits and, consequently, what he intended to use that profit for: purchasing new shoes. Perhaps those shoes were for the son, who by acting carelessly has now indirectly caused a loss upon himself by not getting the shoes he was promised or hoped for.

Yet this is only the direct effect on the individual level. We must also consider the indirect effects. As there are indeed similar "multiplier" effects that arise from paying six francs to either the glazier or shoemaker, very different people get this money. If you are the shoemaker and I am the glazier, whether the shopkeeper's son breaks the window makes a huge difference to us. In this case, it is the difference of six francs' worth of sales: either you sell the shoes (because the shopkeeper has a window without holes in it) or I sell the window pane (because the son has managed to force a rock through the window that the shopkeeper had). Either you get the extra income or I do, which of course affects our choices. Without the extra income, I (the glazier) wouldn't buy ice cream, which means the ice cream maker might not buy the better milk from the farmer, which means the farmer might not invest in a better breed of cows, and so on. Of course, this chain of events is initiated because the shopkeeper's son destroys the window and his father therefore loses six francs. In the original situation, before the son breaks the window, the father values the six francs more than a window (since he has no windows that need to be replaced) but less than a pair of shoes. After the window is broken, however, his preference ranking has changed because his satisfactions—the wants that were satisfied—have changed. Or perhaps we should say: his preferences have been forcefully rearranged, since he's lost a value that he enjoyed. After the window is broken, replacing it becomes necessary or much more urgent and it is therefore worth more to him than the shoes. As he only has the six francs and cannot buy both the windows and the shoes, he might no longer value the shoes more than the six francs (for the simple reason that he needs the window and knows that he can get one for six francs).

So we see how the preferences held by economic actors change all the time, even as a result of rather banal things like a broken window. This is a fact that entrepreneurs have to deal with, and this is why they cannot do better than trying to imagine the future and estimate whether there will be—for wannabe glaziers—enough broken windows to profit from such an endeavor. The shopkeeper's preferences changed quite dramatically, at least from the point of view of the glazier or shoemaker, as a result of the boy's rock throwing.

Considering what we have learned above, the alternative to a broken window should seem a lot better to the observer. Not only is there a fully functional window in the shop, but the shopkeeper buys a pair of shoes as well. So we get the "multiplier" effect as in the previous example but our starting point is at a higher level of wants satisfaction: with a whole rather than broken window. The chain of transactions following the shoe purchase could then seem much more positive and beneficial, and in a sense this is the case. But it is the case only because we focus on the window. The "multiplier" is, as we noted above, approximately the same. But, of course, the revenues will be received by completely different people. The shoe maker, upon making the sale, may buy additional or better leather from the hunter, who might invest in a better trap to catch more beavers, and the trap maker might use his additional income to buy a little ice cream on a sunny day. If this is so, then the ice cream maker makes a sale in both scenarios. But if the trap maker buys less ice cream than the glazier would have, perhaps because his income increases less than the glazier's, the ice cream maker is a little less better off in this particular chain as compared to the other one. Though, of course, he still makes a sale. Yet for the trap maker, the hunter, and the shoe maker it makes a greater difference whether the shopkeeper's son throws rocks through windows.

We cannot, of course, blame the glazier for wanting to sell window panes just like we cannot blame the ice cream maker for wanting to sell more ice cream. As long as the glazier doesn't pay the shopkeeper's son to break the window, the exchange between the shopkeeper and the glazier is voluntary and for mutual benefit: there is nothing fishy going on, no fraud or theft. So there are no moral implications of the "multiplier" effect and therefore of the ripple effects through an economy; they happen because people can improve their lives through engaging in voluntary exchange. But the "multiplier" does affect what choices people are able to make, and who is able to make them. The shopkeeper is left with little choice other than investing in a new window pane when it breaks, so the loss has a very real effect on the shopkeeper's freedom or optionality. Destruction is consequently not a way toward increased prosperity, as we saw above, and cannot be thought of as an empowerment of those directly affected. The same is true for anyone involved in and, perhaps, dependent on the chain of events that doesn't happen because of the destruction. On the other hand, replacing the window pane—which after it is already broken is the better option for the shopkeeper, since he values it higher than the shoes—similarly enables the glazier (and, if the choices are as above, also the ice cream maker, the farmer, and so on) to make choices previously not within reach. Voluntary trade, as made possible by specialized production, facilitates additional choices by those involved by increasing their well-being, but trade also creates a chain of empowering events that "ripple" through the economy.

This is why it is important to understand the "flow" of goods and values through an economy. Without understanding that "one thing leads to another," we cannot trace or assess the effect that both endogenous choices (production, exchange, and so on) and exogenous forces have on an economy—because we don't really understand how the market works. As Bastiat teaches, we need to look at both the seen and the unseen, and understand the overall process within the market. Furthermore, as we will see in later chapters—and especially chapter 9—it is important to recognize the effects of changes on individuals' available options for action: that is, their optionality and thus the "freedom" to choose as follows from the number and quality of alternatives that are realized for the individual.

NOTE

1. This and the next section rely on and summarize the argument originally expressed in Frédéric Bastiat's essay "That Which Is Seen, and That Which Is Not Seen" (*Ce qu'on voit et ce qu'on ne voit pas*) from 1850. The reader is recommended to read the full argument in the original essay, which is available on many sites on the world wide web.

Chapter Six

The Market and Natural Disasters

We have seen how the economy is affected by destruction, and how replacing a value that has been lost gives rise to a different chain of events than otherwise would have been. After a value has been lost, what is seen is the actions taken to replace this value as well as the actions that follow: the glazier's increased business leads to increased profits and thus a different consumption pattern. While this is value created, we cannot when analyzing the market treat it as value gained. Indeed, there is also the unseen, or the economic activity that would have taken place had there been no destruction of value to begin with. The difference between the two chains of events, as we discussed in the previous chapter as arising from the use of income by the glazier and the shoe maker, respectively, lies not primarily in the extent of the repercussions (that is the ripple effects) but in the point of departure. To again refer to Bastiat's example, the starting point is either the loss caused by a broken window, which sets one specific chain of economic actions in motion, or the situation where the value of the window is retained, which *also* sets a specific chain of economic actions in motion. It is a fallacy not to consider the unseen, which is the opportunity cost of what we see happening.

While a market's structure and evolution is primarily endogenously motivated and, consequently, in constant flux, it is also affected by exogenous forces. This is easy to realize when considering such trades as farming, fishing, and hunting, all of which depend on weather, climate, and so on as much as endogenous factors, if not more. The market situation, including both supply and demand, of farm products, fish, and game are endogenous variables, which means they represent effects arising from within the economic organism. In fact, the very reason we can think of them as products, which makes them potentially saleable through exchange, is due to consumers' existing demand and because producers have invested time, effort, and capital into supplying these goods with the intention of satisfying demand through exchange. These are all endogenous to the economy, and therefore cause changes "from within." But production of farm goods, to limit our discussion to one example, is not purely dependent on endogenous effects like supply, demand, and production techniques; it is also dependent on non-economic factors like the suitability of the soil, precipitation, sunlight, temperature, the natural process of growth in planted seeds, and so on. Modern GMO techniques blur the boundaries of what used to be purely endogenous or exogenous, but there are still exogenous elements to them. Also, we have not yet figured out how to replace the sun as an essential input to farming. So while entrepreneurs in farming expect a standard yield from their field, the real outcome of their efforts is subject to exogenous shocks as well as being limited by exogenous restraints such as the natural seasonality of farming: sowing in spring, growing in summer, harvesting in fall.

The farmer-entrepreneur has expectations of standard output quantity from the employed acreage, that is how much (approximately) they expect to grow, but actual production is affected by other things than economic factors such as the occurrence of adverse weather. For instance, the summer could turn out to be unusually hot and dry, or unusually cold and wet, and there may be severe storms or wildfires, all of which would have an effect (in this case, exclusively a *negative* effect) on the farm's yield (its output through production). While much less likely events, a meteor may hit the farm, a volcano may erupt and cover the fields in lava or ash, or a landslide or sink hole could completely undo the farm. These are all examples of exogenous forces that affect the yield of the farm, and for this reason the farmer's return to investment, and therefore contribute to the uncertainty of the undertaking: the farmer-entrepreneur cannot know whether the weather will be beneficial or not—or to what degree. They also originate specifically *outside* the economic system: neither the number of sun hours nor average temperature nor precipitation have economic causes. So while the economic organism overall is primarily an endogenously generated structure, it is also subject to exogenous forces that affect how and whether it works. The question, therefore, is whether and to what degree the economic system—the *market*—can handle, avoid or respond well to exogenous forces that can change the conditions for production. As we know from previous chapters, the economy is already busy responding and adjusting to the numerous changes coming from within.

In general, risk management consists of lowering the cost of negative effects by employing one or a combination of two strategies: preventive action to reduce the likelihood that an event will occur, and responsive action to mitigate the effects of already occurred events. We will look at these two strategies as they apply also to the economy and will revisit Adele's apple-growing undertaking to illustrate. At the time when we come back to see her, the orchard is recently established and has yet to bear fruit. In other words, she's heavily invested and is still expecting the orchard to produce apples that she will eagerly sell to the market to cover her costs and make a profit. But she hasn't had any apples produced yet, and thus she has made no sale. Our focus is on how she acts to handle exogenous events.

AVOIDANCE THROUGH CONTROL

Before Adele decided to go into the apple-growing business, she studied it in detail so that she would know what to expect. Like any other specialized trade, there is a lot to apple-growing that those who are not in the business don't know (or care) about. So there was a learning curve (that is, it took time and effort to acquire the knowledge and skill necessary), but Adele is a thoughtful person who lives by the motto of "better safe than sorry" so she didn't mind investing the time and effort—in fact, she preferred doing so to acting without thinking first. Also, she would much rather spend a little now to limit the possible downside than risk losing it all because she's poorly prepared when an adverse event happens. In other words, she is risk averse and thus prefers little risk to more risk.

When studying apple-growing, Adele realizes that there are many things that can go wrong. As the production process is very long—it takes years from planting the trees until they produce apples—there are many things that can happen. With several seasons between planting the seeds and the first harvest, both very hot or very wet summers would delay the growth of the trees and therefore her return on investment. So she decides early on that it would be wise to invest in an irrigation system to make sure the trees would grow even if there was not sufficient precipitation. It cost her a lot extra to contract with Frank, who is an irrigation expert from the other side of the mountain, to connect pipes to the nearby lake for irrigation. But the cost is worth it, Adele figures, because the cost of delaying income from selling apples by a year or two would be disastrous. It therefore makes sense to shoulder the extra cost up front, even though there is no saying whether there would be enough rain the next few years.

She is also aware of the risk that there might not be enough sun for the trees to bloom and bear fruit. This would postpone her chance of income in the same way as a lack of rain, the sun is much harder to replace. So that risk was one she would have to take despite all the other potential problems that she could have to face. In fact, to Adele the very reason there is no way of insuring the apple-growing business against too little sun made the irrigation system seem so much more worth it. Because the sun hours in the years to come is an uncertainty that she cannot control, the peace of mind from not having to worry about the supply of water to the trees is worth more to her. And she's also made some calculations to make sure the irrigation makes business sense. Her conclusion was that adding the irrigation system and therefore the higher upfront cost for her business means it will take her longer to cover her investment, but that she expects this cost of waiting to be lower than the cost of risking a slowing in the growth of the apple trees—even if the risk of a dry, hot summer is quite low.

So while she has chosen to control water supply to the trees, she has also chosen to bear the uncertainty of too little sun. Both too little precipitation and too little sun are exogenous events that would be very costly to Adele should they occur. Neither can be prevented in any real sense, since we cannot control nature. But the cost of slow tree growth due to a lack of rain can be avoided by investing in productive means that replace the natural process and therefore, in a sense, counteract natural effects. We can see, then, how the innovation of specific productive capital—the creation of *economic* resources—such as irrigation provides a means to make production independent of—and, in other words, control—the whims of nature. Indeed, the economic realm is continuously affected by and ultimately depends on the resources offered by nature, but its productive power is distinct from it. The production and maintenance of productive capital is a means to bring about a permanently higher degree of wants satisfaction. [1]

Irrigation is not the only type of capital that Adele may choose to invest in to increase or speed up production. As we saw in previous chapters, she could invest in labor to clear the land, plant the seeds, and tend to the trees much more effectively—and therefore in a less time-consuming manner—than she would be able to without investing in it. And she could invest in machinery as well to increase the productivity of the employed worker, thereby further increasing the output per paid labor hour or dollar invested. These are all endogenous or economic means to handle both endogenous and exogenous problems, and both using and not using them comes at a cost: to not employ others to help her means she will need to invest more of her own time and labor; to not buy machinery means she will need to employ more people, and so on. Economic decisions are always about tradeoffs between different goods and different costs—and when they are expected to occur. Some things are impossible to control—such as the number of sun hours—whereas others seem too costly to be "worth it," that is the benefit is too low to warrant the cost.

In addition to the irrigation system, Adele invests in pest control. Some pests are too uncommon to be worth the trouble, but others pose real threat to her business. She chooses to set out scarecrows to keep birds from eating the fruit before it is sufficiently ripe to be picked. Scarecrows are not perfect, but will keep the number of birds down—and scare off the worst kinds—efficiently enough to cover the cost of the scarecrows and then some. Again, Adele estimates the cost of the means—buying and setting out several scarecrows—with the estimated benefit—avoiding in part the loss of apples to hungry birds. The issue of scarecrows is a no-brainer, since the scarecrows won't cost her much and will remain useful for a long time—and they will keep plenty of birds off the apples. The benefit of investing in them exceed the cost by so much that there was no calculation necessary.

For other pests, however, it's not as obvious. Apple trees can be infested by moths and mites; they can become the homes of larvae like the Apple Tree Borer; and they can attract scab and other fungi or diseases. For many of these, there are countermeasures available that can help save the trees by preventing infestation or by fighting pests that have already affected the trees. But whether it is a good investment must be decided without the facts known: whether Adele's orchard will be infested is something she cannot know—she can only make educated guesses about the risk and the approximate cost if her orchard is affected by a specific kind of pest. In this case, she decides not to use any countermeasures. With the irrigation system and scarecrows, she imagines that she'll have enough chance of getting a sufficiently large harvest that will produce a comfortable return on investment. Considering the whole undertaking, the risk of infestation is too small and the cost of prevention too high for it to make economic sense, she reasons.

RESPONDING TO "SHOCKS"

We're now a couple of years into the apple-growing business and the orchard is beginning to look like an actual orchard. The trees are growing fast and Adele is happy with how the irrigation system kept the dirt moist when they experienced a couple of very hot and dry weeks last summer. Within a couple of years, she hopes to have a first limited harvest available for sale, and then in a couple of more years production peaks. So far, she's avoided the costs of too little rain because of the irrigation system (which proved to be a prudent investment) and she hasn't suffered much from loss of sun. Moreover, she's had no real issue with pests and only a few birds have dared defy the scarecrows. She is very happy with how things have turned out, even considering that she chose to not employ anyone but is relying on only her own—and a few of her nephews'—efforts. It has been tough at times, but not too much to handle. So she is glad that she didn't take on the extra cost of employing others; as things turned out, it would not have contributed to her bottom line so the cost would have exceeded the benefits.

As the spring nears, she hears reports from other apple-growers in the region that they have seen signs of scab on the trees. Scab is not an uncommon fungal infection of apple trees, but it can potentially kill a whole orchard if it is not properly controlled. The news, therefore, is not good. Adele had actually noticed scab lesions on a couple of her trees in the previous fall, but took action to excise them from the trees. She chose to take other precautions as well, such as removing all leaf litter from under the trees often, but chose not to invest in the potentially harmful chemical controls that can be used to fight apple scab. So she realizes that she might be affected. But as she has seen nothing to indicate that her orchard has been infected, at least not more than the minor lesions she's already dealt with, and has taken all the non-chemical precautions, she estimates that she is comparatively safe. In her mind the reports do not justify the cost and other unfavorable effects.

Unfortunately, the reports were not exaggerated. As spring moves into early summer, it becomes clear that many of the orchards are suffering severe scab infections. The affected apple-growers lose the year's harvest, since scabbed apples are very hard to sell—at least at a price that makes sense. Adele and a few others are lucky to avoid infection, whereas other apple-growers had chosen to apply chemical controls. The latter apples sell at a lower price because of the potential harmful effects, but these growers—in contrast to Adele—have considered the lower revenue to be a worthwhile cost in comparison to the risk of losing a year's harvest or the whole orchard. As a result of the scab, the supply of apples to the market diminishes.

Whether or not consumers are aware of the scab, it soon becomes obvious that there are not as many apples available as expected. Consumers looking to buy apples find grocery stores with empty apple bins, and the stores in turn cannot find apples to fill their bins. As consumers' quantity demanded exceeds the available supply, the price is bid up. The effect is here the same as if consumer demand suddenly increases and entrepreneurs therefore, as a result, make a mistake in expecting to produce to satisfy a lower demand. In fact, the story is exactly the same whether or not the demand changes: entrepreneurial mistakes cause a mismatch between supply and demand, which brings about a price change.

Some entrepreneurs realize that things have changed unexpectedly sooner than other entrepreneurs. For instance, some grocery store entrepreneurs increase their price of apples before the shortage is obvious because they judge or imagine the situation correctly. These stores would at first be avoided by consumers, since their price of apples is higher—apples are available at lower prices elsewhere. But as soon as grocery stores with lower prices run out of apples, anyone who wants apples would need to go to a high-price store. That is, after all, the only place that still offers apples for sale. Of course, those consumers who don't think the higher asking price for apples is "worth it" will not go there. But there may be enough actual customers for these entrepreneurs to sell their stock.

Likewise, some wholesaler entrepreneurs would imagine that prices are traded at a too low price and will therefore raise their prices. Grocery stores too will at first avoid them, since apples are available from other wholesalers at a lower price. But as soon as the shortage becomes apparent, they will consider the higher price—if they think consumers are likely to pay enough for the remaining apples. And the same applies to the unaffected apple-growers—like Adele—who are likely to realize the shortage sooner than those further down the chain. They will require a higher price to sell their apples because they imagine the lower supply is not met by a lower demand which means the market will bear the higher price.

What this means is that a shortage does not necessary have to be realized before the adjustment process begins. In fact, consumers may not see empty bins but only a higher price tag—because entrepreneurs throughout the supply chain will have adjusted their buying and selling in anticipation of how consumers will react to the lower supply. And the consumers may in fact be completely ignorant of the sudden large-scale scab infection of orchards. They don't need to know the details,[2] but need only react to the prices that entrepreneurs ask for apples: if the price is too high, too few of them will buy; if it is too low, too many of them will want to buy. As a result, the entrepreneurs will either realize their mistaken anticipated price and make the proper adjustments up or down, or will end up bearing the full cost of their mistake. The entrepreneur's task, after all, is to attempt to correctly anticipate consumers' true valuation of the good they offer for sale and in what quantity—and bear the uncertainty thereof.

So we see that exogenous shocks to the "economic organism" are handled just as endogenous such as by decentralized, bottom-up adjustments to prices and offerings. In our example, apples were infected by apple scab, which reduced the supply. As the general tendency in any market is to find the proper balance between supply and demand through price, an exogenous shock to supply is not different from an endogenous shock from changing consumer preferences. It is also not different from an endogenous shock to supply through disruptive innovation, which can completely change what is produced and how it is being produced. But can the market's decentralized and "automatic" adjustments be sufficient in a time of real crisis? What if there is not a scab affecting apples, but an earthquake or hurricane devastating a whole city?

DISASTER

A disaster, whether it is devastation due to natural forces such as earthquakes, volcanic eruptions, tsunamis, and hurricanes or man-made destruction from wars or rent control,[3] can, economically speaking, be understood as an abrupt and radical increase in scarcity. While the apple scab is also an increase in scarcity (the scab diminishes the supply of apples), it affects a single good and one that is likely inessential for the population. Disasters, in contrast, have a huge impact on the supply of essential goods such as food, shelter, and power; they greatly reduce the supply—or even wipe it out—and therefore put people in a very delicate situation. In other words, they create abject scarcity of essential goods within a very short time frame.

For it to be a disaster, the change needs to be unanticipated. As we discussed above, market production is continuously adjusted toward the anticipated future by entrepreneurs attempting to outdo each other by finding a better use for resources available or invented. If the supply of essential goods is dramatically reduced but the change is anticipated, then prices and production structures have already been adjusted to account for this change, and the disastrous effects are therefore mitigated if not even avoided. A disaster is therefore different from other radical change because it is rarely anticipated if at all as well as affecting most or all goods across the board.

So how would the "market" respond to for instance an earthquake that breaks bridges in two, wrecks and flattens houses, and causes mayhem? The answer is no different from above: by finding prices where supply meets demand and by reallocating resources toward their better uses. Following a disaster, there are fewer resources available than before but there are still resources. Of course, the initial and direct response to a disaster is likely to be in the form of community and voluntary efforts rather than organized for-profit entrepreneurship: neighborhood communities, churches, families, and other associations, new and old, get together to pool their resources in order to help those in greatest need. For example, temporary hospitals would be set up and run by volunteers, people would get together in teams for organized search and rescue, and temporary shelters would be made for those without. These community and volunteer efforts should not be discounted or underestimated, but they too will benefit from the market response.

At some point, and following a disaster this would happen rather soon, the affected region will fall short of and therefore need supplies from elsewhere—as well as produce their own to the degree possible. Both of these, which aim to increase supply, are primarily economic activities, and can thus be explained using the template from above. Two responses are needed: increased inflow of necessary and needed goods, and reallocation of remaining resources toward the now more highly valued needs (shelter, food, water, etc.).

The increased inflow of goods from elsewhere is accomplished in two ways, both of which are important. First, there is the voluntary and community-based relief efforts through aid: for instance, private people or organizations renting trucks to transport and offer their personal property to those in need; there are also organizations dedicated to relief work and aid like the Médecins Sans Frontières (Doctors Without Borders), and the Red Cross. These organizations are dependent on the charity of those who were not affected, and therefore indirectly on the productive power of economies not devastated. There will likely be campaigns urging donations to help those affected, and as a result new resources are collected to be transferred to the benefit of people in affected areas. Of more direct interest to us here, however, is the incentive-based economic mechanism for directing goods toward disaster areas. As above, this involves adjustments to the prices of goods. As the need increases for certain goods, so does the willingness to pay for those goods and as this leads to a higher price it produces an incentive to increase production of those goods to satisfy the demand.

Antibiotics may serve as an example of this. The need for antibiotics is higher following disaster than before, whereas the demand in other, unaffected areas likely does not undergo a drastic change—if any at all. The price may therefore go up in the affected area, which will attract antibiotics from other regions. As the price goes up, of course, we know that more of the more highly priced goods will be reallocated toward a higher price (the more intense want/need). But how can the price go up in a disaster area? After all, people who have lost everything hardly have money to pay for antibiotics. This may be true, but it is not necessary to have cash in hand to pay the higher price—this price could be paid in many other ways. We should recall that a higher price is the most effective way in which existing antibiotics are directed toward their better uses—and the way to effectively drive up supply by increasing production. What matters is that the higher price is offered in some way, not that cash is provided. So the price can be offered and paid by those donating money for relief efforts, by those needing effort offering future payment (that is, they assume debt), or by suppliers in unaffected areas hoping to increase their customer base by developing goodwill through gifting antibiotics to disaster areas. The effect is the same: the relative price of the good in the disaster area increases, and therefore more of it will be allocated toward satisfying wants and needs there rather than in other places.

But we should not forget that the redirection of antibiotics toward the greater need, whether this is through donations or charitable activities or for-profit market action, also means there is relatively less of this good available overall. In other words, the price goes up as the demand for the good has increased *overall* and this incentivizes producers to increase and accelerate production as well as deplete stocks they have kept in anticipation of higher future prices, and therefore increase the available supply. So even though there may be higher "bids" for antibiotics in the disaster-stricken area, the relative asking price will also increase in surrounding areas and this will bring about increased production as well as inflow from more distant areas. In other words, the price mechanism works to both redirect existing resources toward their greater need from area to area, and increase supply of goods that become relatively less abundant (more scarce).

Price also plays a role in reallocating resources already in use in the affected area. For instance, a single-family dwelling could be used as a hospital. In many cases, owners may recognize the need and therefore offer their space to help those in greater need. Where this is not the case, a higher price—whether offered in cash, goods, service, gratitude from the community, or future payment—entices those in control of the resources to allow them to be used toward the greater good.

This is also about discovery, since resources can have multiple uses. Thus, a resource used in a certain way, and generally recognized as usable primarily in that specific way, may have other uses that directly contribute to satisfying the more urgent needs. These uses are discoverable because the greater needs are identified through the adjustment to prices. Whereas prices may not be determined immediately (or in a vacuum), and therefore may not be of much use immediately following the earthquake-caused disaster, prohibiting prices to be determined can itself bring about a disaster. Prices, as we have noted above, do not need to be cash prices but can be expressed in other goods, in access or other grants of opportunities, or anything else that individuals consider valuable. Indeed, a disaster area may adopt a completely different means of exchange—a different kind of money, as it were—that makes more sense in that unique and terrible situation.

Whereas disasters make it less obvious how the economic organism would properly and without direction adjusts to the new conditions, the mechanisms remain the same. The difference between a disaster area and the examples of "shocks" above is the former's greater magnitude, which calls for faster and significant change, and because infrastructure for communications and power as well as existing institutions, such as money, may have been affected or even destroyed. Such changes indeed hinder the economic organism from effectively responding, but this does not change the fact that better ways are hard to come by—if at all possible. Whereas the immediate relief may be charitable and in the form of aid, this effort depends on market mechanisms for its ability to function and—more importantly—continue to provide relief. The market mechanisms are far from efficient but provide the framework within which individuals' incentives and actions are aligned, and the totality pull in the same direction.

The aftermath of Hurricane Katrina, to date the costliest natural disaster and one of the deadliest hurricanes in United States history, can be used to illustrate the economy's response and effect in the wake of natural disaster. Hurricane Katrina hit the Gulf of Mexico in August 2005 and caused vast destruction and flooding along the Gulf coast from Central Florida to Texas. The most severe flooding, with water lingering for weeks, happened in New Orleans, Louisiana, as a result of extensive levee failure in the city's hurricane surge protection. A large part of the city was evacuated as the destruction made much of the Gulf coast dangerous or uninhabitable, without functioning infrastructure and services. For instance, at the peak of the storm the big-box retailer Walmart closed 2 of its distribution centers and 126 of its stores, of which "more than half ended up losing power, some were flooded, and 89 . . . reported damage."[4] But within ten days 121 of those stores were open again, as a result of corporate resources having been redirected toward preparing for the impact of the storm and more resources allocated toward restoring damaged stores.[5]

Several of the big-box retail chains as well as large fast-food restaurant chains like McDonald's have permanent crisis centers with dedicated resources to prepare for destruction and disasters, and are tasked with quickly re-establishing "business as usual"—to avoid losses and thus maintain profitability. As the storm neared, these businesses directed more of their resources to their crisis centers in order to plan and prepare for impact and thereby minimize the interruption and cost due to destruction. In fact, private enterprises responded quickly to Hurricane Katrina and was overall much more effective than government in providing necessities such as food and water as well as shelter, and restoring supply chains to the affected areas. As reported by economist Steven Horwitz,[6] businesses "responded with speed and effectiveness, often in spite of government relief workers' attempts to stymie it, and in the process saved numerous lives and prevented looting and chaos that otherwise would have occurred." Their responses, both the preparation for and the execution of restoration efforts, illustrate the redirection of resources from unaffected parts of the market toward those parts in greater need.

These efforts were not made merely to quickly restore profitability, even though this was an important reason for repairing stores and re-establishing supply chains. Many of the private businesses took an active part in community efforts to restore normalcy, both through assuming large costs for restoration work, donations to charity, and helping employees and their families to find new or temporary homes. They also provided food and necessities such as water free of charge to those in need. Walmart is credited with providing the local population with water and food, hospitals with medicines and supplies, and providing space in their stores to serve as headquarters for relief organizations.[7]

This private relief effort was not uniquely done by big national corporations, of course, though they were, by their sheer size, and thus the amount of resources they control, able to redirect more resources to the affected areas. The local communities focused their time, resources, and energy toward restoring their neighborhoods and reclaiming their normal lives. Numerous private citizens both in the affected areas and elsewhere coordinated efforts to help those in need by themselves contributing manpower and supplies as well as helping through established charitable organizations. The majority of this work, of course, was carried out by those most severely affected, that is the inhabitants of the flooded and otherwise affected areas, who had their dwellings destroyed, their families split up, and who lost their jobs and incomes. Whereas it took only days for the hurricane to pass, the work to restore the destruction to property—estimated to be in excess of $100 billion—took many years. Upon being evacuated and displaced, hundreds of thousands of the city's previous inhabitants returned to the New Orleans area to rebuild what had been destroyed.[8]

We can see, therefore, how Hurricane Katrina, while a terrible event that killed well over one thousand people and displaced hundreds of thousands, illustrates what was argued above about redirected resource flows and changing preferences in the face of disaster—both in the directly affected areas and elsewhere. Much of the relief efforts—especially the first wave of supplies and restoration—were effectuated by the economic organism in the form of community efforts and private capital owners (both businesses and individual persons). The existing infrastructure, supply chains, and productive capital structure were highly effective at responding to the Hurricane Katrina disaster and constituted an important part of charitable work within and toward local and regional communities. The governmental authorities "responsible" for such efforts were not effective.

DISASTER AND OPTIONALITY

What separates disaster from the destruction we discussed in the previous chapter is the scale and scope of its effects. The destruction of a window pane is very limited and yet it can have a significant impact on the market through the "ripple effects" that change what is being produced and how—even though it is limited in scale and scope. If a broken window can have such an effect on people's choices down the line, as we saw in the case of what choices are made and who makes those choices (the shoe maker versus the glazier, and so on), imagine the potential effects of a large number of windows being broken on a particular day. This could easily change consumption and investment patterns in such a way that the outcome of market production—what entrepreneurs and thus the market end up producing—is different from what it otherwise would have been. Add to this picture that not only windows are broken, but that all kinds of resources are destroyed, worn out, or outdated continuously. It becomes obvious that an economy must deal with and be able to respond to these changes, some of which are predictable while others are not. And this is indeed what we see through supply chains and trade: things break all the time, and this must be considered in the calculations made by entrepreneurs. This is part of the reason they will require a profit margin in order to undertake an uncertain endeavor: to cover for expenses due to unforeseen events. It is also a reason why the economy as an organism produces superior results to any planned structure. Planning only works based on known events or known probabilities of events (that is a known or well understood risk), but with the future being highly uncertain in more ways than we can possibly imagine, a planned system will be too rigid to be able to respond to the myriad minor changes and the number of major changes that affect production. The flexibility of decentralized production and the decentralized decision-making that the market offers is unbeatable, as we saw in chapter 4, because it is highly flexible, include redundancy, and therefore can respond to changes using the information available locally or the imagination of individual entrepreneurs.

Consider the situation where destruction is not limited in scope or scale, as was the case in chapter 5, but where destruction affects production in a great number of ways at the same time. And that this destruction is also widespread, and therefore affects many types of production at the same time. This is the nature of disaster, as was discussed above. It destroys what is otherwise believed to be permanent (or at least long-lasting, endurable) resources and pulls out the rug from under the feet of entrepreneurs' production undertakings. As in the case of destruction, this has an effect on what people need and want, and it often creates an urgent need to satisfy the most basic needs: shelter, food, medicine, safety. In other words, consumers no longer demand the great number of different types of goods that they recently were willing to spend money on buying, but instead focus their attention solely or primarily on reestablishing what we can refer to as "normal life." Needless to say, they are less interested in their optionality—the various different types of goods and services offered—than they are in satisfying the very urgent needs that, due to the disaster, are no longer satisfied.

The fact that a disaster sets society back via large-scale and large-scope destruction, which effectively strips people from the means by which they had been able to satisfy their basic needs, changes people's preference rankings. They will likely still find value in choices as well as in gadgets and goods and services that provide convenience, but these pale in comparison to the basic needs that no longer are satisfied. As the basic needs are not satisfied, they are felt with a great sense of urgency. Consequently, we can say that, to them, what *matters*—in other words, what is much more highly valued—to them is to fulfill or satisfy those needs—not other, and less highly ranked wants. This is the same thing as saying that they feel a strong uneasiness with regard to the basic needs that were lost due to the disaster, whereas the uneasiness they feel with regard to non-basic needs such as convenience is comparatively much lower. While they may have considered upgrading to a newer model smartphone, this value—which could still be a value—is much lower than the now no longer satisfied need for food and shelter. It therefore makes sense to redirect resources to satisfy the basic needs first. Depending on the scale and scope of the destruction, *all* resources may need to be reallocated toward providing shelter, food, security, and so forth.

A disaster, which is in fact destruction of great magnitude, destroys a large part of the capital structure within the economy and therefore inhibits its ability to satisfy wants to the degree previously possible. This is a burden on consumers, but a burden that is at least in part lessened by their changing preferences. As the urgency of satisfying basic needs following a disaster spikes, consumers are no longer as troubled with the wants that used to be their focus—they are now, relatively speaking, much less urgent and therefore of much lesser relative value. So it is not the case that the inhabitants of a city hit by a hurricane, for instance, will strive toward the same goals as prior to the hurricane. And they will not even consider it much of a burden until they have regained their previous standard of living. At the very top of their preference ranking is to satisfy those basic needs that they no longer can satisfy. A disaster therefore impacts the capital structure of the economy while at the same time, due to the loss, effectuating a change in consumers' preference rankings. People in general, when stripped of their means to satisfy basic needs, focus their attention to resatisfy those and therefore, as a result, change how they rank all of their preferences. The loss of capital, in a sense, is met by a reassessment of the importance of wants to a similar degree: with the loss of capital, consumers adjust their preferences to meet the availability of capital.

This does not, of course, mean that consumers are not made worse off by the disaster—the destruction of capital is indeed a loss of much of their combined ability to satisfy wants. This, in effect, is the reason people change their preference rankings. There is no point in pursuing or being bothered with the wants that are now very far from being satisfied. In other words, whereas a person might find the business hours of a nearby 7-Eleven disturbingly limiting, or the lack of a specific color of shirt frustrating, these sources of uneasiness are soon forgotten when there is, for instance, no electric power or one's dwelling is destroyed. The loss is undoubtedly there, and due to the destruction, but many of the wants that consumers were looking to satisfy but are now far removed are of little importance relative the utmost urgency of the much more basic needs, possibly necessary for survival, that are no longer satisfied.

Whereas the disaster is an exogenous event with disastrous effect on the workings of the economy, through the destruction of capital, the endogenous response consists of both reallocating resources and the reassessment of preferences. Both of these endogenous responses serve consumers by readjusting their and the producers' expectations. They re-match, in a sense, consumer expectations and, consequently, their attention to wants, to fit the remaining capital structure and the resources made available from elsewhere, and thus the economy's ability to satisfy the held wants. As the capital structure is rebuilt and reformed, consumers' demand will shift as wants are satisfied. This does not necessarily mean it is reconstructed in the image of what used to be, since the relative importance of preferences may have changed. We saw this above in how more wants can be satisfied as a society's capital structure is expanded and, consequently, value created. This holds true whether or not the economy suffers a disaster. While there is great suffering following a disaster, from an economic point of view it constitutes a temporary setback through the loss of capital—and a shake-up of wants satisfaction. As the destruction inhibits the ability of the market to provide alternatives for consumers, and thus constitutes a loss of optionality, the focus of producers and community necessarily shifts toward restoring the economy's ability to satisfy consumers' basic needs rather than their optionality. To have several alternatives of similar value to choose from is a luxury that can only be afforded when a certain level of prosperity, and thus standard of living, has been achieved.

SUMMING UP

The effect of disaster on the economic organism is similar to the effect of limited destruction or loss of value, but it happens on a greater scale and therefore has implications also on a much greater scope of the economy. For this reason, the effect is not a matter of moving from one simple chain of events to another, as was the case with the broken window pane in chapter 5. Indeed, a disaster is widespread destruction of value and therefore a loss of what facilitates valuable exchange. So the alternative ripple effectsthat we analyzed in the case of the broken window are not possible—disasters affect the economy on a much greater scale than the type of destruction we analyzed in previous chapters. The broken window started an alternative chain of events because its destruction was limited and the loss of value specific. This is not the case with disasters, which entail a substantial loss of value for society overall. So the alternative ripple effects that we analyzed in the case of the broken window as not possible—disasters affect the economy on a much greater scale than the type of destruction we analyzed in previous chapters. The broken window started an alternative chain of events because its destruction was limited and the loss of value specific. This is not the case of disasters, which entail a substantial loss of value for society overall. So the alternative ripple effects may be as impossible as the unseen.

However, as disasters have such widespread effect on the production structure and, consequently, on accumulated wealth, the populations affected naturally adjust their preference rankings. It is no longer a matter of valuing the wants that they otherwise would have acted to satisfy, but a re-ranking of wants based on the fact that previously satisfied wants have become unsatisfied as a result of the disaster. As we all act to first satisfy the most urgently felt, that is the most highly valued, of our wants and needs that it is possible to satisfy, the value we enjoyed prior to the disaster consist of satisfied wants that were (and most likely still are) of much greater value. When those values are lost, we are set back to a previous level of want satisfaction and therefore move to satisfy those more urgently felt needs and wants again.

Disasters commonly take from us the ability to satisfy very basic and therefore very highly valued needs such as shelter, access to clean water and food, means of transportation, and so on. It then makes sense for us to immediately direct our efforts toward restoring our satisfaction of those more highly valued needs than strive toward other and much less urgent wants. As a result, we choose to forego luxury consumption such as technology, conspicuous consumption or vanity products, and vacations. We also forego the relative luxury of leisure time, since we value what can be achieved by using that time working to satisfy wants comparatively much more highly. The setback due to disaster, which of course has a terrible effect on the lives and security of people as well as their ability to economically satisfy wants, is therefore met by a concomitant change in preference for production: from production of comfort and convenience to production to satisfy basic needs and provide us with the necessities of life. As what is demanded changes, production follows suit. The disaster causes a general loss of welfare and wellbeing, but this also brings about a redirection of the remaining productive apparatus toward satisfying those wants that are most highly valued. This is quite different from how taxes and regulation affect market production, as we will see in the following chapter.

NOTES

1. See Hayek (1941).
2. See Hayek (1945).
3. Swedish economist Assar Lindbeck has stated that "In many cases rent control appears to be the most efficient technique presently known to destroy a city—except for bombing." Quoted in Rydenfelt (1981, pp. 213, 230).
4. Zimmerman and Bauerlein, 2005.
5. See Horwitz (2009).
6. Horwitz, 2009, p. 512.
7. See Horwitz (2010).
8. See Storr, Chamlee-Wright, and Storr (2015).

Chapter Seven

Taxation and Regulation

The previous two chapters focused on discussing the effects on and response by the market overall, however as a result of a multitude of decentralized, individual exchanges. The response is undirected and taken by each individual motivated by their perceived self-interest yet seemingly coordinated toward finding a new balance between what is possible to produce—the supply—and what is wanted or sought-after by consumers—the demand. Chapter 5 discussed limited destruction and how this causes a different chain of events to happen than otherwise would have been the case, and thereby shifts the market ever so slightly toward different types of production as well as production of different goods. A broken window, we noted, means we do not get the ripple effects that *would have happened* had the shoe maker made that additional sale, that is, what would have happened had there been no destruction of value. Instead, we got a chain of exchanges following the additional sale by the glazier who earned additional income from replacing the broken window. Chapter 6 focused on tracing the effects of, and the market's overall responses to, changes that are much larger in scale and scope. More specifically, the chapter discussed the effects on value and exchanges due to large-scale destruction. The effect is the same in both cases. They differ only in magnitude, not in principle: the destruction causes previously satisfied wants to become unsatisfied, and therefore redirects economic action and thus reallocates resources toward satisfying those wants again.

In the case of disaster, the wants that are being "unsatisfied" are a set of very basic and thus vital needs such as electric power, shelter, access to food and water, and so on. Until those needs are again satisfied, very few people would waste time thinking about conveniences and the large number of wants that may be relevant or even at the top of the list when survival is not an issue (replacing an older model of a smartphone with the most recent one, for instance). In other words, survival is such an urgently felt need—or, which is another way of saying the same thing, so *highly valued*—that other things don't matter much. For instance, leisure time may be of great value when the fridge is fully stocked and there is electricity to keep the food cool and, when needed, run the stove to cook it—and when other conveniences are readily available. But for anyone struggling for survival, leisure time is not an option. Leisure is valued much lower, relatively speaking, when very urgently held needs are left unsatisfied. This is part of the reason we see so much more economic activity following war and large-scale destruction. People in general find securing their survival and restoring the standard of living made possible by the previous production capabilities so much more highly than they value leisure time without wants satisfaction. The tradeoff is no longer leisure or luxury consumption, two options of similar value, but leisure or survival, which are of course valued very differently: the opportunity cost of not choosing leisure when choosing survival is comparatively very low—the opportunity cost of not choosing leisure when choosing to work for the sake of luxury consumption is comparatively high. So people will choose to work longer hours because the destruction has set them back to a standard of living they are not comfortable with. The loss of standard of living is not by choice, but to put in the work needed to regain the previous level *is*. Though it is a choice made under duress, where all other *available* options are of terribly low value in comparison. And thus they choose to forego the leisure time they could have had.

Some things are of course impossible to do regardless of how much we would value the anticipated outcome. What is possible follows from the productive capital available, which is why destruction sets back the standard of living. In a modern society, producing an automobile is no big problem— most of us don't need to even think about it, we just have to visit a dealership to get one. Neither is, as was the case with Adele's entrepreneurial undertaking, planting an orchard to grow apples. Whatever inputs are needed to establish this type of production process are available in the market. For automobile manufacturing, there are already factories and model designs, supply chains, and productive capital specialized toward supporting the process available. For Adele, this includes anything from apple seeds and shovels to advanced irrigation systems and machinery to pesticides and fertilizer. All these things increase her productivity, since with these things made available to her she can produce many more apples than she otherwise would have been able to. Had Adele instead lived in the eighteenth century or in a very poor or developing nation without the proper institutional support, she would perhaps need to attempt to grow apples without fertilizer and pesticides, and perhaps she wouldn't have access to machinery and irrigation. Instead, she would be completely dependent on manual labor and simple tools such as shovels and hand-made scarecrows. She would need to use buckets to carry water from a nearby stream or lake—or collect rain water—to replace the irrigation system. So she would need to use a whole lot more of her labor and use it in a much less productive way, and she would consequently not be able to grow as many apples as she could with all these advanced tools being available.

Destruction has a similar effect: it sets society back because some of the capital used to increase the productivity of labor, and therefore to produce the output expected, is no longer available. The productivity gain that the now destroyed capital good contributed to the overall production apparatus is lost, and therefore part of the ability to produce. In the case of the shopkeeper's broken window, this may have only a very limited effect on his overall productivity. But in the case of natural disaster or war, the effect can be enormous and actually set back the productivity of a whole society several decades. Imagine the productivity and overall output of a modern city, and then consider the production capabilities of this city after extensive bombing: the difference is obvious. The inhabitants' standard of living is a function of their ability to produce, as we noted in previous chapters, so the city after bombing is much less prosperous—because the capital that is destroyed no longer increases the productivity of labor and consequently labor must be used in less productive ways (or to recreate the lost capital). Indeed, when losing the ability to produce, a society or city loses much of their prosperity. The same goes for individual companies or persons.

So far we have only discussed the market and how it responds to *temporary* changes. We have intentionally left out a specific category of influence that has a large effect on all existing modern markets: government regulations and policy, primarily through taxation and regulation. This type of influence is of a different nature than what we have previously discussed, which is why we dedicate this chapter to discussing the effects of taxation and regulation on production and productivity. The relevance to what was previously discussed in terms of destruction is the following: policy is intended to completely do away with certain types of production, perhaps because they are considered illegitimate or harmful, or alternatively limit their production, and thus steer production toward the production of different types of goods. We will first look at the effectiveness of regulation overall, and then at regulation intended to steer and do away with specific types of production, respectively. The next chapter is dedicated to a discussion on policy used not to restrict but to improve productivity.

EFFECTIVE REGULATION

Before we venture into discussing how regulations affect production and thereby the valuable choices—optionality—that consumers enjoy, it is necessary to distinguish between effective and ineffective regulation. Ineffective regulation would be policy that has little real effect and therefore does not effectuate the level of change that was intended. Indeed, the purpose of regulation is to change completely or influence behavior in some specific way to thereby cause a different outcome of the production and activities that take place in the market. Were this not the case, then there would be no purpose to the regulation. It is intended to do something—to have some effect—which means it must also *change* something. Ineffective regulation fails to bring about change, and therefore has no effect.

There are several reasons why regulations may be ineffective, but the outcome of ineffective regulation is the same: no or at least insufficient change. Consider for instance regulation intended to force certain production techniques to be adopted in apple growing. The regulation is effective if it actually changes Adele's behavior away from the technique she is currently using (if we assume it is an unwanted technique) and instead toward techniques that are considered better from the point of view of policy-makers. We would consider the regulation ineffective if it does not change Adele's behavior at all or if it changes it too little to accomplish the intended outcome. The regulation would be a failure if it changes behavior in the wrong way.

The regulation does not affect how Adele does business if it simply doesn't apply. A real life example of this, often used in economics courses, would be a legally mandated price floor such as a minimum wage that is set lower than the going market price. So enacting a law prohibiting employment at wages lower than $1.00 per hour, for instance, would have very little if any effect on existing employment and wages. It certainly doesn't bring about the type of change intended by enacting and enforcing a minimum wage at that level. The reason is obvious: there may be no jobs that pay less than $1.00 per hour, so the regulation does not apply to any (or only very few) real cases. If the minimum wage, on the other hand, is set to $100 per hour, then it will have a significant effect since there are many jobs that pay less than this new mandated minimum. As all jobs paying less than $100, according to this hypothetical minimum wage law, are prohibited, anyone paying or making less in the present will be affected. In order to avoid breaking the law and risking penalties or other consequences, either employers must raise the wages to the legal requirement, or the jobs will be terminated (that is, people will be let go). It is reasonable to expect both to happen so that some jobs disappear whereas others pay more, but we cannot be sure which will happen in what quantities.

Let's look at an example to illustrate how and when regulation will be effective and ineffective: if Adele grows Granny Smith apples and the law states that apple-growing must use a certain technique but the law does not include this type of apple, then it is ineffective with respect to Adele. The same is true if the law is written to apply to all orchards, regardless of cultivar, located in the valley but Adele has established her orchard on the mountain side. Perhaps it is instead the case that the law defines an orchard as a continuous piece of land with at least 25 apple trees used for production of apples to be sold in the market place. In this case, the law does not apply if Adele's orchard has less than 25 trees, if it has more than 25 trees but on two separate and non-adjacent pieces of land, or if she has 30 trees but uses 6 of them for non-business purposes (since the law specifies 25 apple trees used for production of apples to be sold). In this way, it is possible for businesses to avoid specific regulation by making sure that they fall just outside the law's scope. It is also possible for policy makers to tailor regulation to penalize specific sets of businesses and thereby, as a consequence, favor other businesses.

But even if the regulation formally applies to apple-growers like Adele and there are no loopholes, it may still be ineffective. Examples of this include laws that are unenforceable because they mandate something that is very difficult or even impossible to measure. It could also be the case that it is very costly or impossible to uphold the mandates in the regulation so that the authorities tasked with enforcing it in practice have very limited (or no) ability to do so. For instance, what if apple-growing is regulated in such a way that those orchards producing more than 1,000,000 apples are affected by a certain type of policy? Does Adele produce 1,000,000 apples? It may be very difficult to count, she can easily claim she doesn't, or eat a few to make sure her orchard makes less than the stated number available for purchase. Do apples that are half eaten by birds or larvae count as full apples or half apples or no apples? It could also be the case that there are plenty of orchards of a size that produces approximately 1,000,000 apples, which means the authorities need to physically count the number of apples produced in each orchard. This may not be possible, perhaps because there are not enough bureaucrats to count all the apples. Or the apple-growers are mandated to report the number of apples produced, and policy enforcement is based on those numbers. Why would anyone report just over 1,000,000 apples when they might as well report just under that number and thereby avoid being regulated?

Such "toothless" regulation will not cause actual change even if it is formally applicable, for the simple reason that the threat of consequences for actions violating the regulation is not credible. This is not only the case if the authorities are unable to enforce the regulation because they lack the necessary resources, power, or are limited by the practical possibility of doing what is stated in the law, but there can be political pressures that undermine the regulation. For instance, the only large employer in a small town burdened with high unemployment rates could likely "get away with" violating certain regulations because the community, and therefore the politicians in charge, are dependent on the jobs it supplies. If there is a risk that this business could either move elsewhere or close its doors if the regulation is enforced to the letter of the law, the authorities may choose to indirectly allow them to violate the regulation by simply not enforcing it. This may also be the case where this business has contributed to the campaigns or otherwise helped get influential policy-makers elected, so that they may feel obliged to return the favor by looking the other way or pulling strings.

In particular situations where the authorities lack the trust of the general population, it may be impossible for them to enforce any laws, including regulations, even when they want (or try) to. Where the people hold such deep skepticism toward those in power or do not accept a specific (or type of) law, the authorities cannot rely on the implicit support of the population, meaning any action that triggers dislike or contempt among the populace would endanger the position and influence of the policy-makers. In these situations, any indiscretion could potentially cause uproar and upheaval and this may be sufficient reason for policy-makers to tip-toe and self-regulate their behavior in their official capacities. In any event, an apparent trespass or action taken beyond what is recognized as legitimate by the populace would endanger the continued influence and position of the policy-maker. We see this in some nations where the population has no or very little trust in politicians and officials of government. For regulation to be effective, the political apparatus, and its dealings, must be considered legitimate by a large part of the population. If this is not the case, then it will be very difficult to enforce regulations. Very often, governments are unable to enforce their rules on a citizenry that is not willing to be subject to those rules—or at a minimum is willing to resist them. Indeed, the effectiveness of government, and therefore its attempts at regulation, is dependent on the silent majority sanctioning or at least accepting its claim to influence.

For what is discussed below, therefore, we consider only situations where government is deemed sufficiently legitimate to not be challenged by large sections of the populace, and where the regulation in question is effective.

IMPACT OF REGULATION

The type of regulation that is intended to *steer* rather than prohibit production consists of what we might refer as both "carrot" (incentive) and "stick" (disincentive). As a carrot, different forms of subsidies are used to make specific types of production, the production of certain goods, or the use of certain production processes more attractive. This can be done in one of two ways, since what matters is the *relative* attractiveness, and therefore value, of choices.

The most intuitive form of steering production is to offer positive payments, that is financial contributions made available to the actor following certain choices, which help cover the expenses—fully or partially—and thereby lessen the real cost borne by the actor. For instance, if policy-makers consider investments in solar power to be comparatively advantageous for electric power production, for environmental or political reasons, those investing in such production could be offered a financial contribution. This, of course, changes the choice situation by making solar power production relatively more lucrative than other types of production. This is the means by which subsidies are used in favor of certain production. This type of outright subsidy in the form of positive payment is not as straightforward as one might think, however. Any such subsidies must *follow* regulation (rather than vice versa), since positive payments necessitate that government has already acquired the funds offered. As government is not the typical economic actor in our model, but has primarily a restricting role on the economic organism either in the form of market-supporting institutions[1] or outright prohibition or by adopting means in-between the two, it does not create economic value through production and exchange. For this reason, whatever positive payments offered must first be seized by government from economic actors, for instance through taxation or other types of confiscation. We will therefore discuss subsidies as part of the next chapter, when we discuss attempts to perfect or improve the market through policy.

As we have already stated, any act intended to make a certain type of production, or the production of certain types of goods, more attractive is a relative measure. To that end, government can offer *implicit* subsidies by easing the restrictions generally in place, thereby making certain acts more advantageous by virtue of less-burdensome regulations. This is not an actual "carrot" even though its effect will be similar. In the case of solar power, for instance, rather than offering outright subsidies, policy-makers can support this type of production through either (1) lowering existing taxes on production for the favored kind, or (2) introducing extra taxation on other kinds of production. In terms of the former, we could consider a situation in which the production of electric power is taxed but an implicit subsidy is offered by explicitly lowering the existing tax rate on production specifically from solar power. In terms of the latter, government can introduce new taxation on all types of electric power production *except* solar. In both cases, the result is that the production of solar power becomes comparatively cheaper (that is, more profitable) than the production of other types, and for this reason we would—all else equal—expect more entrepreneurs and businesses to pick solar power over the alternatives. This is, after all, the intent of steering through regulation.

Note, however, that these methods, while the starting position is different (with or without regulation), amount to the same thing: creating incentive by making a certain type of production, or production of certain types of goods, relatively advantageous (less costly) by lowering the regulatory burden on that wanted type. Both create an uneven regulatory burden across the market borne differently by different actors in the market, and it is this difference that creates the incentive. However, if we look at the effect on prices and resource allocation—the real object of this chapter and the book—the effects are different because they have different starting positions: for a starting position with relatively burdensome regulation across the board we would assume that prices and thus resource allocation have already adjusted to the new situation, and then the regulatory burden is lowered on some type of action such as solar power production. For the alternative view, we start with no or comparatively little regulatory burden, and then introduce regulation unevenly so that it affects all types of production except the ones that political decision-makers want to make more advantageous.

Both of these methods of regulatory change through policy attempts to steer the market indirectly by offering differential, or skewed, incentives. The resulting regulation therefore distorts the playing field where the entrepreneurial "game" takes place. The intent is, after all, to have entrepreneurs willingly choose what's politically preferred because it is in their (financial) interest to do so, and this interest—the incentive—is created politically. Such regulation is an attempt to nudge the market in a certain direction without excluding any options by force, that is, prohibition. A potential side effect of this type of regulation, therefore, is the discovery of the real value involved in *not* choosing a certain alternative. So, if we again consider implicit subsidies for solar power production, a minor difference in regulatory burden between solar and other types of power might or might not nudge a sufficient number of entrepreneurs or investors into solar power. If the difference is not enough, this indicates that the economic disadvantage of solar power, as anticipated by entrepreneurs, exceeds the regulatory "discount." A greater differentiation in regulatory burden would be required to reach the political goals. This could potentially help policy-makers discover the market valuation of the alternatives. Or, more specifically, by varying regulatory burden over time, policy-makers can, at least in theory, discover the real cost that entrepreneurs anticipate from choosing solar over other types of power production. There is a limitation to using this method, however, since frequent adjustments to regulatory policy—which, after all, is coercive on all actors—would increase the policy-based or *regime uncertainty*[2] of entrepreneurship in this market sector. If regulations have changed frequently, this may cause entrepreneurs to anticipate frequent future changes and therefore strongly discount the value of investments in this sector. The result could be a sharp drop in investments.

As we discussed in previous chapters, entrepreneurs invest in production based on their anticipated value, measured after the fact in profit, which is generated by satisfying real consumer wants. When regulation is added to the market place, this constitutes a burden by increasing the cost of affected types of economic action. The cost may be both explicit, as is the case in added taxation or fees, and implicit, as would be the case for instance if certain measures restrict the entrepreneur's ability to properly and at will respond to changes in the market place. What matters for economic action and thus our analysis of the impact of regulation is not the specific tax rates or fees or the specific restrictions placed on entrepreneurs, but how entrepreneurs assess the burden. In other words, where they see regulation as a burden on their undertaking they will discount the net present value of their anticipated return on investment, which is the same as saying that they will see the regulatory burden as an added cost, and it will therefore appear as less valuable relative to other available alternatives. This is, after all, the intent of regulation: to steer economic activity by offering relative financial incentives and disincentives, and thereby produce a certain result in terms of changed economic outcome. To deny that regulation is a burden while espousing regulation as a means to change behavior in the market is a contradiction, since the latter depends on the former being true.

If we again use our little society as illustration, let us trace the effects of regulation as it is introduced. We have Adele the apple-grower, Becky the maker of three-inch nails, Bart the baker, and so on. We also have David, Deborah, Eric, and Edda, the nail smiths in Becky's employ, as noted in chapter 4. For our purposes, let us assume that David, Deborah, Eric, and Edda have started their own businesses as nail smiths and that there is a sufficient demand for them all to stay afloat in their preferred line of business. Add to this picture two more bakers—Bob, a new acquaintance, and Charles, the consumer bidding for nails in chapter 2—and Fred the construction worker. In all, we have five nail smiths (Becky, David, Deborah, Eric, and Edda), three bakers (Bart, Bob, and Charles), one construction worker (Fred), and one apple-grower (Adele). We also have the city councilman Luke, who's the sole policy-maker and a millionaire by inheritance, which means he doesn't have to live off tax revenue. Our starting point, therefore, comprises a pure, unregulated market where each of the market actors (all citizens except Luke, that is[3]) produces for consumers and where each is able to sell enough to establish sufficient purchasing power. That is, they are all able to lead comfortable lives based on their own production for the market.

One day, Luke notes that the work of the nail smiths emits quite a bit of smoke and that this smoke causes a layer of soot on buildings that turn into a thick, black mud when it rains. This is ugly, and this is a problem for the little society, he concludes. He then goes to work authoring an ordinance to help with the soot. He realizes that simply prohibiting nail production would be a bad idea, since it constitutes most of the citizens' trade—and because consumers prefer buying the number of nails produced at current capacity. So he figures that he can use the ordinance to nudge the nail smiths toward using higher chimneys so that the wind can transport the soot elsewhere. Consequently, he produces an ordinance that provides the nail smiths with an incentive to increase the height of their chimneys. He does this by requiring a fee, the collection of which will be used to cover the extra cost associated with cleaning the buildings affected by the soot. Specifically, the ordinance states that owners of chimneys under the height of 20 feet that emit smoke from producing nails must pay a fee of an amount equal to no less than 5 nails for each 100 produced. The reason for this is that he figures that the more nails produced, the more smoke would be emitted. So he proudly writes the ordinance on official letterhead paper and posts it on the door of city hall.

When the nail smiths see the ordinance the next morning, they are all a little upset by having to pay a penalty for producing nails the way they've always been produced—and the way preferred by consumers, as far as they can tell. Becky is more upset than the others, because she's the most productive nail smith and can produce many more nails than the others—upwards of 4,000 each year—and she therefore is burdened with paying the highest fee. This is unfair, she thinks, because she doesn't keep the forge burning longer than anybody else—in fact, she uses this "dirty" resource much more effectively than anyone else since she produces more nails using the same heat as everybody else and thus emits less smoke per nail. But she has no say in the matter and no choice, of course, but to pay the fee stated in the ordinance. With the fee set to 5-of-every-100 nails produced, all of the nail smiths are burdened by what can be thought of as a 5 percent tax on the business of nail smiths—unless they increase the height of their chimneys. If no one chooses to make their chimney higher, then prices of nails would need to go up by 5 percent to cover the cost of the new fee. But at the higher price, consumers would not be willing to buy as many nails as they bought before, so total sales would go down.

Of course, the fee of flat 5 percent affects all nail smiths equally in nominal terms. But they are not equally affected by this fee. Some of them are not as productive as the other ones and therefore have narrower margins and lower profitability. They cannot lower the price much without suffering losses, and they don't have the additional capital necessary to pay Fred to make their chimneys higher. Becky, who's by far producing the most nails and has the highest margins, quickly decides that it is a good investment for her to contract with Fred to make the chimney higher. Fred would only charge her the equivalent of 50 nails to do so—equal to the fee she would need to pay on producing 1,000 nails, only a quarter of what she produces every year. So in 3 months she would make up for the cost and after that she could continue to produce just like before. It's a temporary setback of the 50 nails, but one that she can take.

For Eric and Edda, the least productive of the nail smiths, the fee is not a temporary problem that can easily be overcome. In contrast to Becky, Eric and Edda cannot find a solution to the problem: it will take them two or more years to cover the 50 nails Fred charges to make their chimneys high enough, and this will eat up all of their profits during this time. But the option of paying the fee is equally bad—the fee is so close to their profit margin that they would struggle to break even when paying the fee. Even with the higher price, they would not be able to get back to the standard of living they were able to support as nail smiths before the ordinance. So they both choose to close down their businesses and seek employment elsewhere. David and Deborah are better off, since they are almost as productive as Becky and can pay off the higher chimneys in much shorter time than Eric and Edda. And with the fewer producers the three of them—Becky, Eric, and Edda—get larger shares of the market and can actually increase their profits. They can also buy the equipment and other resources previously used by Eric and Edda, since this equipment is no longer of use to them. This, in turn, also increases the productivity and possible output, so Becky, David, and Deborah end up making money as a result of Luke's ordinance—as Eric and Edda are forced out of business because of it.

While the ordinance changes the structure of nail production quite drastically, it is easy to see that there are other effects as well. While Luke doesn't get the additional income he might have hoped for, since nobody ends up paying the fee, he gets the higher chimneys and—perhaps—this means less soot on buildings and elsewhere. Also, Fred increases his sales by being able to construct three chimneys that would otherwise not have been wanted. So Fred, just like the glazier in response to the added sales as the broken window needed to be replaced, starts a different chain of events by earning and spending his new income. It is highly unlikely that he would spend this revenue in exactly the same way that the five nail smiths would have if there had been no ordinance, so this changes price signals accordingly: the effects where the nail smiths would have spent their money will not appear, the effects of Eric and Edda staying in business, including their suppliers and however they would have chosen to spend their profits, also will not happen, but the ripple effects following Fred's new income now come into being.

But what about Eric and Edda? Being nail smiths was their number 1 choice of all alternatives available to them, which is after all the reason they were nail smiths. In the new situation, this option is not available to them anymore so they must choose something else. The options available may be different from what they were originally because of the ripple effects coming from all the changes due to the consequences of Luke's ordinance. So what would have been their second best may no longer be an option either. But perhaps something else, that they consider a little bit more valuable, would be. In either case, they will choose the best option available to them in this new situation. Perhaps Eric can get a job in Bart's bakery while Edda gets hired in an administrative role in Fred's booming business. This, in turn, increases the output of Bart's bakery while Fred gets more time to work on construction and he can therefore increase his output as well. As they choose to employ Eric and Edda, they consider the added manpower worth the additional cost (the salaries they have to pay). This means, of course, that they anticipate that there is sufficient market demand for them to sell the additional output.

As the supply increases, the price tends to fall in order to cater to more consumers. So when Bart increases his output of bread, which is possible because he hires Eric, he can sell more—possibly all of it—if he charges a slightly lower price. In other words, this affects the other bakers, Bob and Charles, who must also lower their prices. If they don't, they might not sell as much as they used to.[4] As Bob and Charles have not changed their production methods, their costs are the same as before and therefore, at the lower price, their profit margins decline. If one of them, say Charles, already had low profit margins because he was comparatively bad at baking bread, then the lower price may not make it worth his while to be a baker anymore. This means both Bart and Bob get larger shares of the market, can increase their prices or sell more at the present prices, and therefore make larger profits. Charles, on the other hand, needs to find employment elsewhere. The effect of Luke's ordinance can therefore have ripple effects of its own and cause changes to the structure of production as well as overall employment throughout the economy. The exact changes are of course very difficult, if not impossible, to predict. But that there will be effects, and that such effects could potentially be far-reaching, should be evident.

The little "nudge" by Luke, intended only to limit the soot from nail production, has thus caused a much greater impact on the economy than simply limiting the emission of smoke. Indeed, we saw that it can cause a whole chain of events that can potentially change the structure of production throughout the economy. Not only are Eric and Edda forced to leave their preferred jobs while Becky, David, and Deborah increase their market share and profits, but the result of this change itself forces change to other market sectors—in this case, construction (Fred's increased output after employing Edda) and baking (Charles is forced out of business while Bart and Bob increase their respective market shares and profits), which leads to further changes elsewhere. This reinforces the view of the market as an interconnected economic organism involved in decentralized production for individual consumption—just like we discussed in the previous chapters. It also shows how this organism responds to change by adjusting all affected production in stages just like the waves on a pond upset by a stone.

IMPACT OF PROHIBITION

A similar but larger effect is caused by regulation in the form of outright prohibition of certain types of production. Regulation forces entrepreneurs to redo their economic calculations and revisit their choices with new and different values. This is how Luke's ordinance with the chimney height requirement caused direct and indirect effects, and how the added cost forced marginal entrepreneurs out of business. Even a small change can reshape the cost structure in such a way that entrepreneurs make different choices, which is of course the intention of the regulation. But core to this type of "nudge" is to allow entrepreneurs to make the choice, despite changed variable values or added variables to consider.

Prohibition is different because this type of regulation not only changes the cost structure but in fact affects the overall choice set: the alternatives available for entrepreneurs to choose from. One way of restating prohibition in terms of cost is to say that the prohibited options come with infinite (or close to it) cost. But doing this makes the distinction unnecessarily ambiguous, since a cost can be overcome—and matters little if the anticipated value from assuming it is much greater. Prohibition is not in actuality a cost in the same sense as a tax or fee or required actions, because it shifts the boundary of what is legitimate or lawful action. By prohibiting a certain action, there is indeed a cost to taking it: not only the cost of avoiding enforcement of the law, but also the cost of not acting within the market. But this cost is not a matter of degree in terms of the profitability calculus of the venture, as is the case with other types of regulation. Those acting in violation of outright prohibition act in a different market, one which is outside the law, and this choice is in this sense a "black or white" issue rather than one of comparing costs. It is rarely the case that a proper and legitimate business, when facing prohibition, simply compares benefits and costs and then decides whether to continue or change its line of business. For this and other reasons, the "black" market tends to be populated by other types of actors than those dealing in the "white" market. In other words, it is not a matter of degree but one of kind. For this reason and for added clarity, we'll treat prohibition as a separate phenomenon, and we'll contrast it with the regulation discussed above using the same example. But note that prohibition can be combined with a certain threshold, thereby making it a hybrid type of regulation. The minimum wage, for instance, is a prohibition of employment *under a certain wage*. Employment at higher wages is allowed, at lower wages it is disallowed. This means entrepreneurs, when considering employing labor, must consider not only the value of adding an employee but must also consider only positions and potential employees that will generate enough value to warrant a wage above the legal minimum. This effectively shuts out less productive labor workers, for instance immigrants and minorities or those without specific education or experience, as well as less productive employment opportunities, that is, unqualified jobs.

As in the example above, Luke finds a problem in the smoke and soot emitted from the forges used to produce three-inch nails, and he finds a solution in political measures. But rather than adding a cost to "nudge" the nail smiths toward picking, from Luke's perspective, a better solution (the higher chimney), he drafts a city ordinance to prohibit the forges. This will undoubtedly take care of the problem of emitted smoke, since the forges will not be permitted to continue and therefore will not emit any smoke at all. (We will here ignore the potential side effects of such a prohibition, such as "black" market or underground forges and the increased importation of nails from adjacent cities.)

Following the new ordinance, Becky, David, Deborah, Eric, and Edda have no choice but to close their businesses and find a different line of work. The immediate effect, therefore, is different from the regulation discussed in the previous section, in which only Eric and Edda chose different employment. It also means that our limited society now is left without production of nails, which could in turn cause problems. As forges are prohibited, the option of selling the forges to other actors is not available. Instead, the equipment can only be sold if there are *other* uses for it. This can be the case for hammers, tongs, and similar tools, but the forge itself can only be sold in the market for used materials, scrap metal and so on. In other words, the prohibition causes a fall in the value of the resources bound in forges—a loss of value that affects the owners as it limits their ability to free the capital and invest it in other businesses. For instance, a functioning forge could be sold for a sum equal to several years' worth of output in the market, say, 5,000 nails, but following the prohibition there is no permitted use for forges so the price other entrepreneurs are willing to pay for forges is based only on their *other* and consequently, as we saw in the discussion in previous chapters, necessarily lesser valued uses.

The prohibition thus changes the value of forges back to the value of the resources that they're built out of. Whereas the forge, before the prohibition, was a better use for the resources, which is evident from their higher price when combined into a forge, this is no longer the case. A forge, in fact, has practically zero value, since it cannot be operated. So after the prohibition, the value of the resources *combined* is lower than the resources themselves, so they must be separated. Undoing the forges consequently maximizes value among the available uses, but of course still sets back their owners—they lose the value that was there when they were running the forges (and would still be there were they allowed to continue).

By prohibiting forges, Luke forces a value loss on the nail smiths while at the same time forcing them into different lines of employment. Whereas the nail smiths personally suffer the loss of value as their resources' market price drops as a result of the prohibition, there is also an *unseen loss* in the value that would have been produced for consumers had the former been allowed to continue producing nails for sale. This value is no longer created, at least not by our local nail smiths, so the consumers lose out. In addition to these losses, both seen and unseen, Becky, David, Deborah, Eric, and Edda now need to find employment. This process is identical to what was discussed above, but of course here involves more people. Now five of them, rather than the two above, need to find employment. All of them, of course, will need to find lines of employment that they value less than being nail smiths. If this were not the case, they would not have chosen to become nail smiths in the first place. So whatever they choose now that being a nail smith is no longer a viable option is something they would have valued lower. This too is an unseen loss to be added to the loss faced by consumers of nails.

In the case we discussed in the previous section, the construction worker Fred received additional business and could therefore expand and employ Edda. Whereas the additional business was not value creating in the strict sense, but rather the result of nail smiths attempting to avoid the larger cost of regulation (the fee), it was still a redistribution of value. The price charged, equivalent to 50 nails, is value that would otherwise have been created and earned by the nail smiths. But the regulation redirects this income to Fred, which is the reason—at least in our example—he can employ Edda. With prohibition, however, there is no redirection of value since the market directly affected by the prohibition is destroyed as it is not permitted to continue—and with it, any value it contributed to consumers and therefore the standard of living of anyone affected. This loss is seen in the discrepancy between the value of a forge before the regulation and the value of the resources after it. It is also observable in the loss in consumer welfare as they cannot buy locally produced three-inch nails. So while the regulation we discussed in the previous section caused an inefficiency by forcing some profitable nail smiths out of business by forcing upon them an additional cost, which redirected value to the more productive producers, prohibition causes a loss of value to be borne by the entrepreneurs in the specific market sector affected and a loss of previously realizable value for the consumers who demand the product in question. Prohibition thus has a much greater effect on the market's ability to satisfy consumer wants than the type of regulation discussed above, since some goods or services that could have been the actual choices made by consumers are forcefully removed.

Prohibition, therefore, has a much more pervasive effect by restricting the optionality of consumers, whose choice sets are restricted as products they valued are banned, as well as producers, since banning a certain type of production makes their preferred production impossible. The value that this would have generated is lost, but could partially—but not fully—be made up for by increasing other types of production. The difference is lost. Regulation that increases the cost rather than prohibit certain production, in contrast, redirects value within production so that some producers (the "insiders" or beneficiaries of that piece of regulation) gain while others lose. It may lead to restricted supply of goods, but the exact effects depend on price elasticity and the competitive situation after the change.

Both types of regulation—added cost and prohibition—cause responses within the overall structure of production, as discussed in the previous section, because some actors need to find employment in other lines of business than their preferred choice (which is now either restricted through policy or altogether prohibited). The flow of labor into some specific industries changes the balance in the market by causing the relative wage rates and/or profitability in those industries to go down. In other words, there are ripple effects in response to regulation just as there are ripple effects to any other change. The difference between regulation and destruction, as we discussed in previous chapters, is that regulation necessarily is a restriction on market action and is likely to remain in the longer term—with a constant, and perhaps *increasing* effect on the economic organism. While destruction causes reallocation of remaining resources to make up for the loss and incentivizes people to choose labor over leisure and therefore invest more of their time and effort, it is temporary destruction that could potentially cause long-term effects in lost standard of living or growth potential. Unlike regulation, a market suffering destruction can recover what was destroyed—a regulated market is continuously hampered by the regulation. This will affect the optionality of anyone affected, but as we saw in chapter 6, for destruction there is a concomitant increase in the relative urge felt for some wants that used to be satisfied (such as shelter, food, etc.). Regulation, in contrast, causes a cost by restricting what production is carried out by adding artificial costs of outright prohibition, affecting choices of both producers and consumers— *while consumer preferences remain largely the same.* In other words, the response to regulation is not an increase in the labor invested in production to make up for a loss, but an overall and continued loss of value available for consumption.

It follows, then, that it is important to treat destruction and regulation differently, because they are different phenomena with different effects on the market. What we've discussed so far, however, are restrictions only— temporary setbacks through destruction or disaster, and longer-term restrictions through policy. We'll now discuss what appears as positive rather than negative influences, which are taken to improve or even perfect the market.

NOTES

1. Institutions, such as property rights protection or contract enforcement, are in the words of Douglass C. North the "humanly devised constraints that shape human interaction" (North,

1990, p. 3). Their productive, if not empowering, influence on the market are therefore through restricting what is legitimate action.

2. See Higgs (1997).

3. Luke is not exempted from the rule that one must produce in order to consume. He consumes his inheritance, that is, what his parents produced in excess of their consumption and then transferred to Luke for his benefit. He is, in other words, consuming the value that his parents produced.

4. If Bob and Charles sell exactly the same types of bread as Bart, then they might not be able to sell much at all unless they lower their prices to match Bart's. If they sell different kinds of bread, then their sales depend on consumers' valuation of the different kinds of bread in the new price situation.

Chapter Eight

Attempts to Perfect the Market

So far we've noted that unhampered markets function as economic organisms with endogenous causes of growth and respond in a seemingly coordinated manner to changes both from within and without (chapter 4). We have also seen how economic action causes ripple effects through an economy, and how destruction (chapter 5) and even disasters (chapter 6) cause setbacks in terms of value creation but that the economy is still able to respond properly by reallocating resources on the supply side to adjusted value rankings on the demand side. A similar story was told about the effects on the economic organism by regulation of markets through restrictive policy, either as taxation or prohibition, which causes a continued setback by restricting or prohibiting certain types of actions (chapter 7). Throughout this discussion we have explicitly focused on policy as restrictions and have intentionally excluded policies intended to provide support for certain actions, that is policy that tries to "nudge" entrepreneurs in what's considered the "right" (or better) direction by offering extra benefit rather than add penalties for unwanted actions. These positive "nudges" include subsidies, different types of corporate welfare, and supportive public investments in infrastructure and similar things, each of which is intended to make a specific action or class of actions more profitable and thereby induce more entrepreneurs choose this course of action—because it, with the subsidy included, appears as a more profitable alternative. If you subsidize something, you generally get more of it.

The previous chapter discussed how policy can be made to indirectly subsidize certain actions by adding costs and thereby penalizing all other alternative types of behavior with respect to a certain industry or product. This of course raises the *relative* value of the preferred action, for instance the production of three-inch nails using chimneys of a certain height, but this

117

does not of course mean that this action becomes profitable. We can think of many examples where a certain type of production is so costly compared to the produced output that they're hardly profitable on their own, so even if the relative cost of alternative actions is higher this does not mean entrepreneurs are willing to act in this realm. Such claims have been made with respect to for instance solar and wind power, which have been relatively more expensive than alternative sources of electric power, such as nuclear power or coal-burning plants, and at the same time not profitable on their own. Where this is the case, it is no solution to add taxes or other penalties to coal- or oil-burning, nuclear power plants, and the other alternative means for the production of power. The effect of "penalizing" those alternatives would not be a shift of production toward the more preferable (but still not profitable) solar and wind power, but a drop in overall energy production: rather than move into solar and wind power, it is possible that entrepreneurs would shift their attention toward different industries altogether. Unless the intention is to cut production of energy, this would be a failure of policy. In these situations, when the goal of policy is to increase the share of renewable energy production, such as wind and solar power, it would make sense to enact policies that support the preferred behavior by helping to cover part of their cost. In other words, policy can be used to *raise* this type of economic action financially in absolute terms rather than raise it relative to *other* types by placing costly restrictions on them. The aim and effect of this type of policy, then, is to lower the costs of certain economic actions to thereby make them the better alternative by making them (1) profitable in absolute terms, and (2) less costly relative to avaliable substitutes.

IMPACT OF SUBSIDIES

Let us again revisit our little society to illustrate the impact of subsidies—and contrast it with the restrictive regulation discussed previously. We use the same starting point, so the economy's production apparatus consists of five nail smiths (Becky, David, Deborah, Eric, and Edda), three bakers (Bart, Bob, and Charles), one construction worker (Fred), and one apple-grower (Adele). As before, we also have the city councilman, Luke. Rather than regulating to restrict entrepreneurs from certain actions, as we discussed above, imagine that Luke has identified that the society sometimes runs out of bread, that bread prices are a little too high for everyone to afford as much bread as they would like, and so on. Consequently, he wants to make sure that bread production increases and that the price of bread goes down. This could be easily done through decentralized entrepreneurial action, of course, but neither Bart, Bob, nor Charles anticipates increased production to be profitable. That is, after all, the reason they have not already chosen to expand their output. In other words, in our current market situation it doesn't make sense for them to increase their output, which suggests that consumers actually value the use of productive resources in other types of production, so they refrain from further investments. Luke disagrees with their decision as well as their assumption and wants to make sure more bread is produced—either by the three existing bakers or by another entrepreneur entering bread production. So he intends to offer a subsidy for bakers. The subsidy needs some sort of basis to target bread production rather than allowing it to become a general hand-out to anyone producing. For example, Luke can offer payment based on the use of a certain input, for instance wheat flour, so that anyone who uses this input—or perhaps above a certain quantity of it—receives a payment from the government (Luke, that is). Or it can be offered based on output of bread, perhaps of a certain kind or above a certain quantity. Or it can be granted to anyone who is a baker to support their line of business in general.

A subsidy is an additional income, which is why it provides an incentive. In other words, existing and entrant entrepreneurs will find ways of making sure they get the subsidy and get as much as possible from it as long as doing so is not too costly. So if Luke, for instance, formulates the requirement to receive the subsidy as based on the quantity of flour used, we would likely see an overall increase in the use (or at least purchase) of flour. However, you get what you ask for, and with a subsidy offered for the amount of flour used, this does not necessarily mean more bread will be produced: it could also mean more waste, more flour per piece of bread, and perhaps a secondary market where bakers sell excess flour off the books to create an illusion of using a lot of flour (which means they're still getting the subsidy) while they are not. Likewise, if Luke formulates the requirement as a payment based on the number of pieces of bread sold, we should expect Bart, Bob, and Charles to soon figure out that they can get a greater subsidy by making more pieces of but not total volume or weight of bread out of the dough—that is, by selling a larger number of smaller pieces of bread. Specific requirements, as with specific regulation in the previous chapter, constitute specific incentives and would change behavior accordingly.

Considering these potential problems, Luke decides to introduce a subsidy available to any entrepreneur who is solely or primarily in the business of baking and selling bread. By specifying that the business must solely or primarily be in baking, he hopes to avoid anyone acting to take advantage of the subsidy rather than getting into the baking business because it is their most profitable type of production. To make sure that the subsidy is paid only to bakers, he takes on the task of certifying their business himself; so he expects to spend many hours analyzing what entrepreneurs do and how they do it in order to make sure the subsidy is specifically for bakers. And to make sure he targets the right entrepreneurs, he sets up formal rules for how to be considered a baker: he will look at their input costs, their labor hours, and their sales, respectively. Of these three, to be considered a baker and thus eligible for the subsidy, the entrepreneur must have at least 51 percent of two of the three directly related to baking bread. He also produces a definition of what is to be considered bread and what inputs are considered to be directly for baking. These rules are necessary not to create any grey zones, where the ambiguity would require arbitrary decision-making on his part. So he must create a costly bureaucracy and a separate set of definitions and rules to be able to process applications.

Of course, Luke still wants the subsidy to have an effect by attracting more entrepreneurs into baking, so he must find a balance between making it attractive enough—that is, to push entrepreneurs already considering the bakery business to take the plunge—while not being too attractive—that is, to attract entrepreneurs more interested in cashing in on the subsidy and other types of rent-seeking activities than in actual production—yet at the same time not too costly in terms of fees and time required for applying. He chooses to offer a subsidy of 0.5 percent of net sales to make baking a bit more profitable, payable every month. And the fee for applying is kept low; he'll cover most of the cost of bureaucracy himself, so bakers only need to fill out a simple form to make him aware of their business. This means there will be less money available for actual subsidies, but as Luke is wealthy he thinks he will be able to offer enough subsidies to increase bread production for several years.

The immediate effect of the subsidy is increased profitability among the existing bakers Bart, Bob, and Charles. After all, they get an additional 0.5 percent on top of their existing sales, which immediately translates into profits for them. As profits increase, this signals to other entrepreneurs that there may be an opportunity to share those higher profits—which serves as an incentive for others to move into baking. At the same time, however, the incumbent bakers—Bart, Bob, and Charles—may earn profits that exceed their preferred profit levels, which in turn could cause them to cut down on production. The reason for this is that as profits reach a certain level the added value of additional work, or the work already carried out, is of lesser value than the value of the leisure time those entrepreneurs could enjoy instead. Indeed, it is easy to see that Bart, for instance, was perfectly happy with his earned profits, which provided him with a standard of living he finds convenient and satisfying, and therefore that he'd rather work a little less while maintaining this standard than work as much as before while increasing his money income. Consequently, he chooses to limit production and instead spend a few hours every week in the sun relaxing in his hammock, which means total bread output goes down. This, of course, is the exact opposite of what Luke wanted to accomplish with the subsidy. So we can see that in order to produce the intended result—increased bread production—

Luke will need to offer a subsidy that is sufficiently high to increase the profitability level among incumbents so much that others enter this line of production—and thereby bring about a competitive reduction in price.

Let us assume that the 0.5 percent subsidy on net sales that Luke decided to introduce is sufficient to incentivize at least one entrepreneur to enter the bread-baking business. The most likely entrepreneur to leave his or her current position is the one with the least profitable undertaking, since this entrepreneur would have most to gain. But, in fact, *all* entrepreneurs with lesser profits would anticipate becoming bakers since doing so will provide them with greater profits. Whether they actually choose to move into baking however depends on their anticipated ability to capture those profits and the cost of making the move; for some entrepreneurs, the cost of shifting away from their current line of business may be prohibitively high. Since these entrepreneurs considering entering baking base their decisions on subjective appraisements of alternatives, which is always the case, it is impossible to tell beforehand how many, and with even less specificity, which entrepreneurs will make the move. So as long as the increase in profitability that is brought about by the subsidy is high enough, we'll have an inflow of entrepreneurs—but there's no saying if this flow will be a drop in the bucket with minor impact on the baking business or an overwhelming wave that completely restructures it or somewhere in-between.

The extent of resource reallocation toward bread-baking of course matters, since the impact on other lines of business as well as the output (and thus profitability) of bakers overall depends on the magnitude of the change. So we must keep this in mind when tracing all effects as a change makes ripples through the market: while we cannot tell the extent or magnitude of the change, which means we cannot say exactly what will be the outcome, we can trace the effects in general. In our example, say both Eric and Adele are attracted by the new and higher profitability levels of baking with the subsidy. Eric, who made a decent living as a nail smith, but came nowhere near the profits of Becky who is his superior across the board in that line of business, sees in bread-baking the possibility of increasing his standard of living. Adele, who has experienced a couple of hard years with pests and bad weather, and with fluctuating and unpredictable apple prices, is attracted by bread-baking because it is less affected by weather and other exogenous, uncontrollable forces—and would offer a steady stream of income to replace the highly seasonal market for apples.

As Eric the nail smith moves into baking, the supply of nails diminishes and thus Becky, David, Deborah, and Edda, the remaining nail smiths, would be able to either raise their prices or increase their sales even if the prices remain the same. For example, with Eric still in this line of business, Edda was able to make a living but not much more. She happens to be a terrible sales person, so she was unable to sell her preferred quantity—but she could still sell enough nails to make meager profits, enough to make a living but not to make her rich. With Eric out of the picture, she's able to sell to more customers, reach her preferred output level and sales, and therefore increase her profits. The same is true for the other nail smiths, who can also increase their sales, however disproportionately. The increase is disproportionate because they have different cost structures—their businesses do not work exactly the same, and therefore reach a productive maximum at different quantities. As we have already seen, Edda's maximum was at a higher quantity than she was able to sell, which is why she increases her profitability by increasing her sales volume. To Becky, the gain from selling more nails at the cost of putting in more hours is not worth it—she already makes enough money to lead a good life. So she raises the price of her nails, which are generally recognized as being of the highest quality. As the quantity demanded in the economy is about the same as ˙before, but the number of suppliers has diminished, Becky is able to sell as many—if not more—nails at the higher price. Her profits increase, and this leads her to decide to take some additional time off—leisure and time with her family is more valuable to her than the additional income from working the same hours as before. So she produces less and chooses to sell at a higher price, while Edda is now able to produce and sell more at a slightly lower price. They can charge different prices because their products—the three-inch nails—are perceived by consumers as of different qualities. David and Deborah follow Becky's lead and raise their prices a little to increase their profits too. The nail-producing business has therefore changed from a standardized product into two separate quality levels: the higher-price, higher-quality product produced by Becky, David, and Deborah, and the lower-price, lower-quality product supplied by Edda. This change, while it could have happened for other reasons as well, was here caused by the subsidy that made Eric leave his trade as a nail smith, which caused a drop in supply and therefore diversification among the remaining nail smiths.

Adele the apple-grower also makes the transition to baking. As she was the only local producer of apples in our little society, she leaves the market without a source of (locally grown) apples. She only made a meager living off the orchard, so even though she abandons a profit opportunity (for an anticipated better one, due to Luke's offered subsidy) it is not of sufficient magnitude to attract other entrepreneurs to leave their current trades to become apple-growers. After all, the subsidy for bread-baking means entrepreneurs overall may expect higher profits, and they have no reason to choose lower profitability over higher ones. The result of this, as Adele leaves her orchard, is that consumers will lose the option of purchasing (locally grown) apples. As we know that they previously chose to purchase apples—the reason Adele's apple-growing business made a profit—even though they had many other alternative ways to spend their money (or not spend them), this is a loss of value: their preferred option is no longer available. So consumer optionality is impacted by Adele's response to the subsidy of bakers, and because she enters a market with several incumbent entrepreneurs her becoming a baker to supply similar types of bread doesn't increase consumers' ability to satisfy different kinds of wants through access to a greater variety of products. They will potentially have more bread to choose from as Adele starts baking along with Bart, Bob, and Charles, but it is safe to say consumers likely consider apples to be a different category of product and therefore assigns bread a different value. And as apple-growing was a more lucrative business than baking, at least to Adele, it constitutes the better way of satisfying consumer wants. Indeed, we saw in previous chapters how profitability approximates, or at least signals, the real value contributed to consumers. The subsidy, since it attracts entrepreneurs from other types of production, produces a shift in overall market production toward lesser value creation. However, while there is less value created for consumers, the value produced by increased bread-baking is the one that is preferred by Luke the policy-maker: indeed, the reason for the added incentive is that he considered bread-baking an undersupplied and, therefore, by entrepreneurs underappreciated (undervalued) economic activity. The subsidy attracts resources (primarily labor) from other types of production—with the result of Eric leaving the trade of nail smith and Adele her chosen trade as apple-grower. This was after all, externalities aside, the intention: more bread.

The shift in production caused by the subsidy is therefore misaligned with consumers' revealed preferences through their actual exchanges and actions taken in the market, since they—through entrepreneurs' productive efforts in anticipation of sales and profit—preferred apples to the increased supply of bread. However, the shift *is* aligned with Luke's preference for a greater supply of bread. (But we do not know how Luke feels about the loss of local apple production or the change to the production of three-inch nails caused by his subsidy.)

The orchard that Adele carefully established and invested funds in loses its usefulness, at least in its present form, as Adele moves into baking bread. The orchard was valued because it contributed to satisfying consumer wants and was expected to continue to do so, but as Adele no longer pursues apple-growing and, as a result, apple-growing is no longer a trade in our little society (as there is no one who chooses to take over this line of business), the effect on its value is akin to the forges in chapter 7: the value of the combined resources after this change is lower than the sum of the value of the separate resources. In other words, the only value available from the orchard is the value of its land, the value of the wood (if sold for fuel or carpentry), and so on. The irrigation system loses its value to the degree it cannot be shipped and installed elsewhere or used as materials or parts in support of other production. This loss of value, as was also the case of the forges, is borne by

Adele as she moves into bread-baking. But as she is not prohibited from continuing to run the orchard but merely chooses to do so as the subsidy is introduced, her choice to move into bread-baking suggests that the subsidy is sufficient to cover this loss. In other words, Adele anticipates that the profitability of becoming a baker, with the subsidy in place, exceeds the profitability of apple-growing by at least the loss of value of abandoning or finding a secondary use for the orchard. Had the subsidy been lower, this may not have been the case.

Our analysis of this loss of value in the orchard as it is taken out of production is parallel to that of the forges above. But it is not the result of an outright prohibition or an in practice prohibitive regulation-incurred cost, but follows from the subsidy-based "nudge" that changes Adele's calculation of anticipated value. She's "lured" to shift her production to another line of business because of the increased profitability brought about by the subsidy. The effect on the specific resource—the orchard—is the same as with what was discussed above, which means the direct cost through loss of market value is borne by the entrepreneur in question whereas the indirect cost, due to the loss of valuable options made available in the market, is borne by the consumers who can no longer make those choices. Indeed, had bread-baking been the better option in terms of value creation, then Adele would have chosen to go into that line of business instead of apple-growing. As she didn't, and she instead earned sufficient profits to keep her in apple-growing rather than shifting toward baking, it was the more highly valued use of her labor as a productive resource from the point of view of consumers—at least as far as Adele could understand her options and anticipate their profitability. To put it differently, consumers found her efforts more valuable as an apple-grower than as a baker, which is why the former paid better than the latter—and this is also why Adele got into apple-growing and stayed in that line of business. The subsidy changed this calculus by adding a benefit to baking that is not provided by consumers through their buying decisions, but an effect specifically caused by the subsidy. This added benefit—the subsidy—is an income made available when engaging specifically in bread-baking and is separate from satisfying consumer wants.

Adele's move from apple-growing also affects bread production, as was the case with Eric's taking up baking above, by increasing the supply of bread offered to consumers. This was the intention of Luke's subsidy, after all, and is also a result of it. With both Eric and Adele adding their breads to the supply and competing for customers, their bidding for sales will force them to lower the price to undercut the incumbent bakers Bart, Bob, and Charles—and the latter are likely forced to follow. This too was the intention of Luke offering the subsidy, since he considered the bread supply too low and bread prices too high in the little society. With lower prices, more consumers are both willing and able to purchase bread. This added sales volume, which is a result of the higher quantity demanded at the lower price, means more consumers—including those who were not willing (or able) to purchase bread at the previous price—have access to bread. But it also means that they do not have access to the apples that they used to be able to choose. Overall, the value offered to consumers is reduced as they as a group placed greater value in Adele's apples (and Eric's three-inch nails) than the bread they are now offered.

If we deconstruct the group of consumers to get a more nuanced picture, we can see that consumers indeed are affected by this change in created value—but in different ways. The consumers who preferred to use their funds toward buying apples are now stripped of this alternative, as it is no longer made available to them, and thus have to make due with something they deem of lower value. This group loses from Luke's subsidy. The consumers who previously purchased bread at the higher price, that is those who considered bread to be worth more to them than that asking price, can now buy bread at a lower price and thus have funds for other kinds of purchases (or to save for future consumption). This group is made better off. The consumers who previously chose not to buy bread because they were unwilling or unable or both, but who are able to buy bread at the lower price, now gain from the additional available alternative for their purchases: bread at an affordable price. This group also benefits from the subsidy. But there is one other group who is affected by this change in their consumptive behavior, and that follows from the lower price being charged for the bread: the incumbent producers. In our little society, this would be Bart, Bob, and Charles, whose production now generates lower income that used to be the case, and unless it is fully covered by the subsidy this loss of income affects their ability (and possibly willingness) to consume. Were they to have employees to assist in baking, these employees would be affected in a similar way (likely by lower wages or cut benefits).

The reader may recall our discussion about the ripple effects that cause changes through the economy due to any choices made, as we discussed following the broken window in chapter 5. This applies here as well as in any other actions taken (or actions not taken), and it too affects consumption patterns. As Adele chooses to close the doors to her apple-growing business, this constitutes a loss of revenue for all entrepreneurs who produce supplies that Adele used when producing apples. This loss of revenue effectuates a reduction in volume and, likely, in profitability, which therefore has an effect on the entrepreneurs' respective ability to consume. If they have employees, they too are affected either by commanding lower wages or by some of them being left without work. A similar effect strikes any laborers previously in Adele's employ, who are left without employment and therefore income. Their ability to consume diminishes with their loss of income, and this has an effect elsewhere in the economy depending on their preferences and the

previous consumption behavior. All of the entrepreneurs and laborers making a living directly or indirectly from Adele's apple-growing business face a
reduction in income and therefore lose some or all of their previous ability to
consume.

The subsidy therefore creates several winners and losers among consumers. This is different from the market responses to changing economic
conditions, whether it is changing consumer preferences, destruction, or productive innovation, because such changes are in response to or happen together with changing consumer valuations. The subsidy, as was the case with
different types of regulations in the previous chapter, does not change what
consumers actually demand but causes a reallocation of productive resources
by changing the conditions of production without consideration of and therefore directly in contrast to consumers' revealed preferences. We can think of
the subsidy as an artificial increase in the profitability of bread-baking; it is
artificial as it has no economic origin but is a policy-created condition. The
creation of winners and losers from the shift from nail manufacturing and
apple-growing therefore constitutes a redistribution of wealth in our little
society: from the losers to the winners.

While we assumed above that the subsidy that Luke offers is a payment
made using his personal wealth, this is rarely the case in real policy making.
We therefore have yet to elaborate on the source of this type of subsidy that
brings about the change we've already discussed. In the case of a policy-
maker's personal wealth, which in an unhampered market such as our little
society's economic organism must be accumulated from previously undertaken successful entrepreneurship (that is, the successful use of productive
resources to satisfy consumer wants), such a subsidy can be considered consumption of capital by the policy-maker. It would then be a use for the sake
of satisfying the policy-maker's own wants, which in Luke's case would be
to see a greater availability of bread. In this case, the effects remain as we
have discussed above and it is likely that the policy-maker will, eventually,
run out of funds. The subsidy is thus a temporary measure. But even if it is
not, it is an influence on production based on consumption of the value that
was produced, only without gaining personally in terms of goods and services. If Luke, as a multi-millionaire, chooses to consume this wealth by
paying bakers to make more bread available, then this is akin to regular
consumption. In fact, one way of understanding the subsidy in terms of
consumption is that Luke implicitly picks up the tab for some of the bread
sold—0.5 percent of the price, to be exact. And this, of course, has an effect
on the structure of production as well as prices throughout—as revealed
consumer preferences always have.

But, as we noted, this type of charity is rarely the case when governments
use subsidies to encourage certain types of behavior. Government is not an
economic actor, which the multi-millionaire Luke is, but an exogenous force

on the economy. It does not produce using economic means and benefit from sales, but relies on a monopoly of force to make the rules under which entrepreneurs act. For this reason, government cannot offer subsidies to economic actors without first extracting the funds from the economy. This is why we, in a previous chapter, noted that subsidies must *follow* regulation (taxation, usually). In other words, for our analysis of the effects on the little economy to make sense from the perspective of our modern, real-life markets we would need to first introduce a regulation that redirects funds from production and consumption within the economic organism toward the regulating government, and then add to this the effects of subsidies. In order to add value to an economy, a government must first extract that value. We can see, then, that this would have vast distortive effects on the structure of production in the economy—both through the extraction and the subsequent addition. We can also see that it would be very difficult to trace the real effects, as they cause ripples in numerous stages, throughout a modern and highly complex network of specialized productive efforts throughout the market.

IMPROVING ON THE MARKET

What we have seen so far is how the different kinds of regulation affect the market's allocation of resources, and how this has implications throughout the market especially with regard to its ability to satisfy consumer wants. We will now reiterate a point made in chapter 4 whether regulations and other coercive measures through policy can be used to improve the market's performance and structure of production. As we noted in chapter 4, the market is not efficient in the sense that it can at any point in time be made more effective by putting the available resources into what would be more efficient uses from the point of view of consumer wants in the immediate present. Indeed, if all resources were dedicated to producing what was requested in the present, society would reach a higher standard of living. As we stated in chapter 4: "the market will not ever fully utilize all the productive resources available toward providing satisfaction in the present, because some of them will necessarily be dedicated to uses in production processes that will be concluded at different points in time." This means markets aren't—and cannot be—efficient in an allocative sense at any specific point in time, but must be evaluated as time progresses.[1] The reason is that entrepreneurs accumulate and orchestrate resources to produce in anticipation of creating value for themselves by satisfying consumers' wants at future points in time. The entrepreneurs do not focus on concluding their efforts at the exact same point in time, and they're also not always accurate in how they assess, plan and time their undertakings, which is why the market at any moment includes a large number of production processes that have not been completed and certainly have not been optimized to satisfy wants in that specific moment of time.

It is into this highly dynamic and ever changing process, which has no end goal and therefore no aim, that policy is introduced. There can be many reasons for policy, but we will here focus on policy intended to improve the market, its functioning or outcome, in some specific way. Policy can from this perspective be used to "nudge" or otherwise direct entrepreneurs away from or toward specific industries, lines of business, or the production of specific goods and services. Our interest here is the overall effect on the market, and especially how policy affects individuals and groups in society—that is, the people that comprise the economic organism.

In order to improve any process, it must have a purpose or aim against which its performance can be measured. If it doesn't, then any counterfactual—that is, benchmark or measuring rod—is arbitrarily chosen. Economists look at the economy as a system that satisfies wants through economic and mutually beneficial actions with the purpose of getting as much as possible out of scarce resources. What matters, of course, is that what we get out of it is something that is of value to us. In other words, economists look at the amount of satisfaction or contentment achieved by markets and compare markets operating under different institutional settings, markets that utilize different productive structures, and so on. Of course, as we saw above, the problem is how and when to assess the efficiency of the market in using scarce resources to achieve satisfaction, or, to put it differently, how to say when or if a market is "efficient." Indeed, as Joseph A. Schumpeter astutely put it, "the problem that is usually being visualized is how capitalism administers existing structures, whereas the relevant problem is how it creates and destroys them."[2] Indeed, as we've seen throughout this book, the "administering" of "existing structures" will not be very helpful, at least not on an economy-wide scale, but would be a proper measure within a business venture; instead, we must view the market as an ever changing and open-ended process. We therefore cannot assess the efficiency of markets at any point in time but must look at the market's ability to, over time, find better ways of producing value by adjusting to changing conditions and responding to new or shifting preferences among consumers. Or, in Schumpeter's preferred phrase, to assess the market's functioning over time in terms of "creative destruction"—how new and better production technologies, organizational structures, and goods and services are introduced and replace those that are less effective. This is what we saw in chapter 4, in our discussion about the division of labor, comparative advantage, and innovation.

From our point of view, then, to improve the market a policy must assist in strengthening or achieving what can be referred to as *adaptive efficiency*, that is, efficiency in production over time and therefore including the dynamic adjustment to changing conditions, by inducing innovation and facilitating the risk-taking and creative activities that help find solutions to problems and thereby create value for society over time.[3] Whereas the market is a process, with entrepreneurship as its driving force, the task of policy intended on improving the functioning of the process must be to help entrepreneurs carry out their function. We learned above what entrepreneurs do and how they attempt to accurately anticipate what will be the most highly valued use of resources by seeking profit from satisfying consumers in the best way possible. As acting on anticipation necessarily means bearing the cost of uncertainty, an endeavor fraught with mistakes and failures, one possible approach is for policy to target reducing the cost of uncertainty. This can be achieved, theoretically speaking, by helping entrepreneurs avoid mistakes or by lessening the burden of uncertainty on the undertaking. The latter would be similar to subsidizing entrepreneurs who undertake pursuing novel ventures or attempt to realize productive innovations in the market. To put it simply, government can incentivize entrepreneurship by covering part of the cost if the entrepreneur fails. This would, as in the example of the baking subsidy, increase risky undertakings by entrepreneurs, which is not necessarily a productive use of scarce resources. Also, we saw in the discussion above that subsidies imply regulation, primarily in the form of taxation, to cover the cost of the subsidy—and this causes distortions in the economic organism's ability to satisfy consumers' wants and needs. The subsidy itself would then "nudge" entrepreneurs toward assuming more risk rather than less, to pursue novelty rather than better uses for or improvements to existing production structures, which could end up being wasteful by redirecting productive resources from wants satisfaction in the present or near future toward a more distant and lesser known future.

A more fruitful approach, it seems, would be to assist entrepreneurs who choose to undertake uncertain projects for profit by helping them avoid mistakes. As the future is uncertain, however, it is impossible for policy to direct entrepreneurs toward the "better" opportunities. Which ones will actually turn out to be the better ones will not be known until after the fact, that is the realization of profits, so this is not a way forward. Instead, to avoid mistakes would likely be a more practical and indirect matter of learning best practices and rules of thumbs for identifying and preparing for problems and errors. It is likely that education can be of assistance here, especially in the sense of education in the real workings of the market, as we have briefly discussed thus far in this book, since it offers entrepreneurs a framework for thinking about the market and the role of the entrepreneur as embedded in a social and economic situation. Such efforts will not do away with failures, but may reduce them. Yet it is important to note that even such educational and preparatory efforts require resources to be carried out—at a minimum the labor of the educator—that could otherwise be used to directly assist entrepreneurs in their businesses. Like anything else, resources in education have opportunity costs and this reaffirms the points made above. If resources are redirected toward education, whether formal education or practical on-the-job training, we necessarily forego their alternative best uses. It follows that if those other uses would have contributed to creating *more* value than education, then this type of policy is not value-maximizing but in fact constitutes poor use of those resources. If it is due to a political decision rather than an entrepreneurial undertaking for personal profit, there is also the risk that the opportunity has not been thoroughly analyzed and that the implementing of the project may be burdened with overhead costs. All of this causes distortions to the market's ability to satisfy real wants.

We can also think of improvement as attempts to steer market production toward *other* goals than the "blind" satisfaction of wants among consumers. For instance, there may be more socially beneficial outcomes, politically identified and preferred, than what the market spontaneously produces. Note that such values, which do not follow from consumers' actual economic actions and therefore their use of resources in exchange, are necessarily different from what consumers would choose and entrepreneurs anticipate that they value. It places an unreasonable trust in political decision-makers or experts to accurately identify what should be done instead of satisfying consumer wants the way consumers themselves see their wants. It also raises questions about how to define a "social good" and a "social value" that do not emerge from the actions of individuals engaged in social cooperation through production under the division of labor and, as a result, facilitate consumption to satisfy their own wants. To the extent that this is possible, an issue we will not dwell on here, such efforts still fall into one or both of the categories discussed above: regulation that restricts action or subsidies that incentivize certain action (following regulation). Both necessarily bring about distortions with respect to consumers' preferred actions.

Nevertheless, policy makers can make use of measures that increase costs for or even prohibit certain actions that are considered socially unfavorable or perhaps destructive. For instance, the outright prohibition of narcotic drugs, often considered a proper policy intended to reduce their use, causes resources and therefore entrepreneurial endeavors to be redirected from the production and distribution of such drugs toward other activities. Policy makers can also rely on subsidies to bring about an increase in politically preferred socially beneficial outcomes, such as fighting unemployment by creating jobs. In our analyses above, we have assumed full employment, but this is hardly ever observed in modern economies. This is problematic since without producing and therefore earning an income, those without income also lose the ability to acquire goods and services necessary to satisfy wants. Unemployment is therefore, as well as for other reasons, considered a social bad that requires a political solution. Political solutions, however, like other actions, use resources and are therefore necessarily burdened with opportunity costs—they cause distortions by taking resources from other uses. Whether fighting unemployment is a social good or bad is not relevant to our discussion here. However, it is relevant to consider the discussions above in light of available resources—how do our examples of entrepreneurship and social cooperation change if there is an unused stock of resources available for use? After all, we assumed full employment, which is why for example Adele's giving up apple-growing to become a nail smith led to the society losing their supply of locally grown apples. If there are people under- or unemployed, it seems intuitive that they would be able to take over the orchard that Adele leaves behind. And if that's the case, then the consumers who preferred to purchase apples could continue doing so even after Adele becomes a baker. In other words, this group would no longer be on the losing side. We will now look at this issue in detail.

UNEMPLOYMENT IN THE MARKET

Unemployment is another way of saying that there is an existing supply of a productive resource that is currently unused, fully or partially. To see how such underutilization of labor affects how we understand the market process, let's consider a variation of a previous example. To recapitulate, the total production apparatus in our little society consists of five nail smiths (Becky, David, Deborah, Eric, and Edda), three bakers (Bart, Bob, and Charles), one construction worker (Fred), and one apple-grower (Adele). To study the impact of unemployment, we add three underemployed men and women: Gina, Gordon, and Gregory. Gina works part-time with Fred to assist in house building. She specifically is responsible for new-building foundations—performing the excavation, then mixing and placing the concrete. In other words, she does the heavy lifting necessary to get started with construction, while Fred does the rest of the work. As Fred only rarely gets contracts for new construction, Gina only works half as much as she would like to. In other words, she is *under*employed but not unemployed. Gordon and Gregory, in contrast, are *un*employed.

Before discussing the effects of a change such as the subsidy for bread baking that "lures" Adele to give up on apple-growing, we must ask why it is the case that our three new friends are under- and unemployed. After all, the arguments presented in the first few chapters established that production precedes consumption and that in an unhampered market people produce to satisfy their own wants—that is, they work to facilitate their own consumption. To do this, they either produce goods and services that can directly satisfy their own wants or that satisfy the wants and needs of others (thereby generating a profit that can indirectly satisfy their own wants). Those who do not produce consequently cannot facilitate consumption and thus fail to satisfy their own needs and wants. Whatever you consume that you have not produced, directly or indirectly, is necessarily offered to you by someone else and taken out of their belongings, and thus out of what they have produced, and provided without requesting the reciprocal offer of value. It is therefore a charitable contribution—a gift—rather than part of an exchange, since only one party has value to offer, and consequently the receiving party has little bargaining power. An individual's independence and sovereignty are in this sense "earned" by engaging in the production of value, particularly highly specialized production in the form of social cooperation through the division of labor.[4]

So far in the discussion our little society has not suffered from a lack of natural resources to sustain its members. While this may seem unrealistic, it is not. The reason is that natural resources are only resources in so far as they are *economic* resources. The example of crude oil illustrates this point. Before the process of refining oil into petroleum, and the innovation of the internal combustion engine, there was no economic use for oil. It was as much a natural resource as it is today, but was not an economic resource—it had no value in production and couldn't be consumed. In fact, oil was just a gooey substance that at best was a nuisance but oftentimes incurred a burdensome cost on the poor fellow being so unlucky as to have oil on his or her property. Ranchers raising cattle, for instance, need to dig wells to water the animals, especially when the weather is hot and dry. Striking oil instead of water, which today would be considered good luck and would make you a fortune, was for cattle ranchers the worst kind of luck: it made the newly dug well, and likely any adjacent wells, unusable by poisoning the water—and at the same time making the land unfit for both cattle and crops. Finding oil, therefore, was an additional cost on their business, and as the oil restricted the usefulness of the land—in more than one respect—it also caused a drop in its market value. What this serves to show is that no society runs a risk of running out of economic resources, as the supply of economic resources is limited only by the extent of human ingenuity—the ultimate resource.[5] If the availability of a natural resource that is the basis for a specific economic resource diminishes, the market responds by increasing the price and thereby produces an incentive for alternative means to the same end—or alternative ends altogether. We saw this above when we discussed how an economy responds to destruction and natural disaster, and the same applies when natural resources are used up. As a result, the economic organism does not cease to function but shifts production toward the best uses of the resources available. In other words, the only way Gina, Gordon, and Gregory can be held outside production in the economic organism for any extensive period against their will is if they do not have and cannot gain access to economic resources.

This is however an impossibility, since it is not true that economic resources in the unhampered market are available only to "the rich." Instead, economic resources—capital—are available for those who will accumulate wealth *in the future*. This may seem unintuitive, but it follows from our discussion above. We argued that prices as well as production undertakings are based on anticipations about the future rather than facts in the past or present. The same is true for the availability of capital for investing in entrepreneurial undertakings. This availability is not dependent on how much value one has already accumulated, which says nothing about one's future performance, but is rather a function of the anticipated value that one can generate by using a specific resource. As we concluded above, economic resources for entrepreneurial investments are awarded to those who are willing to outbid other entrepreneurs for those resources. The same is true for the investment necessary to make a credible bid, which does not need to consist of payment in the present but could include a credit arrangement. In other words, entrepreneurs can offer owners of capital payment of a specific amount at a future time, or part of profits to be earned, for the present use of resources. Whether capital owners, themselves entrepreneurs with past success(es), accept a bid depends on how they subjectively estimate its value and whether it exceeds the value of other bids.

This applies to Gina, Gordon, and Gregory as well, who could compete with other entrepreneurs for economic resources to use in their entrepreneurial undertakings even if they themselves lack capital on hand. But even if we, for the sake of argument, assume that something makes it impossible for them to get access to capital. This can be the case for one of two reasons: either all resources are already occupied in entrepreneurial undertakings of very high anticipated value, or very few economic resources exist in this world. In the former case, this means the economic resources are employed in endeavors that could employ Gina, Gordon, and Gregory and pay them for their supplied labor. It should also be the case, since there is plenty of capital, that their labor is highly productive because of this—and therefore more valuable. In the latter case, with very few existing economic resources, the value of our three friends' labor should be much higher, relatively speaking, simply because there is very little productive capital. They should therefore be able to sell their labor services to assist in production. In both cases, therefore, the conclusion must be the same as with respect to entrepreneurship: there is nothing preventing Gina, Gordon, and Gregory from partaking in production. It may be the case that they do not find what they would consider to be sufficient remuneration for their services, that is they're offered a wage they consider too low and therefore choose to not work. But that is a choice based on their assessment of the available alternatives.

This conclusion, that unemployment in the unhampered market is voluntary, may seem crass, but it is the only reasonable conclusion considering our discussion so far. In an economy without artificial restrictions there is only one reason why valuable—that is, *productive*—resources are not used, and that is because they are anticipated to become even more valuable if instead used in the future. This is true for Bart when he finds flour at bargain prices and therefore buys to store for baking in the future rather than in the immediate present. It was true for Adele buying tools and machines for her orchard before the apple trees were ready to bear fruit, because she expected them to increase her productivity or solve problems later on. It is true for Becky holding on to part of her stock of three-inch nails because she anticipates the price will rise and that she will then be able to make a greater profit. It is also true for someone like Gordon, who chooses not to become an entrepreneur yet still turns down chances for employment, because he believes better opportunities will present themselves in the future.

But what we have said here about unemployment is true only in the genuine and thus unhampered market. As we will see in the next chapter, it is not necessarily true in a distorted or artificially restricted market.

NOTES

1. Schumpeter notes that "since we're dealing with a process whose every element takes considerable time in revealing its true features and ultimate effects, there is no point in appraising the performance of that process *ex visu* of a given point in time; we must judge its performance over time, as it unfolds through decades or centuries. A system—any system, economic or other—that at *every* given point of time fully utilizes its possibilities to the best advantage may yet in the long run be inferior to a system that does so at *no* given point of time, because the latter's failure to do so may be a condition for the level or speed of long-run performance" (1942, p. 83).
2. See Schumpeter (1942, p. 84).
3. See North (1990, pp. 80–82).
4. We look specifically at the economic implications of production, which is the subject matter for this book. A society may include many other dimensions, such as personal and social ties, including friendships and family, and belonging to a community, in addition to the social cooperation through specialized production that we discuss here.
5. See Simon (1998).

Chapter Nine

The Unrealized

Our discussion so far has established how the economic organism responds to changes both from within and without, and how it encompasses as well as encourages entrepreneurs to find ways to satisfy more highly valued consumer wants. We have also looked at the effects on the functioning of the market when affected by artificial restrictions through policy, and how such influences create distortions in resource allocation as compared to what otherwise would have been—and therefore limits decentralized production efforts throughout the market. We saw how the effect of policy is similar to that of destruction, but without the concomitant change in preferences: policy is a one-sided change, which makes it extra costly, by causing distortions—a mismatch between supply and demand.

While distortionary when viewed from the point of view of the unhampered market, and thus costly to society in lost wants satisfaction, policy-based restrictions are not necessarily only or even primarily a cost on society. The reason any policy is introduced is, of course, to attempt to solve one or more problems. If the policy is successful, the value of solving that specific problem should be recorded as a benefit to offset the cost of distortion and loss of productive capacity.

Policy introduces a different problem, however, that we noted briefly in the discussion above on Luke's attempt to solve the apparent issue of too little bread being produced. Policy tends to solve problems that consumers through their actions have shown are of overall less value than what is provided by the market. As we observed above, Luke considered the supply of bread to be too low and therefore attempted to solve this problem by offering a subsidy. The effect, in that case, was indeed an increased supply of bread—but at the expense of reduced supply of other goods, which consumers more highly valued. Indeed, the shift of resources from the production of three-inch nails as Eric leaves to become a baker, and from apple-growing as Adele similarly leaves her trade to instead bake bread, solves the problem that Luke considered more important—but at the same time means the problems already solved by nail manufacturing and apple-growing become "unsolved." As Eric and Adele in this example go to different trades, they do so not because they anticipate that they will serve consumers better by doing so. By making the move, they do anticipate their profits to become higher, which in the market signals that one has offered valuable service to consumers, but the profit actually generated by the market—that is by consumers through buying goods and services offered at prices that are lower than the value that is gained in return—is in fact *lower* than in their current professions. If this were not the case, the subsidy would not be needed. The subsidy makes the difference and thus makes baking more profitable. In other words, their move to other occupations—and therefore the economic organism's overall productive shift from nail manufacturing and apple-growing to baking—is not a move that solves problems that consumers are willing and able to pay for, but solves a problem that Luke is more interested in (too little bread).

Similar to what was the case in chapter 5, in which we discussed the effect of the shopkeeper's broken window and the "ripple" effects caused through the economy, the policy-induced shift changes consumptive behavior. But, as we noted in chapter 8, the shift sets other chains of events in motion by *shifting production*, not—as was the case with the broken window—consumption. When consumption shifts this is an indication of consumers' value rankings having changed, such as the shopkeeper who values replacing the window pane higher than buying shoes, and when market production shifts it does so in anticipation of shifting consumer demand or an increased ability to satisfy consumer wants. Indeed, we saw in the early chapters of the book that production in the unhampered market facilitates consumption—and that production is undertaken specifically to meet anticipated demand. In other words, production tries to find consumption, and as consumption changes production thus follows.

A policy-induced shift in production is different, since it restricts or distorts wants-satisfying production in order to solve a politically valued problem. Consumers' preference rankings may not have changed as a result, but what set of goods and services that are made available to them *have* changed. Production does not facilitate consumption but is restricted from doing so in the way entrepreneurs think proper—this is, after all, the intent and implication of policy—and thus forces them to choose other ways of satisfying consumer wants, which are consequently are less valued since the most valued and thus most profitable are chosen first. This loss of ability to satisfy the more highly valued wants makes consumers as a group worse off as they will be able to satisfy only less highly valued wants. Consumers have different preference rankings, of course, so some of the consumers may be better off while others are worse off, depending on—in our previous example—whether they prefer bread or nails or apples.

We identified the effect of the subsidy on several groups within consumers in chapter 8. In this chapter, we will focus on the effect of policy on individuals' optionality—the choices *that can be made*. More importantly, we will discuss what choices *cannot* be made anymore because the means to make those choices remain unrealized.

LIMITATIONS OF THE PURE MARKET

We noted in chapter 4 that markets, even when they are not affected or distorted by regulation, are hardly efficient in the regular usage of the term. Part of the reason for this is the ignorance we suffer with regard to the future: we cannot foresee what will be supplied or demanded in the future, and therefore it is impossible to perfectly fit production to the wants and needs that will emerge in the future. This problem is due to consumers' ignorance of what they will want, which partly depends on what wants they will discover as entrepreneurs make new types of goods and services available, and producers' ignorance of what they can and should produce, which depends on limited technological knowhow and incomplete understanding of what problems consumers face today and in the future. The latter is also due to the fact that even if the demand situation is perfectly predicted, which is impossible, the supply situation isn't. Consumer demands are not only dependent on the problems consumers want to solve, but also on what problems they have already solved, the manner they are to be solved, and what problems consumers anticipate that they will be able to solve—and at what cost. Take a problem like transportation, for instance. It was solved by walking, running, riding horses and carriages before the advent of the automobile and, more importantly, when Henry Ford made the automobile available to a larger share of the population. The automobile proved to be a much more effective (and, just as if not more importantly, *cost* effective) solution to the problem of transportation, so this innovation replaced what was previously the obvious and generally accepted solution. With the highway system, which was a government creation and thus a distortive subsidy to favor automobiles and similar types of transportation, and improved comfort and speed, consequently making automobiles an even more regular solution.[1] This does not mean, of course, that there won't be an innovation to replace the automobile. So even a solved problem can be solved again, if entrepreneurs find better ways of solving it.

It is quite conceivable that there were innovative entrepreneurs introducing new and better carriages, better and more effective stables and horse-feeding, breeding, and training operations, better horse feed, improved buggy whips, and so on as the automobile was introduced. These innovations are all improvements of what was, and in this sense create value—but they are misaligned and misdirected attempts to create value, since consumers are about to change their behavior with respect to transportation. The market for horse-drawn carriages, horse feed, and buggy whips will shrink dramatically as consumers shift their demand from horse-and-carriage toward automobiles. Entrepreneurs who didn't see this coming failed because they were competing for a share of a shrinking market. Other entrepreneurs, who anticipated this change much more correctly, may have invested in oil refineries for petroleum production or gas stations or steel plants or rubber ersatz for the production of tires. These undertakings would have been complete and utter failures had the automobile not been invented and adopted by consumers. In other words, to be successful in production, one has to anticipate the supply situation.

The supply situation is less straightforward than one might think, however. It is obvious that the production of substitutes—like the horse-and-carriage to the automobile—and complements—like gas stations for automobiles—are affected by the supply situation. Without automobiles, producers of horse-drawn carriages would have the whole market, and these entrepreneurs establishing gas stations along the roads would be hopelessly malinvested. With automobiles, the situation is quite different. But what about shopping malls? Shopping malls were not possible before automobiles were adopted by the general population and thus had become a common means of transportation. Suddenly it made sense to collect different stores in a single place—located far from the city center. With the automobile, it suddenly became sensible to place housing outside of cities as well, thus creating urban sprawl, giving rise to the phenomenon of commuting to work, making daycares necessary for double income households. One change, therefore, caused numerous adjustments to consumer behavior that triggered responses by entrepreneurs in the market. Many of these responses in turn produced other changes to behavior, which caused other responses, and so on. It is in this highly dynamic, ever-changing situation that entrepreneurs attempt to anticipate whether they and their intended good have a place. Whether they actually do, and can make a profit from it, depends on how both supply and demand evolve between now, that is what is known in the present, and when the good is finally produced and made available to the market.

As the market situation at any point is caused by the interplay of supply and demand, that is by the entrepreneurs' production undertakings and consumers' wants, the evolution or process of the market is extremely difficult to foresee. Because supply and demand are mutually constituting, the economic organism is *endogenous*, which means the reasons and ways in which it changes over time comes primarily from within. An economy is of course affected also by exogenous changes (such as disasters or other externalities) but the market process is not dependent on but only reacts to such events. While endogeneity means it is very difficult to predict the course of change, it is not random. We have already established that the market consists of production efforts intended to facilitate consumption, which in turn satisfies experienced wants and felt needs. As such its direction—the market's progression—is clear: it tends toward the greatest possible want satisfaction, because this is where the profit is.

Progression toward is not the same thing as attainment of the aimed for end, however. The market process is always in disequilibrium and thus—for that very reason—inefficient: it is constantly *moving toward* higher states. Since it is composed of only decentralized decisions, but those decisions are incentivized by satisfying real wants, the market process typically reaches higher levels of want satisfaction as capital is produced and accumulated, productivity strengthened, and investments are made to support innovations that challenge the status quo by offering further improvement. Real economic growth through the satisfaction of a greater number of and more urgent wants and needs is accomplished through competition for profit, and the mutual discovery that follows from offering competing products intended toward consumption for given ends, and the absence of artificial barriers to entry.

The reason *all* wants and needs are not and will never be fully satisfied is a result of human nature and facts of reality. Economics generally assumes that consumer wants are insatiable, which means there is always something that could be made better or improved; we do not live in the garden of Eden, but in a real world of scarcity. And this points to the limitation of economy due to the fact that goods are scarce, which is also the reason there is such a thing as economy. In a world where no resources are scarce, the resources have no value. Their value, after all, is imputed from their contribution to satisfying real wants—but if all wants are being satisfied, which is the implication of all resources existing in abundance (that is, they're non-scarce), then there is no choice toward which want they should satisfy and, as a result, nothing has a cost. Without cost, then, resources aren't valued. The economic organism responds to changes, but its main feat is to produce ever greater satisfaction of wants and thus limit the effects of scarcity on people's lives.

We see this lessening of scarcity in the form of increased convenience and comfort in our daily lives—that is, our standard of living increases as our wants are being satisfied.

While the effects of scarcity diminish with innovations and increased productivity, it cannot be fully abolished. It is conceivable to eventually reach a level of prosperity where everybody can afford whatever stuff and gadgets they could wish for. But even in this situation, some wants remain to be discovered as entrepreneurs offer new types of goods and services that shatter consumers' ignorance about their real wants and preferences. Also, time and space cannot ever be anything but scarce for a living being: even if we live forever and have colonized the universe, it is still the case that we cannot do everything we would like to at every moment. We cannot eat and sleep at the same time, for instance. This is due to time and space limitations that amount to scarcity: had we had non-scarce access to both time and space, we could do both—and all other things we would like—at the same time. As the saying goes, we cannot have the cake and eat it too—but that's exactly what we would need to be able to do, for cakes and everything else, in order for us to not be affected by scarcity. Scarcity in the colloquial sense can be abolished, but not in the sense that makes economy irrelevant: the choice will always be there, and the choice necessarily means choosing something over something else—the choice has an opportunity cost. This cost indicates the presence of scarcity, and the only way of lessening it is by economizing—that is, by finding out how to better use existing resources, and thus to allocate resources toward more highly valued uses. This is what is done "automatically" in the unhampered market, since production precedes and facilitates consumption and because specialized production for the benefit of others is a more effective way of gaining the means to satisfy one's own wants. Our incentives are in complete, or almost complete, alignment.

What this means is that the market, when left to its own devices—and thus unaffected by imposed restrictions or large-scale destruction—tends to reach higher levels of want satisfaction by developing the means necessary. Why? Because a situation where the chooser has one highly valued alternative and all other alternatives are of significantly lower value is an opportunity for profit. If the problem to be solved is shared by more people, the fact that there is only one solution—or only one provider of solutions—means their profits are likely higher than the market average. After all, consider a situation where a person is looking for transportation across the Missouri plain from St. Louis to Kansas City and there are only a few alternatives available: walking, traveling by horse and carriage, or taking the train. The entrepreneur operating the train can, because the train is the much faster and more comfortable means of transportation, charge a high price. This is the obverse of a situation without optionality: the higher price can be charged because travelers value taking the train so much more than the other means available. So from the travelers' perspective, the situation is one where the opportunity cost of taking the train is low, meaning the value anticipated from walking and traveling the distance by horse and carriage is significantly lower than riding in a train car. As the train entrepreneur offers a much higher value, he or she can benefit by charging a higher price.

But this is also an incentive for other entrepreneurs to develop competing means of transportation that provides them with a share of the profit. They can build railroads or roads or fly the 250 miles between the two cities, all of which would make them able to compete for the profit—by offering consumers value that is at least as high as is already offered. And by adding to the supply of highly valued transportation services between St. Louis and Kansas City, the number of similarly valued alternative means of transportation that consumers can choose from—their optionality—increases. It also means the opportunity cost of the choice increases because the value foregone by, for instance, choosing to drive on the newly constructed highway instead of riding the train is much higher than the value forgone when choosing to travel by train before the highway was constructed (that is, the value of walking or traveling by horse and carriage).

We discussed this in chapter 4, where we noted that a relatively high opportunity cost implies real optionality: a situation where choosing takes place between several alternatives of similar value to the chooser. Because entrepreneurs compete for profit by satisfying consumer wants, they individually attempt to outdo the competition by adopting productive innovations and, as a group, attempt to keep up with the front runners. The result is continuous progress and, which is another way of saying the same thing, higher levels of want satisfaction.

Innovations that reshape the market, or even create new markets, are still always in some sense improvements of what already exists. This may sound paradoxical, but the explanation is simple: an entrepreneur who innovates a new type of good, previously never imagined, will still rely on the existing production apparatus to implement this innovation. Even highly disruptive innovations like the printing press and the Internet built off and therefore improved on other, and already existing production methods. They use tools, knowledge, and infrastructure in a different way, but these resources are in existence before the innovation can be realized. An innovation that doesn't build on what already exists would need to not rely on anything at all in existence: no tools, no machines, no materials, no knowledge, and so on that is already in use. Whereas this may be theoretically possible, it is difficult to think of how anyone could imagine an innovation that does not make use of but rather is completely new in every sense and in every part of the production process. It is much easier to use what we know and have than to come up with completely different methods and tools. And since the diversity of tools and services and knowledge in an economy's production apparatus were developed because they are of value in production, it would make very little sense to start anew. So even though the market may be "disrupted," that is, its productive structure and "direction" are changed fundamentally by the introduction of a previously unseen and unimagined product or service, there is continuity. An economy's productive achievement is cumulative—innovations build on some of the previous successes but challenge others. They must, since not building on what already exists is too limiting: it would be like becoming the entrepreneurial equivalent of the shipwrecked Robinson

Crusoe, and we have already established that specializing is an important means to become more productive.

This means there is a boundary to what is possible in the market, since each person in his or her endeavors is limited by what already exists; to add the market's production apparatus, a person can only add to it by challenging parts of it or the way some resources are put to use. In other words, even innovative super-entrepreneurs cannot go too far from what already exists, because doing so will make their attempts incompatible with all the means of production existing and created in the market—making them as inefficient as the unspecialized, self-sustaining Robinson Crusoe. It is not a means toward success, but a sure way of failing and thus losing one's investment. To be successful, therefore, innovations must break new ground without going too far: they cannot go so far that they end up being significantly incompatible with the production structure already in existence.[2]

Economic history is littered with examples of innovations that went "too far" in some sense, often because they were before their time—consumers were not ready for the innovation. A recent example is the tablet computer, which is a modern-day version of the age-old tablet for notetaking. Even so, the success and disruption of the computing market by the release of Apple's iPad tablet in 2010 was preceded by similar innovations that turned out to be complete failures for the simple reason that the timing was wrong: the MS-DOS-based GRiDPad in 1989, Apple's Newton in 1993, the Microsoft Tablet PC in 2002, and the Android-based Archos 5 in 2009. The failed attempts at devices introducing tablet computing were different but were similar to the iPad in their defining characteristics—their failure was to launch too soon.

The boundary is therefore not simply a limitation of what can be produced, that is what tools, machines, techniques, and materials are available, but is also the set of what consumers are willing and able to comprehend as means toward satisfaction. Unless consumers are able to see how a specific good can provide for the satisfaction of certain wants, they will not see it as having value. Where this is the case, the good will not have a price on the market or will only be sellable at such a low price that it fails to cover the costs of production—and therefore the venture fails. This confirms what was stated above about production facilitating consumption as well as being intended to satisfy wants, and that the value of the means of production is imputed from the value contributed to consumers. And if consumers are not convinced of the ability of a new product or service to satisfy real wants, it will have no value—the market is thus, due to this limitation, conservative in its progression.

This also means that the major shortcoming of the economic organism— that it is inefficient, since it does not satisfy all wants—cannot be thought of as valid criticism, since the wants and needs not yet satisfied are either not technologically feasible, not cost efficient and therefore a poor use of resources, or simply have not yet been discovered. Due to these three reasons, a market will never reach a general equilibrium—that is, full contentment will not ever be in reach.

THE PURE ECONOMY AND THE REALIZED

The previous section focused on the limitations and "inefficiency" of the pure market. This model of economy—the unhampered market process—used in this book differs significantly from what is commonly used to assess the efficiency of economic states. Our focus is the market as an economic organism, a process that is constantly undergoing change brought about by entrepreneurial discoveries, innovations, and investments for profit—indeed, entrepreneurship is the driving force of the market process. This model, as we concluded in the previous section, is not an efficient system in the strict economic sense, that is as compared to the model of perfect competition. The latter assumes, among other things, that actors have perfect information—that we know everything about the present, including what others know, imagine, and plan to do, as well as the future, and therefore can use re-sources, which are mostly homogeneous (there's only capital and labor, not different types of tools, machines, expertise) and transactions therefore aren't very costly, in an optimal, maximizing way. Perfect competition therefore excludes entrepreneurship and change, since they are neither needed nor of value if there is perfect information. Indeed, the very existence of entrepreneurship suggests that the market has *not* reached full efficiency but is in an inefficient state, because otherwise there would be no (profit) opportunities to better satisfy consumer wants. The model of perfect competition thus *by design* excludes uncertainty and discovery, both by producers and consumers, by assuming that the economy has already reached a state of maximum performance. Improvements *cannot* be made since the system is without flaws, so entrepreneurs would only—if they acted—cause inefficiencies. Therefore, entrepreneurs have no place and no function in the model.

To assess the functioning of a real or proposed economic system, a model based on foreign or even outrageously unrealistic assumptions is a poor benchmark. All real economic systems are necessarily inefficient, since there is no such thing as perfect information. The problem of imperfect information *per se* is not a problem that can be solved economically (or in any other way). Thus, critique of any real economic situation based on such assumptions is falling victim to the nirvana fallacy[3]—it presents as relevant the comparison between something ideal (and out of this world) and a real, and therefore imperfect, alternative. Setting up the problem using such false alternatives isn't without consequence: it can misdirect our attention to problems that may not be possible to solve—and may actually be unimportant in the real world. In other words, such a benchmark can potentially do more harm than good for the simple reason that the real problems may become over-shadowed by the more unrealistic ones. Indeed, the real and solvable prob-lems may seem of only marginal importance or peripheral from the point of view of the "perfect" model, so the focus of improvements may instead fall on what's either an impossible or unreal real problem that may very well be both these things. The real is compared with a fantasy world.

The proper benchmark to assess the functioning of real economic sys-tems, such as those including attempted corrective policy or those that in-clude an element of central planning, is a model of the unhampered economy as we have discussed above. This model is realistic in the sense that it does not assume actors to be omniscient or are motivated only by pecuniary bene-fits like profits. Instead, the model stresses real issues caused by ignorance and discovery; it places production, entrepreneurship, and uncertainty at the heart of the analysis; and it indicates why it is necessary that a society accumulates productive capital to be able to generate higher standards of living—that is, to experience sustainable economic growth. The model also includes a logic by which the market process can be properly understood, and effects consequently traced from causes, which in turn facilitates detailed and exact analysis of the unfolding of events, their consequences, and interac-tions and interdependencies in the market. This is what we did in previous chapters, where we traced the effects of changes by walking through how one change generates shifts and changes elsewhere, and how those in turn pro-duce a change elsewhere.

What matters to us here is not efficiency of the overall system in an abstract sense, as is the intent of the model of perfect competition, but how the system affects the actors that comprise it. More specifically, we are interested in the extent in which an economy empowers people by producing valuable goods and services—and by offering optionality. The discussion has so far focused on the issue of production, since production is what facilitates consumption and therefore is the means by which actors satisfy real wants—the wants of others, and thereby indirectly their own. Optionality, however, is a matter of independence and autonomy for the individual in a choice situation—it is restricted neither to production nor consumption. An entre-preneur can experience (and thus benefit from) optionality by choosing be-tween several suppliers, inputs, production techniques, locations, expertise of employees, and so on of similar value; likewise, a consumer can experience (and thus benefit from) optionality by choosing between several products and services that equally or to similar extents satisfy a specific want—either perfectly or imperfectly.

The fact that a choice must be made, which implies that at least one alternative option *cannot* be chosen, does not necessarily indicate a problem. For instance, we can easily think of a person hungry for dessert choosing between different alternative baked goods, ice creams, chocolates, Jell-O, etc. Perhaps this person realizes that he or she does not have room for more than one serving, or maybe they are really hungry for dessert but cannot, for whatever reason, justify taking more than a couple of bites to taste. In both cases, getting all the desserts on the menu is not an option because that does not contribute value—only the first serving does. So the choice is positive in the sense that it entails picking out the one dessert to satisfy the want best, rather than not being able to choose the other desserts. Of course, it may also be the case that this person would like more but cannot afford more than a single serving of dessert. This would seem to be a less positive situation, since the person is primarily choosing which desserts *not* to order. While this may appear to be more problematic, as we discussed in previous chapters, this really means that our dessert-hungry person was or is not willing to give up what it would cost to buy more than one dessert—because the non-dessert alternatives are worth so much more. Alternatively, not having enough money in one's pocket to pay for two desserts, even though two (or more) would be preferred, should be a result of previously not having produced sufficient value and therefore not having generated enough buying power—for instance by choosing leisure over labor or failing in one's entrepreneurial undertaking. The lack of ability to satisfy a want in the present—more than one dessert—is therefore a result of a value achieved in the past—leisure instead of labor. As we noted in chapter 8, there is only voluntary unemployment in an unhampered economy, since there are no restrictions on one's options except the physically impossible and the willingness and ability to put in the effort.

Actually having the choice, especially if it is a tough one because the alternatives are of similar or equal value, is a luxury. It indicates prosperity. Such a choice situation suggests two things: that very basic needs for one's survival have been properly met, that is a basic standard of living has been accomplished, and that market production offers alternative and competitive solutions to the present single problem, which of course also indicates a high standard of living. So finding yourself in the situation where you need to (can) choose between two delicious desserts, and neither appears as the obvious choice but both seem delicious, is an indirect measure of wealth since those alternatives—optionality—are made available to you by the combined productive apparatus of the market.

We can therefore assess a market's performance by looking at the choices people can and might have to make—and especially the options they're presented with in the choice situation. Societies with abundant choices are, all other things equal, more prosperous than those that offer very few real alternatives and thus limited optionality. Though this is an indirect measure of prosperity, it tells a story of how well people are doing within an economic system. It is very difficult to measure directly, since it isn't possible to see how people value the alternatives—we can only see what they end up choosing. We can potentially list the contents of a person's choice set, that is the number of possible options, but whether they are similarly valued or very far apart in terms of the person's actual valuation is hidden to the observer. This valuation that the chooser makes in that moment is not simply a ranking of the present options, but is also affected by anticipations of what options may be made available later on—and the value they will present at that future time. The choice is also tainted by the perceived cost of already exerted effort, that is the labor already invested in production to facilitate the choice of means for consumption, even though this cost—from an economic perspective—is sunk and therefore irrelevant. In other words, it is impossible to separate the individual's choice at any moment in time from both the situation's temporal and spatial context: what happened before and is anticipated to come about, and what the options actually perceived by the person are.

The good news is that we don't have to put together a complete picture of the choice situation in order to analyze it. Instead, we can return to the logic above and look at what alternatives are realized in a certain economic system—and by walking through the logic we can trace what goes wrong in the systems that offer very limited choice situations. The question we ask is thus: compared to what options could reasonably be available or even expected, how many—and which ones—are made available in this specific economic system?

To answer the question, we must first establish a baseline, and therefore analyze the options realized in an unhampered market. This is, as we noted above, the model that is unbeatable in terms of value creation and, therefore, the one that should present individual actors with better optionality. It is theoretically possible, of course, that we can, when walking through the logic of different economic systems, to find a system that is better at providing individuals with alternatives in every choice situation than the unhampered market. The discovery of such a system, and how it is or can be structured, would be a very important finding indeed. The working hypothesis (though it is actually of little importance), considering what we have learned above, is however that the unhampered market should be maximizing in terms of optionality due to its matchless ability to create real value through production that facilitates consumption.

Consider again our chain of events from chapter 5, but this time we add our friends from the discussion on production and market responses, and add their consumptive behaviors, to get a fuller picture. As we argued in the very beginning of the book, production facilitates consumption and therefore every consumer is also a producer. There are potential exceptions from this rule, such as small children and sick or disabled adults, who may not be able to produce sufficiently to facilitate their own consumption. But unlike many streamlined models used in economic analysis, the model of the unhampered market process is compatible with treating individuals as embedded in a social context such as community and not simply instances of the economic caricature *homo economicus*, who responds atomistically and only to pecuniary benefits. Individuals are social beings and are always embedded in a social context, which means it is possible to survive and lead a good life even if you are a small child, sick, or disabled. We should note that the fact that production facilitates consumption doesn't mean "everyone for his or her own" without exception. But it is nevertheless true that even if an individual doesn't produce the value that facilitates what he or she consumes, *someone* has—it is impossible to consume what has not been produced, and it is equally impossible to consume a value that has not yet been produced. This allows for some redistribution between individuals—through community pooling of resources, joint savings initiatives such as workers' unemployment or health care funds, or simple charity—and this suggests a simple and down-to-earth solution to both temporary and permanent economic setbacks. However, it is not possible for a whole society or community to consume more than they have produced. It is thus not possible for a population to live beyond their means, which suggests a limit to how many net consumers, as compared to net producers, can be supported over time. To live beyond one's means, to consume more than what is produced, means that one's savings (if any) are depleted and then accumulated capital is consumed, which in turn inhibits productivity in future value creation. It is not a sustainable state of affairs and therefore requires a swift solution: either by increasing production to a level that at least equals consumption, or decrease consumption to no more than the level of production. This rule applies to both individuals and communities.

Let's revisit our little society to illustrate the complexity of the economic organism. Adele is, as she was from the very beginning, an apple-grower, Adam produces and sells soft drinks, Becky is the nail smith, Bart and Bob are both bakers, and Fred is a construction worker. The others have found their way from previous employment into roles from our discussion on the seen and the unseen in chapter 5, as well as some additional roles: Charles is now a shop keeper, David and Deborah are both farmers, Eric is a cattle breeder, and Edda is a hunter. Also, the previously underemployed Gina, Gordon, and Gregory have found new occupations: Gina combines her part-time employment for Fred with making ice cream, Gordon competes with Gina's business and is a full time ice cream maker, and Gregory has become a cattle breeder. In all, this little society consists of 14 people, all of whom are engaged in specialized production to facilitate their consumption. None of them produce exactly and only what they themselves use, which means whether or not the 14 members constitute a community (or several communities), the society as a whole is engaged in social cooperation through the division of labor.

The degree of optionality experienced by the population is realized because the producers create and offer goods and services valued by others in exchange for goods they themselves value. This optionality is evident both in production and consumption, and is increased by having higher purchasing power. Indeed, the richer a person is—that is the more capital he or she has accumulated through working and saving—the more wants can be satisfied at will in the market and, consequently, the less restrictive are the asking prices for the desired goods and services. To put it differently, with greater purchasing power there are more options available within a price range that can be afforded as well as considered worth it. This is a simple, valid conclusion in our model as well as in our everyday lives: with more money, we can afford to buy goods in greater quantities and also goods that are sold at a higher price. Optionality, therefore, is partly a function of one's purchasing power, which in an unhampered economy is a result of one's contribution to satisfying the wants of others. It is also partly a function of the success of others in producing goods and services that we find of value and therefore find worth acquiring, which in turn increases those producers' purchasing power and thus optionality. [4]

Of course, as this little society is indeed *little*, we cannot expect a huge number of choices—after all, there are only 14 people to produce and consume so it isn't possible for them to produce hundreds or thousands of different products and services. We will therefore look at purchasing power as a proxy for optionality. We will also look at the effects of a change, since this is where the results are most easily recognizable.

To illustrate our baseline, we will start with a seemingly well-functioning unhampered market and walk through the effects of a change. So our starting point is as described above: 14 fully employed people working in specialized trades. In this example, Gregory the ice cream maker was rather recently married to Deborah the farmer, and they live together in the small hut on the farm (as this is a rather small and limitedly developed economy, they all live in huts rather than houses). They've just learned that Deborah is expecting their first child, so they need to add a nursery to the hut. Fred the construction worker advises them to instead consider tearing down the hut and replacing it with a house. It will be more work and a little more expensive, but it will keep the whole family warm during cold winter nights and protect them and their belongings from rain and humidity—thereby saving them a bunch of money over time. It could also provide Gregory with a shop for ice cream production and sales, right next to where Deborah keeps her cows and therefore with excellent access to fresh milk, which would make his life a whole lot easier and probably increase his business. A house will also provide them with enough space to have a nursery and a guest room, and they wouldn't need to add more rooms for future additions to the family. Gregory and

Deborah are immediately sold on the idea, and start working on the plans with Fred—and Gina, working part time as Fred's assistant, helps as well.

At about the same time, Gordon the cattle breeder decides to contact Fred and ask if he could build him a house. Gordon doesn't have a dwelling of his own so has been sleeping in Bart's bakery at night. Even though the bakery is nice and warm—and Bart is kind enough to allow him to live there at no cost for as long as he'd like—the very early mornings (Bart starts baking around 3 am to have fresh breakfast bread for sale) and constant smell of bread are beginning to become more than a nuisance. Also, he doesn't want to be more of a burden to Bart than he already has been, so he has been trying to save as much as possible of his earnings from the cattle in hopes of being able to purchase a house of his own. When Gordon sells his next couple of fully grown cows, he anticipates having enough saved to buy a house. So after watering his cows in the early evening, he takes a walk to Fred's hut to discuss this matter with him. But when he gets there, Fred already has visitors—and he is halfway through drafting blueprints together with Gregory and Deborah, and Gina is there too cheering them on. Gordon quickly realizes that there is no way Fred will be able to help him build his house, at least not until he is done with Gregory and Deborah's house, which would be at least a year from now.

Understanding there is no way he can live with the early mornings and constant bread smell for another year—or maybe even two—Gordon decides to look for alternatives. He knows Edda, who earns a living by hunting, is very handy, so he contacts her to inquire about the possibility that she would be able to build him a house. Surprisingly, she accepts. She's been considering other trades for a while, and while she makes a decent living off hunting she realizes that she would easily make more in construction—and working on Gordon's house is a great way to get started and gain a reputation as a quality builder. So she gladly accepts.

As the two construction projects begin, the demand for Becky's three-inch nails sky-rockets. She has a hard time keeping up with the new demand, and raises prices to lessen demand somewhat and provide her with a decent profit. Bob notices this drastic increase in profitability from nail manufacturing, and as he has played with metals as a hobby (he made his own steel oven, for instance) he can easily switch from baking to nail manufacturing. He anticipates that he'll be able to get enough of a market share to make a nice profit in excess of what he's making as a baker, so he eagerly closes his bakery and starts working on nails.

Also, the demand for building materials increases as the two major construction projects pick up. Previously, Fred has, with the help of Gina, visited a nearby forest to cut down the trees necessary for the huts he was building. But for houses, timber isn't enough—he (and Edda, of course) needs planks. Making planks out of timber is time-consuming and adds a lot of time to building the houses, so Fred talks with Adam the soft drink maker about possibly going into the business of making planks (for him). Adam has been struggling to sell his sodas ever since it became fashionable among the men in our little society to adopt a low-carb, high-fat diet, so he doesn't need much time to consider shifting. He lives by a forest with very tall and straight pine trees that he could use. Learning about Edda's new line of business and her contract with Gordon, he talks with her about supplying her as well. She's thrilled to not have to make planks herself, so even before Adam starts his new line of business he has two customers signed up for large quantities of planks.

The result so far is a shift toward house-building, caused by Deborah, Gordon, and Gregory's revealed preferences for houses. To satisfy the demand for houses, Edda was attracted from hunting to the more highly valued work in construction, Bob went into nail production from his previous trade as a baker, and Adam was attracted from soft drink making to plank production. Each shift implies an increased value-creating capability in the economy, since Edda, Bob, and Adam contribute greater value in their new positions than they previously did. As such, they are also made better off themselves, allowing their respective purchasing powers increase. The same is true for Becky, who was able to make more profits in her line of business because of the greater demand (at least until she started facing Bob as competitor), and Bart, who is the only remaining baker, can sell more bread or raise the price—or perhaps both. And, of course, Fred, who landed a much greater project than he had previously. It is also anticipated that the output and quality of ice cream will increase when Gordon establishes his production in the new house; this too is a value created.

The losses, or the opportunity cost for the little society, is the loss of game as they're now out of a hunter, the loss of one of two bakers, and the loss of soft drink production. The opportunity to buy game meat, cheap bread, and soft drinks are now unrealized options—they cannot be chosen. Each of these lost choices, however, is the result of productive activities being replaced by other types of production that produce more value in the eyes of consumers. The opportunity cost of instead keeping any or all of these productions would therefore be higher than their actual value.

In terms of optionality in production, house construction has become a longer process because Adam is now specialized in plank production and both Fred and Edda therefore have the choice to build using timber they gather themselves or build using planks—that they either produce themselves or purchase from Adam. Fred and Edda also have the choice to buy nails from either Becky or Bob, whereas they used to be dependent on Becky's ability and willingness to spend time in the forge. Also, as both Fred and Edda now offer construction services, there is greater optionality for anyone interested in building a new house or hut, or perhaps just getting an addition to their existing dwelling. Of course, the losses also affect optionality: it is no longer possible to buy sugary soft drinks, the price of bread has gone up, and buying game meat is not an option anymore. On the other hand, the quantity and variety of ice cream is likely to increase.

While what's been stated summarizes the supply situation, that is production, we have not considered the effects that the shifting prices might have on consumptive patterns. For instance, it is quite possible that Adele the apple-grower gets a share of Bart's increased profits. It is also likely that Eric and Gregory, the society's cattle breeders, will experience increased demand and therefore, potentially, higher profitability. Why? Because when Bart increases his prices as he is the sole baker, those who used to buy bread may choose other types of food: apples and beef, for instance. While apples and beef aren't perfect substitutes for bread, they are close enough to be considered—depending on how much Bart anticipates that he can charge for bread.

Just like we've shown in previous chapters, a change has ripple effects throughout the market which thereby adjusts to the new situation by reallocating productive resources toward production of the most highly valued goods and services. What was discussed here is the addition of more highly valued production, which causes shifts throughout the economy—all of them are caused by more valuable options being made available: Edda acted on the opportunity to better serve consumers by shifting her efforts from hunting to house building; Bob similarly gave up baking to produce nails, and Adam quit making soft drinks to instead create a new trade: plank production. While these and the other changes are all important to understand, our intent here is to use this as a benchmark when we now turn toward assessing the effects of regulation.

THE UNREALIZED IN THE REGULATED ECONOMY

Let us now turn toward analyzing the same development as above but in the context of a regulated economy. We use the same starting point as above, with our 14 specialized producers and the added demand for houses, but this time we also have Luke the policy-maker and his private subsidy, paid for by personal wealth and intent to increase the production of bread. In this market, therefore, Bart and Bob—our bakers—already benefit from the subsidy by being slightly more profitable than they were in the example above. Rather than work through the effects of introducing a subsidy, as we did in chapter 8, we assume that it has already been put in place and that what we see is therefore the structure of the market after the effects of the subsidy have played out. The market starting point, when Gregory and Deborah go to visit Fred to discuss construction of their house (and Gordon soon does the same), is thus the exact same as above in terms of the structure of production. But a subsidy is supporting Bart and Bob's bakeries.

As was the case in the previous section, Gregory and Deborah, our expecting couple, visit Fred to have him build their new house. Slightly thereafter, Gordon visits Fred only to learn that he will need to find another builder. Also as in the previous section, Gordon makes an offer to Edda that she gladly accepts, with the result that Edda shifts her efforts from hunting toward construction. Edda and Fred, our two house-builders, get started on their projects and, just like before, convince Adam to give up soda production for the new trade of plank master to supply both of their businesses with the proper materials. So far the effects remain the same as in the example above.

Due to the increased demand for resources going into the construction of houses, Becky's business as a nail smith is booming. She raises prices because the demand is overwhelming, and the increased profitability that the higher prices provides makes it easier to put in the necessary hours. Also, with higher prices, both Edda and Fred are more careful with the nails they purchase—so they won't waste as many. At this point, in the previous section, Bob was attracted from bread-baking by the higher anticipated profits in nail production, which increased the supply and thus made house-building easier and a less costly endeavor. Now, however, since both Bart and Bob benefit from Luke's subsidy, it would take very high profits in nail-making to lure Bob into that line of business. It turns out that the profitability Becky enjoys, or more accurately the anticipated profitability that Bob expects to capture from the market share, is not sufficient for Bob to leave his subsidized bakery to produce nails.

The result of this is that the houses become much more expensive than was previously the case, which of course affects both Edda and Fred in their undertakings as well as any of their continued efforts as builders. Edda, as we know, is hoping the house she's building for Gordon will be the start of a career as builder, but with the high prices for nails—profits that go directly into Becky's pockets—it is no longer as clear whether this may be possible. Edda and Fred will also, because of the higher price of three-inch nails, try out other methods than nailing the planks together. For instance, they might experiment with different types of glue, special cutting of the planks and timber to make them fit together without adhesives, or simply tie the planks together using string or industrial-strength rubber bands. Some of these methods are poor solutions that would not have been considered at a lower price for nails, whereas others were previously considered but deemed to be too costly—that is, they could not sufficiently contribute to satisfying consumer wants and are therefore poor uses of available resources. With the much higher price for nails as Becky is the sole supplier—a monopolist—these methods are no longer out of reach. The implication, as we have learned in previous chapters, is that house-building—the type of production preferred by consumers—becomes less efficient as it now requires more resources to complete such projects. To put it much more briefly, the little society gets less house construction as Becky enjoys artificially high profits. The profits are artificial because without the subsidy of baking Bob would have chosen to go into nail manufacturing, which would have increased supply and decreased price, which in turn would have provided the society with more housing.

But the effects don't end with these indirect but still easily recognizable implications of Luke's subsidy in support of baking. As Bart and Bob are partly supported by the subsidy, they have comparatively little incentive to produce the quantity demanded by consumers. They also have less incentive to put in long hours to meet spikes in demand or try new techniques or develop different types of bread. In other words, baking as a protected trade is less innovative and less efficient than it otherwise would have been. It is also more profitable because of the subsidy, so Bart and Bob are comparatively more wealthy than they otherwise would have been. Bob, as we noted, makes enough money to not want to shift into nail manufacturing. Bart, on the other hand, makes a decent living as it is, partly because of the subsidy, but had there not been a subsidy he would be the only baker—and could possibly make even more money. So even though baking is a protected business and those in that line of business profit from it, the effects are not the same: Bob earns more than he otherwise would, even including his alternative income as a nail smith in the unhampered market, whereas Bart actually makes less because baking is less efficient because of the subsidy—and because it keeps Bob in baking bread.

As both of them are still in bread baking, their combined output is likely higher than the quantity supplied by Bart after Bob decides to become a nail smith. The higher quantity suggests a lower market price, and the subsidy certainly makes a lower price possible as it covers the bakers' actual costs. For this reason, the increase in demanded quantities of apples and beef that we saw in the previous section does not happen. This opportunity for Adele, Eric, and Gregory to expand or refine their businesses simply isn't realized. They remain unaffected by the boom in house construction, except for the higher price of nails were they to require nails for some project, whereas they would otherwise be winners. Their standard of living is therefore, relative to what otherwise would have been the case, lower—and so is their purchasing power.

Furthermore, as Bob does not become a nail smith, which leads to a relatively higher price of nails and therefore the cost of building, it may be the case that for instance Gordon no longer has enough capital to contract with Edda. So he must postpone his house-building plans and thus continues to live in Bart's bakery while saving for his dream house. Say that he needs to save for another year and a half to be able to afford the more expensive (but otherwise the same) house. This means Fred may no longer be busy building for Deborah and Gregory, but could take on Gordon's house as well when his savings account has reached a sufficient balance. And if this is so, then Edda may never get the chance to move into house building. Instead, that value ends up in Fred's hands as the only builder in our little society. In fact, the higher cost of building may also lead to Deborah and Gregory choosing to build a slightly smaller house than they would otherwise have preferred because they get less house for their money.

The result of the subsidy, then, is higher profits for Bob without moving into nail manufacturing, higher profits for Becky in her established line of work, and higher profits for Fred. But the result is also the loss of those opportunities that would otherwise have been realized: Edda, who will then remain a hunter; Adele, Eric, and Gregory, who won't get a share of the increased profit from demand shifting away from bread; Bart, to the degree he would have earned more as a monopolist baker than a subsidy-supported competitor; and Adam, if his specialization into plank making cannot be supported with only Fred as builder. They are all losers as the opportunities they had been offered in an unhampered market are left unrealized in the wake of an artificial, subsidy-induced house construction boom.

These effects are all caused by the added subsidy but not by adding the subsidy itself. Note that we used the same starting point when walking through the economic changes, with the only difference being that baking was a fully market-based business in the baseline (the previous section) but subsidized in the discussion in this section. We did not consider the distortive effects of adding the subsidy, but focused on tracing the effects of having a subsidy in place when other change occurs. What we find when comparing our current scenario to the baseline—the unhampered market—is that simply having a subsidy in place creates a plethora of deviations, each of which has an effect on people's lives and wellbeing. There are both winners and losers, but we should keep in mind that even though we tracked the different effects and found both who benefits and who is set back by what remains unrealized there is one difference that is economy-wide: the impact of implementing the subsidy. We left that out, since we walked through that logic in a previous chapter. But it should be noted that this society with a subsidy is comparatively less well off than the society without a subsidy to begin with. The problems that we saw appear when the market with a subsidy responds to change—primarily through the opportunities, both in production and consumption, that remain unrealized—are an additional burden. The overall cost is higher.

We could add to this picture the type of regulation that was discussed in chapter 7. For instance, Luke's dislike for soot emitted from nail manufacturing and therefore the legal requirement to have tall chimneys on all forges. If we would walk through the logic following a boom in housing demand where Luke has already regulated against low-chimney forges (and the subsidy for bread-baking is also in place), we would find that the cost of construction would be much higher since the regulation increases the cost of producing nails. The result is a higher barrier for Bob to enter the nail-producing business since he would expect lower profits when and if he makes the shift. With this regulation and the subsidy, the price of nails would need to increase a great deal to incentivize Bob to leave his subsidy-protected occupation as baker for the regulation-burdened occupation as a nail smith. As these barriers exist, Becky would be able to charge an even higher price (though not so high that Bob decides to make the shift), consequently increasing the cost of house building. There is now no chance at all for Adam to move into plank making, which will remain an unrealized trade, and Edda would continue as a hunter. Overall, even less value would be created in the society and the inhabitants' combined standard of living will as a consequence not increase as much as it otherwise would have. This, of course, means they have fewer opportunities to make different choices, fewer alternatives will be made available, and they will likely work longer hours to reach the standard of living they otherwise would have enjoyed.

We could also add taxation to this picture in order to finance the subsidy, if Luke either didn't get his hefty inheritance or simply isn't interested in paying for the subsidy himself. He is, after all, a policy-maker and doesn't have to foot the bill himself—he can with simple means push the cost onto others. So Luke, who has regulated the chimney height on forges and thereby increased the costs on nail production, and has introduced a subsidy in support of bread production, also introduces a tax to pay for the subsidy. He decides on a 5 percent tax on all profits, applicable for all businesses, which he thinks should be enough to pay for the subsidy as well as the cost—his own salary—of weeding through subsidy applications and inspecting chimneys. This tax makes any business 5 percent more costly, since only 95 percent of any profit earned is kept—but all of the cost still needs to be covered. This raises the bar for any investment to become profitable, and entrepreneurs would therefore tend to invest less often and they would also not invest in technology, production, and so on that is sufficiently profitable in itself but falls below the threshold because of the tax. Each investment, even those with anticipated very high profits, becomes riskier due to the added cost. As a consequence, the economy will develop at a much slower pace, and with less value creation there is a greater risk for distortive effects: the number of opportunities that will never be realized—*the unrealized*—increases with the artificial burdens on economic action.

NOTES

1. The automobile, as many other innovations of political interest, is hardly an innovation and product of the unhampered market. But we will here treat it as such to illustrate the point about the unrealized.

2. How this can be accomplished is discussed in Bylund (2016).

3. See Demsetz (1969).

4. The perceptive reader notices that this affirms what was stated in previous chapters about the economy's endogeneity: none of the variables mentioned are exogenous or even with an exogenous cause.

Chapter Ten

Implications for Our View of Society

The previous couple of chapters demonstrated the far-reaching implications of changes that at first sight appear to be local and limited in both scope and scale. In our example, adding a subsidy—even if we for simplicity assume that it is financed privately rather than through taxation—to increase the production of bread completely changed the market's response to the new revealed demand for house building. Indeed, we saw that walking through the responses to Deborah and Gregory's and Gordon's demand for houses showed that the outcome between the unhampered market and the subsidy-affected market is very different. This difference can be measured in terms of aggregate economic growth of the little society as its Gross Domestic Product (GDP). But doing so necessarily hides the details of the change by focusing on the net observable value.

What is not shown in GDP is, to borrow the language of Bastiat and as discussed in chapter 5, the "unseen"—that which didn't happen. But the discussion in chapter 9 showed that there is more to it than simply an unseen chain of events resulting from, as in the case of Bastiat's original illustration, some destruction or hindrance. The chain of events that happen (or events that do not happen) facilitates not only consumption but also production: choices throughout the market are affected by a change by making specific alternatives available or unavailable. The point of analyzing the "unrealized" alternatives—the lost optionality—was that even a limited restriction placed on the market can have far-reaching effects in seemingly very distant and different parts of the market. Who would have guessed, for instance, that the subsidy for bread would mean that Adam will not move into the new occupation of plank maker? Luke certainly didn't see this and didn't intend for it to happen. The intention with subsidizing bread making was to get more bread, nothing else. But there are unintentional (and to some extent always unpredictable) consequences to any apparently limited economic action for the simple reason that the economic organism is endogenous and all types of production undertakings are interdependent in productive social cooperation. We can see how things are connected and therefore affected when walking through the changes and their implications logically, but this is not observable in aggregate statistics. Looking at the statistical data shows neither the unseen nor the unrealized—in our example above, the data would show that the economy with a subsidy would also get one new house (Deborah and Gregory's) but would not show that Gordon isn't getting one, that Adam doesn't go into plank making, that Bob doesn't become a nail smith, and also not that Adele, Eric, and Gregory will not experience increased demand for their food products (that is, bread substitutes). The unseen effects are hidden, and the alternatives that are unrealized affect people's behavior by removing potential choices that would have been made without the regulatory burden.

The unrealized affects individual persons in a very real way by limiting their scope of action. As they are not provided with options that they might have otherwise chosen, their potential for value creation is limited compared to what otherwise would have been the case. In other words, their standard of living, and thus ability to lead their lives as they see fit, is restricted. This, in turn, means the alternatives that would be presented to other actors also are not realized. While a restriction on the unhampered market is a net overall loss, the effect on specific individuals could be anything from disastrous to limiting. At the same time, others—such as Becky and Fred—benefit from the artificial restriction by experiencing higher demand and, consequently, greater profitability. This profit, while it is the result of satisfying real wants, is made possible because the means for satisfying other and more highly valued wants is not realized. The loss for society consists of these unrealized want satisfactions, which would cause responses reallocating resources throughout the market and thus not provide some of the now experienced profits for Becky and Fred. In some sense, we can say that they profit from the fact that other people no longer can satisfy highly valued wants since those means aren't made available.

This, of course, happens in the unhampered market as well—it is not perfect in the nirvana sense. But the unhampered market places no arbitrary restrictions on people acting in their own best interest and thus, through the workings of the market, facilitate other people's consumption and wants satisfaction. The unhampered market has limitations, but as it has no specific aim but is rather involved in continuous discovery, and is highly interdependent through production and exchange, attempts to correct, rectify, adjust, and redirect the market will almost exclusively result in failures to attain the end that is attempted. Not only will added restrictions such as regulations and taxes, or the support that can be offered as a result, produce a shift in *whose* wants are satisfied—from individual actors' to those preferred by the policy maker—but the outcome is a net loss in value creation. The effect is also that winners and losers are created, either directly by receiving a subsidy or being burdened by regulation, or indirectly through artificially high or low profitability—or loss of well-being due to unrealized alternatives that would or would not have been chosen.

So what does the issue of the unrealized tell us about the real market and suggested or already implemented policy? Firstly, it redirects our attention to looking at the direct and indirect effects on real individuals—and their ability to make choices that improve their standard of living. By doing this, we can identify the real winners and losers, and thereby also identify the real extent of the consequences of certain policy measures. And secondly, it allows us to trace the real effects—whether intended or unintended—of policy. This is not restricted to assessing a proposed policy measure by estimating the effects and their scope, but the unrealized can serve as a lens that allows us to analyze any real situation after the fact. We will now turn to a real world example with the purpose of illustrating the power of using the unrealized as a lens.

THE SWEATSHOP AND THE UNREALIZED

The term "sweatshop" is often used pejoratively about a production facility, commonly located in developing countries, where working conditions are harsh—at least from the point of view of us living in developed economies. These factories provide jobs, but those employed often have to work very long hours in potentially dangerous jobs without much protection and in poor working conditions. The wage offered for workers in these positions is often ridiculously low, at least compared to what a worker in North America or Europe would make in similar occupations and types of production. For these reasons, sweatshops are described as a symptom of unbridled capitalism, where the underpaid workers (and their health) are readily sacrificed by profit-hungry corporations eager to make short-term gains that boost their income statements, increase the stock market value, and thereby earn their executives excessive bonuses. Consequently, the modern sweatshop—while in many ways similar to the work in factories in the West in the nineteenth century—is often rejected as exploitative and a horrible fate for those ending up with such a job. Indeed, long hours at low pay and with terrible working conditions is hardly a dream job, and many Westerners of today would never accept a job like that. This is the seen.

As we discussed in the previous chapters, however, the seen is hardly sufficient for analyzing a situation. In line with our analysis in chapter 5, a common retort to the rejection of the sweatshop based only on what is seen utilizes the unseen. This argument thereby contextualizes the sweatshop economically by pointing to the facts of the situation: the sweatshop may be bad or even horrible, but it is the better—or even best—option available to poor people in poor countries. Indeed, it is often the case that workers in sweat-shops make more money than their peers, have better (and sometimes *much* better) working conditions, and benefits. Even though each of these as well as the combined picture is socially unacceptable from a Western or devel-oped-world perspective, it provides a valued means toward wants satisfaction to the people in poor countries and significantly raises their purchasing pow-er. But, as is often claimed to be the case, the possibility of being employed in a sweatshop is often considered a boon for the people living there. The reason for this is that their real alternatives are rarely (if ever) the type of employment that is taken for granted in the West, with higher salary, better working conditions, and perks and benefits. Instead, the alternative they're presented with may be starvation, toiling with manual labor in the fields for very limited harvests, or sending sons and daughters to make whatever mon-ey they can through selling themselves (that is, prostitution). The rejection of sweatshops based only on what is seen is therefore a conclusion based on the nirvana fallacy: if we consider the real alternatives, calling for the prohibition or boycott of sweatshops is certainly not in the interest of the people working in sweatshops. Rather, such measures would seem to harm the very people they are intended to help.

Indeed, it can even be argued that the sweatshop may be a means toward economic development in developing countries.[1] Work in sweatshops pro-vides a higher—and sometimes *much* higher—standard of living for those who are employed and their families. This, in turn, frees up their time to do other productive work, provides capital to invest in productivity-increasing production or education, and their increased purchasing power soon benefits others in the community as those benefitting directly from sweatshop em-ployment increase their consumption through more frequent and qualitative exchange. For instance, those employed in sweatshops can make enough money to repair and even expand their dwellings, purchase better foods and means of transportation. The money spent is somebody else's income, and the flow of value follows what we have discussed above with respect to the economic "ripple effects." In this sense, sweatshops can provide a well needed push for a local economy toward capital accumulation and specializa-tion under the division of labor. Consequently, as the new wealth spreads throughout this economy, the sweatshop could indirectly increase every-body's standard of living. It is from this perspective that we should under-stand Harvard economist Jeffrey D. Sachs's statement that his "concern is not that there are too many sweatshops but that there are too few."[2]

Whereas the analysis of sweatshops is indeed better when considering both the seen and the unseen, as opposed to focusing only on the seen, it is incomplete unless we also consider the unrealized. Focusing on what is seen, we would reject the sweatshop; adding to the picture and even focusing on the unseen, we see sweatshops in a much more positive light. This more nuanced image doesn't mean that we must love sweatshops, of course, but it means we must take into consideration their real effects on real people. The realized changes our analysis yet again and adopts a different perspective by looking not at the effects of the sweatshop per se, but what may be the cause of the situation in which the sweatshop is the better alternative. As we have discussed in the chapters above, what matters to real people is their situation in terms of optionality or, on the other side of the coin, the opportunity costs in their choice situation: what alternatives do they actually have, and what is the value of these alternatives?

If we first look at the choice situation, Rashid, who lives in a rural village in a developing nation, has a very limited number of alternatives to earn a living. For instance, these alternatives would include producing rice by toiling on the family's small piece of land, entering into an apprenticeship with the village's blacksmith or house builder, weaving baskets by hand to sell at the side of the road to passersby, and moving to a large city several hundred miles away to try to get a job. Neither of these alternatives offers much reward, so they are similar in terms of the value created for Rashid and thus the wage he earns. In other words, the opportunity cost is relatively high whereas the absolute outcome is not. This is expected in a situation characterized by equality in poverty: there are no obvious alternatives that will take you out of poverty, so the effort is intended to secure your own and your family's survival.

Enter a sweatshop in the form of a factory in the textile industry in a nearby small town, which offers employment for low-skilled labor to carry out repetitive tasks such as sorting and packaging produced goods, refilling cotton used in spinners and yarn used in looms, and unpacking delivery trucks, restocking and reshelving inventory of produced goods, and so on. Production takes place in a newly built warehouse, which is simply four walls and a roof made of steel. There is no air conditioning but only a few fans in the wall. The building is hot, humid, and noisy, and the workers must work quickly to not stall the production process; the risk of being injured by the large machines is high because of the lack of safety measures and the high pace of the job. Workers are paid $0.25 per hour working 12-hour shifts six days of the week but receive no benefits or insurance, so if they're injured or cannot keep up with the expected, very demanding pace they are readily fired and replaced.

For Rashid, however, the sweatshop offers an opportunity for income that vastly exceeds what he would be able to make toiling in the field or weaving baskets by hand. In other words, his opportunity cost for employment in the sweatshop—the highest value of alternatives foregone—is comparatively low. By getting a job in the sweatshop, he would be able to support his family—and then some. So it is obvious to him that he must attempt to secure employment in the sweatshop, which in fact offers an opportunity to improve his own and his family's situation. Rashid doesn't have a problem with getting up early in the morning, so he manages to be one of the first seeking employment when the sweatshop opens for job applications. And as he is a strong and healthy young man, the sweatshop managers eagerly offer him a job with the task of moving delivered cotton from the dock to the spinners. It is hard labor and he needs to be quick to make sure the machines always have enough cotton fiber to keep spinning. He gets a lunch break if he can work up enough cotton during the morning to keep the spinners busy while he devours the rice leftovers from yesterday's dinner that he brings with him.

Rashid leaves home before 5 am on work days to begin work at 6 am, and returns home just after 7 pm after finishing his shift at 6 pm. His "commute" consists of biking on mud roads and takes about 45 minutes when the weather is very good. During the monsoon season he needs to walk, which takes him 3 hours—if it is at all possible to get to the factory. But so far things have worked out well for Rashid. Needless to say, when he gets home from work he has little energy to do anything but have dinner with his family and then go to bed to regain some of his strength for the next day. Despite the long days and hard work, both Rashid and his family are happy that he has the job. His mother even hopes that his younger brother Hiran can get a job at the factory when he gets a little older. The factory hires boys and girls from the age of 12 if they're strong and hard-working, so Hiran still has a couple of years before he's eligible for employment.

So far, Rashid's story is a story about the seen and the unseen—but not the unrealized. Though his starting point—before the sweatshop—was one with optionality according to our definition (the opportunity costs of the alternatives were approximately the same), it was also a situation in which the family was utterly poor. The sweatshop was not yet an available choice, since the textile factory still hadn't been established. Yet the sweatshop cannot properly be thought of as an unrealized opportunity in the sense we're using the term here, for the same reason that buying a Volvo or Mercedes luxury sedan was not an "unrealized" possibility in the eighteenth century—or a week-long vacation to an all-inclusive resort on the planet Saturn is not an "unrealized" possibility today. If the reader recalls, we specifically refer to opportunities as unrealized not simply because they have yet to emerge but because they are options that *would have been available* had the economy not been distorted. The unrealized alternatives are therefore the options we don't have but could or *should* have had. So the fact that the sweatshop entrepreneur (or, which may be as likely, the management team of the corporation owning it) had not yet made the decision to establish the textile factory does not itself imply that there is an unrealized opportunity—even though it does not yet exist and is about to emerge.

The opportunities that are unrealized for Rashid, therefore, are the opportunities that would have been available in the absence of restrictions on the market. Such restrictions include regulations that are common in developing nations, such as barriers to trade raised as protectionist measures (both by the governments in developing nations and by governments in the developed world), difficulty and wait times when starting a business (due to both bureaucratic requirements and corruption),[3] monopoly privileges, and redistribution of funds from taxpayers to representatives of the regime. We cannot know what exact alternatives would be available for Rashid had the economy been unregulated. However, the fact that a sweatshop is established provides a good indication of what is possible but isn't realized.

As the textile factory can be built and starts producing suggests that there are no economic limitations to this type of industrialized production. Indeed, even if this sweatshop is subsidized, it is embedded in an economic reality that supports the operation of this type of factory. So there is sufficient infrastructure for delivering inputs and shipping outputs, available building materials and power, access to underutilized and willing labor, and there is even access to capital in the form of machines used in manufacturing (the spinners and looms). The subsidy could have caused the factory to be built in this specific location, or perhaps sooner than would otherwise have been the case, but the fact that there are no economic limitations, except for the ever present profitability concerns, means the market is mature enough to support this type of production. We can therefore conclude that the standard of living in the village would likely have been at par with that which is offered through employment in the sweatshop. In other words, the poverty experienced by the villagers is to a significant extent artificial, as is Rashid's choice situation when he chooses between the comparatively high-paying job in the sweatshop and toiling in the fields or weaving baskets by hand.

Considering what we know about how the economic organism functions, it should of course be the case that an economy that can support sweatshop-level technology in production would be able to equally support competition on this particular productivity level. If one sweatshop is economically feasible with respect to the existing level of economic development, but not considering profitability (which is a function of entrepreneurship, not development level), there could as easily be many. But whether or not this would be the case, the fact that this *could* be the case combined with the fact that there are no artificial barriers to entry (such as regulation) in a unhampered market, suggests that the sweatshop would face competition—either competition by existing firms or by potential entrants. With competition, the sweatshop would need to compete not only to sell what is produced but also for

inputs, including labor. In other words, we should expect to see higher salaries and/or better working conditions than is the actual case in the sweatshop.

Indeed, the new textile sweatshop that we discussed above in reality
competes for labor only with the other choices available to Rashid and the
other villagers: toiling in the field, weaving baskets by hand, or moving to a
large city in hope of employment. As these alternatives are so much less
valued by Rashid and the others—which we know from the obviousness of
the choice, that is the much lower opportunity cost of the other choices—
means that the sweatshop is indeed a much better choice. But it is better
because the other alternatives of similar or greater value that would have
been available remain unrealized.

It follows that the villagers' actual situation suffers from the lack of
highly valued alternatives. Even if there is no regulation directly affecting the
villagers, such as taxation or licensing requirements or restrictions of land
use, they are victims of regulation. The reason there is only one sweatshop in
the region, for instance, could be a result of regulations specifically targeting
international trade and that result in forcing wages down below their market
level and keeping them at this artificially low level. This is easy to see if we
apply the logic discussed in the previous chapters. The higher barriers to
international trade, for instance exports of textiles, is a cost on establishing
textile factories (including the sweatshop where Rashid works) and therefore
restricts the number of actors who can profit in this space. For this reason,
entrepreneurs and industrialists with a better political network or a more
extensive lobbying apparatus will be able to exploit the opportunity resulting
from lacking competition: with competition, wages would rise and working
conditions would improve, cost of inputs would rise, and the price that can be
charged for outputs would go down. As there is no competitor—and there
likely can be no competitors, since they're artificially restricted from entering the market—the only existing player gains the type of market power that
monopolists experience and reaps the rewards thereof. In other words, the
poverty of the villagers has the same cause as the low wage offered to them
in the sweatshop: lack of competitive discovery due to the restricted market
and, consequently, malfunctioning economic organism.

In other words, the profits earned by the sweatshop corporation are artificially high despite their business being regulated—the sweatshop is, in a
sense, protected because it is an insider, an incumbent to a protected market
niche, in a market that cannot support more players because of artificial
restrictions. The other side of the coin is the choice situation of the villagers,
which is artificially limited for the same reason. They could potentially have
had a choice between several competitive employers in the textile business or
other manufacturing industries, likely with higher wages and better working
conditions, but are instead left burdened with choosing between comparatively unfavorable employment in the sweatshop and the much worse choices

that entail struggling in outright poverty. The effect of the regulation, by restricting and thus distorting the market, therefore produces a result that is similar to redistribution in how it distorts value creation: sweatshops with poor working conditions earn artificially high profits while people are kept in abject poverty.

Of course, as the illustration above shows, there is no real redistribution taking place—no money is actually taken from the poor villagers and then given to the sweatshop. Instead, the villagers are stripped of the options that they *would have had* but that now remain unrealized; the competitive situation in manufacturing that likely would have emerged and created value also does not take place. But the effect is the same, and this inhibits economic growth and development. The sweatshop is an improvement on what was, but is worse than what should have been.

IMPLICATIONS OF THE UNREALIZED

The example of sweatshops illustrates the power of adopting the perspective of what remains unrealized when assessing a situation in an economy. The discussion about the effect and ethics of sweatshops has primarily been between two camps adopting the seen and the unseen, respectively, as their focus. Whereas the latter may have a more nuanced perspective on the situation by contextualizing the phenomenon rather than looking at it separately and, in a sense, in a vacuum, both perspectives assume that significant portions of the status quo are real and proper points of departure in analysis. But they are not—the status quo is not caused by an unhampered market, but by distortive regulations.

Those focusing on the seen assume that what goes in the developed world is a proper benchmark for analyzing and evaluating jobs in sweatshops, regardless of the economic reality of those accepting such employment. This view looks at phenomena such as sweatshops as though they were not embedded in an economic context, and sometimes even fail to recognize that what's being dismissed is in fact an economic phenomenon. Instead, the phenomenon is taken at face value and evaluated without recognizing fundamental truths about economics, including that of simple trade-offs. As the "seen" analysis of sweatshops shows, the sweatshop is evaluated from the observer's point of view with no consideration taken of the situational conditions of people like Rashid who choose employment in sweatshops. From this point of view, it would be as logically stringent to reject the workers' choice of employment as it is to reject the existence of sweatshops. The reason for coming out on one side and not the other is due to a biased position: from a pro-business perspective, the workers could be blamed for having assumed exploited positions in a sweatshop that, legally speaking, does nothing wrong; from an anti-business perspective, the sweatshops can be blamed for employing workers at low wages under poor working conditions. Neither conclusion accounts for the trade-offs made by the involved parties.

The "unseen" analysis of sweatshops focuses instead on the trade-off as it exists for workers like Rashid (and, sometimes, the sweatshop owners and management), and consequently concludes that the sweatshop offers higher income and better working conditions than all existing alternatives. This, of course, is true, since Rashid and others are presented with the rather obvious choice of poverty and hard, traditional labor in the village or, as an alternative, a higher (perhaps much higher) income and hard labor in the sweatshop. Seeing it from Rashid's and the villagers' perspective, prohibiting or condemning sweatshops would make their situation worse than it already is. So the argument from the perspective of what is seen, often with the conclusion that sweatshops should be abolished, would actually make the situation worse for most if not all of those employed in sweatshops.

Using instead the unrealized as the lens, we look not only at the phenomenon or the trade-off as Rashid and others have to deal with the present as it actually is, but on what caused this choice situation—and whether those causes are market-based or artificial restrictions. In order to assess the real situation, the proper benchmark or contrast is not what we would instead like to see without considering economic reality (that is, the view using the "seen") or the options that have been realized (that is, the view using the "unseen"), but what otherwise would have been. The error of the analyses focusing on the seen or the unseen is that they draw conclusions using improper counterfactuals. They are comparing apples and oranges.

Consider if we are tasked with trying to figure out the value of getting a college degree and that we have John, who just graduated, as an example. Say he makes $35,000 in his job. Is that enough to warrant going through four years of college? It depends on whether we think that is a good salary or not. So maybe we would say that John's salary stinks, because it is less than the average American household income. That statement would be true, but it says nothing at all about whether the college degree was worth it (and even less if it was worth it to John).

Instead, we have to compare the salary after the fact, that is after graduation, to something in order to figure out whether it was "worth it" to John. Looking at the seen, we would compare John's salary after graduation with the salary he earned before going to college. Perhaps he earned $22,000, then we would say that he makes $13,000 more each year because of graduating from college. While the arithmetic is correct, there is nothing to say that it was the degree that made him earn those additional $13,000. Lots of things change in four years: the job market could have changed, the jobs available to John are different with and without a degree, John has matured and has more life experience than before, and so on. So what part of the salary increase is actually due to the degree?

The only way of figuring this out is to look at what John would have earned had he not gone to college: the unseen. This alternative reality doesn't exist, of course, so we need to figure out a way of simulating it as well as we can. One way of doing this is to assume that he would get pay raises at par with everybody else in that particular job category that he was in prior to college, that he would have a similar chance to be promoted as others like him, and so on. So, assuming John is a "standard" employee in a standard job, we can produce a guestimate of what his salary would be if he had stayed in his job instead of going to college. If we are able to think of all the relevant things that would have significantly affected his salary had he not gone to college, then we can with some certainty say, or at least we can with some validity claim, that the remaining difference is likely to be due to his degree. In other words, we compare what actually exists (the seen) with what would have existed (the unseen). This unseen is the proper benchmark since it accounts for time and change, which the seen—at least in this example—doesn't. It is the only way of properly assessing the value of John's degree, since the degree is the one significant difference between the two possible worlds.

While the unseen analysis of John's degree provides insight into the alternatives he presumably faced when choosing to go to college, but with the power of hindsight, it says nothing about what options John *would have had* in an unhampered market. The situation in which he had his job prior to college was to some extent caused by distortive regulation, which we know since it took place in a real economy and all existing economies are regulated. The same is true about his choice of going to college and the job he was offered when graduating. In fact, we can with certainty conclude that the situations were not pure market but *distorted* and therefore that John's optionality while working for $22,000, when making the decision to go to college, and when working for $35,000 after graduation, was restricted. One reason we can make this claim is that others were unable to get jobs and thus were subject to involuntary unemployment in the job market where John earned a salary. This is, as we noted in chapter 8, not the case in an unhampered market, where unemployment is transitional ("between jobs" because you're actually changing from one job to the other) or due to voluntary choice.

So we know there would have been other alternatives available to John in the unhampered market. The problem with John's example is that we have too little information to tell what those alternatives would be. Had we had information about his opportunity cost, it would show that there were few alternatives with high opportunity cost, which we argued above is an indication of artificial restrictions on the workings of the economic organism. His optionality is artificially narrow, just like we found to be the case with Rashid, and with more information about his actual choice set, we could walk through John's real situation. Nevertheless, John acts in a developed economy and this is the reason he is better off than Rashid to begin with, and this explains why his choices are "better." But the valid comparison is not with Rashid but by using the unrealized, even though we lack information.

It is impossible to tell, of course, what John would have chosen had the full set of options been realized. But if we recall the analysis in previous chapters it should appear as quite unlikely that he would have been worse off in the unhampered economy—because value-creating opportunities are relatively abundant in the unhampered market. In the very least, John, while having chosen the standard path of employment, college, and then employment again, should have had several highly valuable opportunities for self-employment, that is entrepreneurship, in an unrestricted market setting. He would also, and partly for this reason, have enjoyed a higher standard of living and more alternative ways to satisfy his wants and needs. Indeed, the economy would be much more developed than the economy in which John finds his job paying $35,000.

These statements may sound somewhat exaggerated, if not utopian. But what we did with respect to analyzing John's situation is exactly what we've done above with the unrealized. We have looked at the choice situation, the presented tradeoff, for people like Rashid, in terms of the sweatshop job, Adele, in terms of the orchard, Adam, in terms of becoming a plank manufacturer, and so on. Their actual choices are of course made in a real situation and thus based on their anticipation of what is to come—that is their judgment about the options, which will become the seen and the unseen after they make the decision and act on it—because that's all the information and optionality they have. But to properly analyze their situation, we must take into account what otherwise would have been: the unrealized.

We saw above that the reason Rashid was presented with an "obvious" choice was that his situation was in fact severely restrained by burdensome regulations in other parts of the economy—he was in a worse position than he otherwise would have been, and the choice presented to him was likely worse than it otherwise would have been. The sweatshop indicated as much. To John, if going to college is an "obvious" choice in order to increase his salary, then it is reasonable to assume there are similar restrictions at play—because a well-functioning, unrestricted economic organism produces optionality. Adele, in contrast to Rashid and John, acted in an unhampered economy and therefore benefitted from a full choice set, limited only by what is not economically possible. We can hardly place blame on an economy for failing to do what isn't possible, but we can use the concept of the unrealized to point to the real causes of suboptimal economic outcomes—what happened to the options that *would have existed*, but are not present in a person's choice set, his or her optionality. For instance, Adam, when the little society in chapter 9 was burdened with Luke's subsidy to increase the supply of bread, was never presented with the opportunity to specialize in plank making and was as a result worse off than he otherwise would have been. Indeed, the whole economy was deprived of value that could have been created.

As for John, we have too little information so we do not know what opportunities he was never presented with. Consequently, we cannot tell the exact extent to which the burden of regulation has affected his situation. But we know for a fact that the choice situation is affected by existing regulation, since production precedes consumption and productive efforts in a developed economy are interdependent. In other words, the economy is much more of an organism than it is a machine, and it is important to recognize this in order to understand how the market works. Even if we disregard the fact that there are regulations affecting the market in which John makes his decisions, we have noted that there are indications that his situation is in fact restricted: the existence of unemployment—especially long-term and involuntary—is a symptom of regulation and policy rather than a shortcoming of the economy.

What our discussion suggests, and the main point of this book, is that the choices that are actually made are not the full story—and may even be far from it. It is obvious that whatever choice we make, when in a choice situation, is the one we think is superior to the existing alternatives. So we always choose in line with our perception of opportunity costs, even if we could change our minds or acquire missing information after the fact. But our opportunity cost is based on the existing choice situation and how we value the presented alternatives; it says little if anything about the choice situation itself, and how it arose. Many of the choices we make are artificial in the sense that we would have made other choices had we not been placed in a disadvantageous situation with a restricted or perhaps completely suboptimal set of choices.

This becomes very obvious in choice situations such as the one Rashid finds himself in above, where there is very limited optionality. Indeed, using colloquial language we would say that there is not much of a choice for Rashid, while in real terms there is of course a choice if there is a tradeoff. But there is "no choice" for the reason that one option is so superior to all other options, that one single value of that choice exceeds all other possible values. Even if Rashid was allergic to cotton, if his health would be seriously compromised by working indoors, if the early mornings would make him have a heart attack, the difference in terms of standard of living between the job in the sweatshop and staying in the village makes it worth it. His choice is still voluntary, despite the downsides, but it is not *euvoluntary*, to borrow a term from Duke political scientist Michael C. Munger.[4] What this means is that the choice is *formally* voluntary because there is no coercion involved in the choice situation and therefore no restrictions on choice-making itself, but the situation is so dire—and the one option so much better—that the choice is in practice reduced to simply acting on it, not actually choosing between valuable options. Our analysis is different from Munger's, however, because we do not here focus on the fairness of the choice, but on the causes of the choice situation. The concept of the unrealized is important because it helps us trace the origins of the choice situation and therefore identify what is missing from it: that is, what choices no longer exist, what choices have been created artificially (that is, through non-economic means), and how this affects the individual chooser and society at large. As in the case of John deciding to go to college, which may have appeared as an obvious or at least highly advantageous choice. But was it really? In the specific choice situation and the alternatives presented to him, this may be the case. But the choice situation itself is artificial and restricting, which means there would likely have been other alternatives that John may have considered—or even chosen—that do not emerge. This is not because the economic organism limits John's optionality, but because regulation has created artificial restrictions that affect the very structure of production in the market and consequently affect John in his choice situation. This is not to say that John necessarily is burdened by regulation, however. There are both winners and losers, and whether the specific outcome is desirable or not is a different discussion. We have specifically discussed only the *economic* implications of policy but not whether those implications are "good" or "bad."

THE UNREALIZED AND POLICY ANALYSIS

The model of the market that we presented in the first several chapters in this book provides a model against which we can evaluate existing situations (as we did above with respect to sweatshops) and attempt to predict the implications of changes such as public policy. By focusing on effects in terms of what options become unrealized, and how the unrealized distort the choice situation, the true cost (and benefit) of policy can be approximated for both individual actors (or classes of actors) and the economy overall.

As is well known, policy tends to produce both intended and unintended consequences, of which the former are the direct and anticipated consequences and the latter are the indirect and unanticipated consequences. The unintended consequences of policy have received some attention, primarily through attempts to explain the highly complex situation in which specific policies attempt to create specific results. Very often, as history shows, the economic organism is too complex and endogenous for policy-makers and analysts to be able to predict the exact implications—one specific policy change doesn't have a specific, limited effect on the market. As we saw above, the effects of policy can be far-reaching, and as each specific effect depends on individual choices in very specific situations, where the individual chooses based on his or her subjective understanding and assessment of the options, it is almost impossible to estimate the effects prior to the fact. And even after the fact, only changes in the aggregate are observable—and they can rarely be traced to a single cause.

Unintended consequences refer specifically to the measurable effects that were not intended and, therefore, not foreseen. This is a very important aspect of analyzing the implications of policy, and the reality of unintended consequences indicates the immense uncertainty with which policy must wrestle. Social sciences like economics and sociology may help in estimating the effects, and even though such analyses are often made they are of very limited value since they tend to be wide of the mark. Indeed, economists can approximate the effect on overall unemployment and employment shifts between sectors of the economy by for instance an increase in the minimum wage,[5] but these approximations should be taken with a large scoop of salt. The reason is that the effects approximated and measured are changes in aggregates in the economy rather than real choices made by economic actors.

The unrealized explains both the intended and the unintended consequences of policy on a so-called micro level by tracing the real effects, step by step, from the changes as they proliferate through the market. What can be measured empirically after the fact as real effects of the policy on an economy are the *net* effects of the unrealized. To illustrate using our example from chapter 9, in which Deborah and Gregory as well as Gordon wish to build new houses, what can be actually collected and measured are aggregate data that are descriptive of the situation. In other words, data collected before the two houses are ordered would include things like how many three-inch nails and how much bread is produced, and what incomes are earned, and so forth. Collection of data after the orders have been placed would show the differences in these figures, which means the economic implications of Luke's subsidy of bread on house-building would never be shown. Indeed, the fact that Adam never specializes in making planks and that Edda never enters the house-building trade cannot be measured. Looking specifically at the measurable *consequences* of policy necessarily leaves out anything that is unrealized. The measures used severely underestimate the implications of policy by failing to measure the potential situation, the state of the market that could or should have been.

To estimate the real effects of policy, it is necessary to trace the effects as they ripple through the economy and not just look at the net effects. It is also important to use a proper counterfactual to assess and determine the real magnitude of these effects. Advanced economic analyses attempt to construct a counterfactual using sophisticated statistical methods that allow us to simulate data describing a plausible alternate reality. However, statistics are necessarily net rather than gross, and they provide a snapshot whereas the economy is better understood as a process. For this reason, sophisticated statistical economic analyses can only provide answers that are wrong, if they are at all relevant.

Nevertheless, even if we accept these sophisticated techniques and assume that they are relevant to analyzing the implications of policy, they are intended only to measure (and simulate) effects in the aggregate. As we saw above, however, the unrealized focuses on the real effects—based on the proper counterfactual—for each decision-maker in the economy. While it is different from standard approaches by acknowledging that an economy is more like an organism than a machine, and that it is an open-ended process rather than a state or circular flow, what really sets the unrealized apart and makes it useful is the potential to identify and explain specific changes as they happen in time, and trace the causal chains of events that make up market responses as well as emphasize the interdependence between actors in production and consumption. While this provides a more realistic view of the economy, it is also a much more accurate analysis of the effect of policy on individuals' economic actions.

As we emphasized already in the beginning of this book, the perspective we adopted that treats the economy as an organism explains both economic growth and development, the structure of production, and the origins and causes of prosperity. It is neither unrealistic nor utopian, but acknowledges that the market economy is very far from efficient. But we also recognized that efficiency—in the sense of theoretically maximized resource utilization—is neither possible nor desirable. It is even a poor benchmark for assessing the present state of the economy and therefore also the implications and effects of specific policy, because comparing what is real with its unrealistic perfect state can only draw our attention away from the real problems and issues that adversely affect people. It is therefore questionable whether economic efficiency serves a purpose in analyzing the economy, especially when attempting to approximate the effects of policy.

What *does* matter is the real effects on people's lives, which is primarily captured by theorizing on what options are unrealized—that is, what options should have been made available but aren't. It is safe to say that very few people are troubled by how far apart their real situation is from an efficient economy as in the model of perfect competition. However, they *should be* troubled by the wealth-diminishing consequences as they are stripped of options that they should have had were it not for the distortive effects of attempted improvements.

The same should be true for policy-makers and their staffs, who after all mostly have good and proper intentions and wish to do good. Had they been aware of the real effects of specific regulations, and the far-reaching consequences of apparently specific regulations, they may have chosen a more conservative approach. After all, our analysis above suggests that the real costs of restrictions placed on the economic organism are hidden for the simple reason that the value that would have been created was never realized—and therefore was also never measured. The choices that otherwise would have been made and that would have served consumers were never realized and thus not chosen. This cost, which is the true burden on society by restrictive policy, is yet to be recognized and fully understood.

NOTES

1. For an interesting elaboration on the implications of the sweatshop, see Powell (2014).

2. Cited in the *New York Times*, "In Principle, a Case for More 'Sweatshops'" by Allen R. Myerson, June 22, 1997.

3. Data from the World Bank shows that it can be significantly more difficult and take a much longer time to start a business in developing as compared to developed countries. See http://data.worldbank.org/indicator/IC.REG.DURS/countries/1W?display=map.

4. See Munger (2011).

5. A policy-mandated increase is often referred to as "raising" the minimum wage, but whereas this suggests that wages will increase the law does not raise wages but prohibits jobs earning a wage lower than the mandated minimum.

Bibliography

Bylund, P. L. 2016. *Problem of Production: A New Theory of the Firm*. Abingdon, UK: Routledge.

Demsetz, H. 1969. Information and Efficiency: Another Viewpoint. *Journal of Law & Economics*, 12(1), 1–22.

Hayek, F. A. v. 1941. *The Pure Theory of Capital*. London: Routledge and Kegan Paul.

———. 1945. The Use of Knowledge in Society. *American Economic Review* 35(4): 519–530.

———. 1978. Competition as a Discovery Process. *New Studies in Philosophy, Politics, Economics, and the History of Ideas*: 179–190.

Higgs, R. 1997. Regime Uncertainty: Why the Great Depression Lasted So Long and Why Prosperity Resumed after the War. *The Independent Review* 1(4): 561–590.

Horwitz, S. G. 2009. Wal-Mart to the Rescue: Private Enterprise's Response to Hurricane Katrina. *Independent Review* 13(4): 511–528.

———. 2010. Doing the Right Things: The Private Sector Response to Hurricane Katrina as a Case Study in the Bourgeois Virtues. In *Accepting the Invisible Hand: Market-Based Approaches to Social Economic Problems*. M.D. White (ed.). Basingstoke, UK: Palgrave Macmillan.

Kates, S. 1998. *Say's Law and the Keynesian Revolution*. Cheltenham, UK: Edward Elgar.

Kirzner, I. M. 1973. *Competition and Entrepreneurship*. Chicago, IL: University of Chicago Press.

Menger, C. 1892. On the Origin of Money. *The Economic Journal* 2(6): 239–255.

———. 2007. *Principles of Economics* (Dingwall J, Hoselitz BF, Trans.). Ludwig von Mises Institute: Auburn, AL.

Mises, L. v. 1935. Economic Calculation in the Socialist Commonwealth. In *Collectivist Economic Planning*. Hayek F.A.v. (ed.). London: George Routledge & Sons.

———. 2008. *Human Action: A Treatise on Economics. The Scholar's Edition*. Auburn, AL: Ludwig von Mises Institute.

Munger, M. C. 2011. Euvoluntary or Not, Exchange is Just. *Social Philosophy and Policy*, 28(02), 192–211.

North, D. C. 1990. *Institutions, Institutional Change and Economic Performance*. Cambridge: Cambridge University Press.

Olson, M. 1971. *The Logic of Collective Action: Public Goods and the Theory of Groups*. Cambridge, MA: Harvard University Press.

Powell, B. 2014. *Out of Poverty: Sweatshops in the Global Economy*. Cambridge: Cambridge University Press.

Ricardo, D. 1817. *Principles of Political Economy and Taxation*. London: J. Murray.

Rogers, R., and Monsell, S. 1995. The Costs of a Predictable Switch between Simple Cognitive Tasks. *Journal of Experimental Psychology: General, 124*, 207–231.

Rothbard, M. N. 2004. *Man, Economy, and State with Power and Market. Scholar's Edition.* Auburn, AL: Ludwig von Mises Institute.

Rubinstein, J. S., Meyer, D. E., and Evans, J. E. 2001. Executive Control of Cognitive Processes in Task Switching. *Journal of Experimental Psychology: Human Perception and Performance, 27*(4), 763–797.

Rydenfelt, S. 1981. The Rise, Fall and Revival of Swedish Rent Control. In *Rent Control: Myths and Realities.* Block W., Olsen E. (eds.). Vancouver: The Fraser Institute.

Schumpeter, J. A. 1934. *The Theory of Economic Development: An Inquiry into Profits, Capital, Credit, Interest, and the Business Cycle.* Cambridge, MA.: Harvard University Press.

———. 1942. *Socialism, Capitalism and Democracy.* New York: Harper and Bros.

Simon, J. L. 1998. *The Ultimate Resource 2.* Princeton, NJ: Princeton University Press.

Smith, A. 1776. *An Inquiry into the Nature and Causes of the Wealth of Nations.*

Storr, N. M., Chamlee-Wright, E., and Storr Virgil, H. 2015. *How We Came Back: Voices from Post-Katrina New Orleans.* Mercatus Center at George Mason University.

Taleb, N. N. 2012. *Antifragile: Things That Gain from Disorder.* New York: Random House Incorporated.

Williamson, O. E. 1985. *The Economic Institutions of Capitalism.* New York: Free Press.

———. 1996. *The Mechanisms of Governance.* Oxford: Oxford University Press.

Zimmerman, A., and Bauerlein V. 2005. At Wal-Mart, Emergency Plan Has Big Payoff. In *Wall Street Journal.*

Index

About the Author

Per L. Bylund, PhD, is assistant professor and Records-Johnston Professor of Free Enterprise in the School of Entrepreneurship at Oklahoma State University. He has previously held faculty positions at Baylor University and the University of Missouri–Columbia, and is an associate fellow of the Ratio Institute in Stockholm, Sweden, and an associated scholar with the Mises Institute in Auburn, Alabama. Bylund's research aims to explain the market process of wealth creation and economic development with a focus on organizations, institutions, strategic management and entrepreneurship. He is the author of *The Problem of Production: A New Theory of the Firm* (Routledge, 2016).

Bylund is a native of Sweden and has decades-long experience in practical politics and policy-making as well as professional careers on three continents within information technology, business consulting, and education. He lives in Tulsa, Oklahoma, with his wife and their dog. His web site is www.PerBylund.com.